ALSO BY JOSIAH HESSE

Runner's High

CARNALITY SERIES

Dancing on Red Lake
Sebastian Phoenix and the Dark Star

ON FIRE FOR GOD

ON FIRE FOR GOD

Fear, Shame, Poverty, and the
Making of the Christian Right—
a Personal History

Josiah Hesse

PANTHEON BOOKS · NEW YORK

FIRST HARDCOVER EDITION PUBLISHED BY PANTHEON BOOKS 2026

Published by Pantheon Books, a division of Penguin Random House LLC, 1745 Broadway, New York, NY 10019.

Pantheon Books and the colophon are registered trademarks of Penguin Random House LLC.

Library of Congress Cataloging-in-Publication Data
Names: Hesse, Josiah, author.
Title: On fire for God : fear, shame, poverty, and the making of the Christian right—a personal history / Josiah Hesse.
Description: First hardcover edition. | New York : Pantheon Books, 2026. Includes bibliographical references. | Identifiers: LCCN 2025010934 (print) | LCCN 2025010935 (ebook) | ISBN 9780553387292 hardcover | ISBN 9780553387308 ebook
Subjects: LCSH: Hesse, Josiah | Ex-church members—Assemblies of God—Biography | Evangelicalism—Iowa—Mason City | Christianity and politics—Iowa—Mason City | Working class white people—Social conditions—Iowa—Mason City | Mason City (Iowa)—Social conditions | Mason City (Iowa)—Religious life and customs | Mason City (Iowa)—Biography | LCGFT: Autobiographies Classification: LCC BX8765.5.Z8 H47 2026 (print) | LCC BX8765.5.Z8 (ebook)
LC record available at https://lccn.loc.gov/2025010934
LC ebook record available at https://lccn.loc.gov/2025010935

penguinrandomhouse.com | pantheonbooks.com

Printed in the United States of America
1st Printing

The authorized representative in the EU for product safety and compliance is Penguin Random House Ireland, Morrison Chambers, 32 Nassau Street, Dublin D02 YH68, Ireland, https://eu-contact.penguin.ie.

To Anna Montoya,
for all the dark nights of the soul we endured
throughout the writing of this book.

Contents

Author's Note

Although this memoir was written following dozens of interviews with friends, family members, historians, farmers, sociologists, and economists, along with countless hours of research and fact-checking, much of it is driven by my own memories.

Nevertheless, I worked hard to make this story as factually airtight as possible. When I mention specific evangelical institutions, such as Open Bible Churches or Assemblies of God, my stories have been confirmed by at least two sources who were there at the time. However, I was attending so many different churches as a teen, there were sermons or teachings I'm confident I absorbed (and others confirmed they heard) but couldn't attribute to any specific church camp or youth group.

At times I use terms like "fundamentalist" (those who believe the Bible to be 100 percent factual, both scientifically and historically), "Pentecostal" (those who practice worship of God through "speaking in tongues" and spastic physical movements), and "evangelical" (Christians defined by their "born again" or "getting saved" conversion experience and proselytization) somewhat interchangeably. These labels do differ from one another, but understanding them is not essential for the purposes of this book. Additionally, I do not dig as deeply into "end times" theology as some academics might desire, avoiding esoteric phrases like "premillennial dispensationalist eschatology."

You're welcome.

I have changed the names of most of the people in this book, and when necessary changed details about their lives and physical characteristics to protect their identities. There are also several minor manipulations of time—placing disparate events in the same moment—for storytelling purposes.

This book is not intended to shame or condemn any of my friends or family.

Though I strongly disagree with Supreme Court Justice Antonin Scalia on nearly everything, I've always appreciated his approach to partisanship: "I attack ideas. I don't attack people. And some very good people have some very bad ideas."

ON FIRE FOR GOD

Introduction: Midwestern Gothic

"Tell all the Truth but tell it slant"

—EMILY DICKINSON

1994

The children are weeping and handing over all their money.

Used tissues litter the church floor, making me think of dead bodies spread across a battlefield. *You'll soon know what that really looks like,* a voice speaks within my head.

I am surrounded by hundreds of other preteens, our faces pale and splotchy from hours of crying. Mascara-soaked tears trickle down baby-fat cheeks. The boys beat their chests, rip at their hair, and scream like they are being dragged through barbed wire. More than a hundred children are laid across the ground of the sanctuary, twitching and flopping about like fish out of water.

It's the last night of church camp, and we've been instructed to give every last dollar in our wallets to tonight's offering. But for me—and likely most everyone else—this does little to soothe our guilty hearts.

We are sinners, and try as we might, we will never feel clean.

"Feel the *Holy Spirit*!" a stylish man with a microphone shouts from the church-camp stage. "*Speak it!* Rebuke the demons of Hell that surround this camp! Belie*eeeeve*, and your mouth will follow!"

I am surrounded by three older male counselors, who are leaning in close to my face, their ears less than an inch from my mouth, also demanding I "speak it!," that I "let it flow!"

I start speaking in a language I do not understand—a gibberish of random syllables—believing my mouth to be taken over by God's Holy Spirit. I will repeat this ritual almost daily for the next decade.

"You must be *on fire for God!*" our camp speaker proclaims, waving his arms over a crowd of moaning children. "In Revelation, we are told God rejects those with weak spirits, saying 'Because you are neither hot nor cold, I will spew you from my mouth!'"

I tell myself I must believe, or else.

Believe, believe, believe.

I believe the Antichrist is coming soon.

I believe the Mark of the Beast is nearly upon us.

If I can be cleansed by the Holy Spirit tonight, my belief will be strong enough to save me from the eternal fires of Hell. The church-camp band plays softly, led by a boy (who reminds me of Jonathan Taylor Thomas) playing an acoustic guitar.

We all sing along, knowing the lyrics to "I Wish We'd All Been Ready" by heart.

It's the same song our parents sang as teens, describing a post-apocalyptic world of extreme violence, starvation, and dead children, reminding those unworthy of Heaven that "there's no time to change your mind, The Son has come and you've been left behind."

I can easily picture the demons that (I'm told) surround this camp, trying to stop us from communing with God's spirit. Large black wings, and eyes with distant fire in their pupils. Demons of lust. Demons of sloth. They want us to sin, to join them in Hell, and will try to trick us through infiltration of our thoughts, which we must guard with furious vigilance.

I dream about them every night, particularly the witch demon named Caldonia, who speaks to me inside my own mind. I've never dared to tell anyone about Caldonia, fearing it would be taken as evidence of demonic possession, leading to exorcism and confessions of all my unspeakable sins.

If you don't believe, you won't be saved, she reminds me. *And then you'll be tortured for all eternity.*

Giant curtains of rain sweep across the Iowa campgrounds, assaulting the tin roof of this church like machine-gun fire.

The man onstage walks down toward the crying children, who are standing shoulder to shoulder in a long line before him. "In the *name* of *Jesus!*" he shouts as his hand shoots onto the forehead of each child, one by one. Each one falls to the ground instantly.

Some laugh hysterically, others scream, all of them convulse involuntarily.

The band plays on, singing about the moment the Lord will allow demons to feast on the flesh of those who did not believe.

I bite my tongue hard enough to bleed, punishing myself when my thoughts stray toward worldly desires of fashion, television, and crushes on girls.

Or, even worse, boys.

"We all know that this life is just a test that determines our lives in eternity!" the camp speaker tells us, eyes closed, sweat dripping from his spiky gelled hair. "One day we'll shed these Earth suits and live in our eternal, spiritual bodies in Heaven. Those without true faith, true *belief,* won't be so lucky!"

I stand at the far end of the line, waiting my turn. A small red-haired girl next to me falls to the ground before the man even touches her. I glance down and notice her sundress hike up slightly, then quickly look away, just as someone covers her legs with a modesty cloth. "Forgive me!" she screams, tears pouring down her face.

I am hyperventilating, certain this preacher will see the demon in my eyes.

The smell of his sweat and cologne fills my nose, and suddenly I can't breathe. The sound of thunder roars through the chapel; dizziness floods my head as my knees buckle.

"The truth shall set you free!" he shouts as his fist punches me in the chest, knocking me to the church floor like a scarecrow in a high wind.

My eyes are closed, but I can still hear the collective moaning, chanting, and speaking in tongues from my fellow campers, growing so deafening the band must play louder to be heard. But then all sound fades away, and I feel myself sink through the carpet.

My body remains on the church-camp floor, but my mind sinks through the concrete, the dirt, the galaxies of insects, rocks, and coal. This vision carries me into a realm of darkness incomprehensible to anyone stuck in an Earth suit.

The sound of agonized moaning returns, multiplied a billion times over, but it's no longer the sound of preteen campers. It's as if the entire global population is shrieking in pain, sounding more beastly than human. In my vision, I continue falling through the darkness of Hell, and then, eventually, hover before a small pit where a boy lies on the ground, weeping. The boy is me, but younger than I am now, maybe six or seven, naked, and covered in blood.

A giant TV screen on the wall of the pit flashes the word LUST, followed by scenes of the boy watching pornography and coveting boys in the school locker room. Watching this, he screeches in agony as his eyes swell and burst.

GLUTTONY is next, and the boy is pelted with snow and hail, as a team of rabid dogs tear out chunks of his flesh. On the screen, we see the boy eating cupcakes and drinking Mountain Dew when he'd promised God he'd be fasting all weekend.

SLOTH follows, and the pit slowly fills with swampy water, mildewed branches, giant mosquitoes, and thick black carpets of moss. The boy is weak and struggles to tread the water, as scenes of him sleeping late when he should be getting up for school, lying on the lawn when he should be doing homework, reading Stephen King novels when he should be reading his Bible, flash across the TV screen.

I am unaware that, in my real body, I am screaming from the church-camp floor.

I see the face of Caldonia from my dreams, gray and wrinkled, with tiny flames whirling deep in her large eyes, looking like the old crone from *Snow White*. The sight of the boy in agony brings her to hysterical ecstasy.

"The soul of the sluggard craves and gets nothing," she says, cackling with laughter as she quotes the Book of Proverbs. "Slothfulness casts into a deep sleep, and the negligent soul shall suffer hunger. Lazy people irritate their employers, like vinegar on the teeth or smoke in the eyes. He who does not work shall not eat!"

The flames in Caldonia's eyes grow like a prairie fire, consuming her face, then rain down on the little boy in the pit as I plead for forgiveness.

2023

I am jerked awake, panting and covered in sweat.

It was just a dream, but I don't yet know where I am.

One moment I'm twelve and at church camp, the next I'm forty and in the sky.

Is this Heaven?

"No, it's Iowa," I hear Kevin Costner's voice from *Field of Dreams* say.

The Costner line in my head is correct. I've just woken up from a dream about church camp (which I have at least once a week) and now find myself flying above my hometown in an airplane full of strangers.

As we descend, I can see the endless tiles of farmland and the enormous hog-confinement buildings, followed by my hometown, looking like a diorama sitting beside a lake. I see the pyramid-shaped building hosting the church I grew up in, and the dozens of factories, puppy mills, and chain restaurants I worked at after flunking out of high school (forty-five jobs in all). "We'll be landing at the Mason City airport in ten minutes," the pilot says into a microphone, "and if you look to your right, you can see the town of Clear Lake, Iowa."

The small plane bounces dramatically as we pierce the clouds, and I think of Buddy Holly. Sixty-four years earlier, he and Ritchie Valens and the Big Bopper were flying through this same piece of sky, in a very similar plane, taking off from the same airport I'm about to land in, before something went horribly wrong and all of them plummeted to their death in a nearby cornfield.

Unlike Buddy Holly's, my plane lands safely.

Perhaps I'm paranoid, but I can feel the eyes of the eight other passengers staring at me as we exit the tiny plane, suddenly feeling self-conscious about the skimpy athletic shorts I'm wearing. I tug them down slightly, attempting to cover the scars of a childhood spent cutting myself.

Mom is late picking me up, making me think of all the years I'd waited hours for her to come get me from school or church, while she worked three jobs and attended night school at the local community college. Standing outside the airport, I'm hit with the noxious smell of industrial farming—the giant warehouses of tortured animals that have sprung up over the last thirty years, producing enormous amounts of waste and toxins that poison our water, contributing to Iowa's profoundly high cancer rate (second only to Kentucky's).

I text my dad that I'm in town and am headed for City Beach.

It's not a far walk from Mason City to Clear Lake (my two home-towns rest side by side), and as I start to hoof it down the highway, a pickup truck rolls up beside me. An old man in a MAGA hat leans out of his window and asks in a Midwestern accent, "You here to work?"

I think for a minute.

"Yes, I am," I say, and I throw my bag and myself into the bed of his truck.

"I have to make a quick stop in Mason City, but I'll get you to the carnival," the driver yells to me through the open window.

This proud Trump supporter thinks I'm here to work the Fourth of July carnival in Clear Lake—when the population of this tourist town grows from seven thousand to thirty thousand for one week a year—and at one time, he'd have been right. When I was twelve, I was hired to run the ring-toss game at the carnival, watching hundreds of overconfident men fling hard plastic rings onto a table filled with dozens of glass Coke bottles, attempting to wrangle just one of them. "It looked so easy," they always said with a defeated sigh, assuming everyone but them won their girlfriend a giant Coca-Cola polar bear.

But no one ever won that game.

And that's kinda why I'm here. Nothing makes me angrier than a rigged game where the participants are told it's easy to win yet end up walking away with their heads bowed in shame. As a journalist who has spent the last twelve years reporting on mental health, poverty, and religion (particularly within the Christian right), I often come across evangelical hucksters telling an audience of poor people that the solution to their problems is simple and easy. It's easy to become rich. It's easy to raise children (especially a ridiculously large number of them) and maintain a healthy, loving marriage. It's easy to find a lucrative, satisfying job. It's easy to understand the will of God, the meaning of the Bible, and your purpose on this Earth. All you have to do is *believe*, surrender to His will, and it'll all work out just fine. You'll be rich in no time. And if you're not, it's your own damn fault, because just look at how easy this game is! Anyone can do it! It's the American Dream!

I've flown from Denver (where I've lived for the last two decades) to my hometown of Clear Lake (where I spent my first two decades) to interview friends and family members about the grifts the Christian right has inflicted upon us. I want to lift the heavy stone of the past and expose to daylight all that has been rotting in the dark.

Iowa became ground zero for the culture wars in 1976, when it was decided that the presidential primary season would begin here. Since then, this "flyover state" has become a target of political manipulation and cultural gaslighting. Utilizing racism, xenophobia, misogyny, Cold War paranoia, and, later, the War on Drugs, hard-right conservatives in the Republican Party have conned rural evangelicals into demonizing the poor and championing the wealthy, trading in their Biblical mandate to care for "the least among you" in favor of materialism, militarism, and moralistic myopia.

We were convinced that the American Dream was an easy game to win; all we had to do was get rid of those pesky unions (i.e., communists), eliminate the social safety net, cut taxes for the wealthy, deregulate the banks and corporations, and dismantle environmental laws, and the economy would erupt like a volcano, raining down currency from sea to shining sea.

In the 1980s, churches like the one my parents helped build were conjuring their own trickle-down economic doctrine in the form of "prosperity gospel." This theology promised that, on top of the weekly tithe of 10 percent of your income given to the church, any additional "gifts" or "seed faith offerings" given to preachers during their endless fund-raisers and telethons would lead to a blessing from God in the form of a literal "tenfold return on your investment."

These magical promises seduced desperate farmers throughout the farm crisis of the 1980s, when the suicide rate in Iowa spiked 400 percent, largely thanks to a massive wave of foreclosures on land that had been passed down for generations. This was followed by corporate agribusinesses swallowing up the farming industry, destroying a centuries-old way of life, polluting the land, and leaving the people without a cultural identity.

My parents gave an estimated $125,000 to our church in less than a decade (and that's not including countless hours of free labor), while we ate burnt Tater Tots bought with food stamps. Adjusted for inflation, that's around $360,000 today. At the time, they could've invested that money in damn near anything else and been better off. They could've bought Apple stock at $.05 a share in 1985, watching its value soar to $221 a share as of this writing. Instead, we had to bankroll Pastor Jim's new cars, designer suits, and tropical vacations.

With this book I aim to unpack all the betrayals, grifts, and lies that animated my family, yet were never discussed. I'll dive into all the topics that, though banned from polite dinner-table conversation, still drive so much of our behavior: politics, money, sex, mental health, and religion.

It's a journey that looks at how evolution, communism, welfare, rock music, abortion, immigration, gay marriage, and trans people using the bathroom became political tools of manipulation wielded by the Christian right, not to mention the impact that the relentless fear of Hell and Armageddon have on a child's future socioeconomic potential. It will also explore how a once-progressive movement of evangelicals became co-opted by wealthy conservatives who fundamentally reshaped the American economy—and what the sixties hippie counterculture had to do with all of it.

I'm also here to explore why my story wound up taking such a different turn from those of my working-class friends in Iowa, many of whom went to prison, or went insane, died of heroin overdoses or suicide, or maintained their drug habits until their minds and bodies became as fragile as eggshells.

As I ride through Mason City in the back of this pickup, I look at the "Trump 2024" stickers plastered across the back window and think of J. D. Vance. Ever since the 2016 presidential election, people like me, from impoverished, working-class communities, have been tasked with "explaining" Trump's unprecedented 81-percent support among evangelical Christians (particularly the poor, white ones).

This is, in part, why J. D. Vance's memoir, *Hillbilly Elegy,* was a bestseller.

I can relate to a lot of the themes and trials of Vance's story: We both come from a community of rural laborers who clash with rich urbanites, are obsessed with not being humiliated in the eyes of strangers, are suspicious of "elites," and often find themselves teetering between stretches of drug use, violence, and madness, followed by sobriety and religious zealotry. We both left our dying hometowns to pursue ambitious careers, and carried with us the tropes of our Protestant Christian work ethic: punctuality, hard work, and a fetishization of exhaustion.

But that's where Vance and I part ways.

I find his championing of payday loans and demonization of marijuana to be distasteful, and since jumping on the Trump train, he's added everyone from immigrants to childless women to his list of scapegoats for what ails America. But the real thorn in my tractor seat is his constant finger wagging at poor people throughout *Elegy,* parroting those old Reagan-era chestnuts about how welfare does more harm than good, that addiction is a moral failure, and that complex socioeconomic issues can be resolved by more church.

In my experience, the rhetoric of rugged individualism espoused by Vance and the Christian right is a kind of gaslighting that only leads to self-loathing and isolation in those faced with the inescapable adversities of the modern era. In his book, Vance ignores all the factors increasingly narrowing the options of working-class people, and recognizes only the shortcomings of the individual. Ironically, the fear and shame this thinking breeds are two of the most essential factors promoting the addiction, chaos, and poor decisions that Vance believes church to be an antidote for.

In the churches I attended, drugs, marital affairs, and misanthropic behavior were not unusual, they were just well hidden. There's a popular belief that small-town people know everything about one another, and though that may be true in some places, in Clear Lake, at Agapé Christian Family Church, the congregation all guarded a wealth of secrets.

Equally well hidden are the economic realities facing working-class people today. When opposing a hike in the federal minimum wage (which hasn't budged from $7.25 an hour since 2009), Republican Senator John Thune of South Dakota proclaimed that as a young man he lived on six dollars an hour working in a restaurant, and that was good enough for him. Adjusted for inflation, he was at that time earning the equivalent of over twenty dollars an hour. There are currently one million Americans living on minimum wage, and nearly a third of the U.S. workforce are earning less than fifteen dollars an hour.

Incomes for middle-to-low wage earners have been stagnant (or in some cases have declined) for the last forty years, while the cost of living has steadily climbed beyond the reach of many working-class families.

The golden age of middle-class prosperity during the mid-twentieth century (presumably the "Again" of Trump's "Make America Great Again") was largely attributable to the progressive policies of FDR's New Deal (though, admittedly, the fact that America's factories were the only ones not bombed into dust during World War II played a large part as well). And the soaring inequality, stagnant wages, and general decrease in quality of life in America can be laid at the feet of the Reagan Revolution's dismantling of unions, deregulation of the economy, and tax cuts for the wealthy, alongside cuts in mental-health care, welfare, and higher-education subsidies.

And yet white, working-class voters continue to flock to conservative candidates. In *Elegy*, Vance says it was when they saw loafers getting handouts from the government that the working class began to abandon the Democratic Party. As I'll point out in this book, however, working-class white men were more than happy to receive government assistance for decades; they didn't denounce welfare until it was extended to Black, Hispanic, and female citizens.

President Lyndon Johnson put it best when he said, "If you can convince the lowest white man he's better than the best colored man, he won't notice you're picking his pocket. Hell, give him somebody to look down on, and he'll empty his pockets for you."

Upward comparisons can be equally toxic.

Throughout the farm crisis of the 1980s, depressed farmers were constantly comparing their failures with the success of their fathers and grandfathers, rarely acknowledging that they were just as good at growing crops and raising livestock but the value of those items had plummeted, along with the value of their land, while the cost of production had skyrocketed. My generation of working-class millennials do the same thing when comparing themselves with their parents and grandparents, who went to college for a few thousand dollars (if that), bought a house for twenty grand, and could raise a family on a single income while Mom stayed home to raise the kids and ensure her husband had all he needed for the day's work ahead.

I was born in 1982, just as this dark cloud began to fall over America.

My parents had three kids before they were twenty-one and lacked the historical perspective to see how different their game was from the one their parents played. They were promised riches by our church, a robust economy by the Reagan administration, and were told they had only themselves to blame if it didn't work out.

As the pickup truck I'm riding in pulls through Mason City on its way to neighboring Clear Lake, I see a giant billboard that reads "Smile, Your Mother Chose Life!" I stare at that sign for a long time and continue to think about it as we enter downtown.

The inspiration for the iconic Broadway play *The Music Man,* Mason City has worked hard to preserve its early-twentieth-century aesthetic and (as with Clear Lake and Buddy Holly) cash in on its pop-culture relevance. Driving through town, I see a mural of the film painted across a water tower. Sculptures of musical instruments are peppered throughout downtown, and the local Hardee's hosts a kind of mini-exhibit featuring actual props, costumes, and posters from the film. The childhood home of Meredith Willson, author and composer of *The Music Man,* has even been preserved as it was during his boyhood in the early twentieth century.

Each spring, Mason City hosts the North Iowa Band Festival, a parade consisting exclusively of marching bands from around the area. Everywhere you turn is yet another tribute to *The Music Man,* one of the last vestiges of regional culture in Mason City—even though it's ultimately a story about how gullible its citizens are.

In case you somehow never saw (or performed in) one of the millions of high-school performances of this musical, or saw the 1962 film or one of the stage or television productions starring Matthew Broderick, Hugh Jackman, or Brian Cox, *The Music Man* is a satirical play about small-town fears of urban vice, and the fast-talking con artist who knows just how to exploit them. (*The Simpsons'* episode "Marge vs. the Monorail" was a loving tribute to this musical.)

The story opens with a group of traveling salesmen on a train, all of them moaning about how the changing landscape of cars, travel, and mass commerce is putting them out of business. And then one of them tells the story of Professor Harold Hill, a prosperous salesman who doesn't worry about any of these changes, because he is selling a product that has remained in demand throughout history: the fear of sin and the purchase of salvation.

Professor Hill arrives in River City (Willson didn't dare use the name Mason City, erroneously believing his hometown would hate him for the play), and meets up with an old partner in crime who's been hiding out in this tiny hamlet of North Iowa. Attempting to devise a grift, he asks his buddy what kind of trouble the town is in.

"River City ain't in any trouble," he says.

"Then we'll have to create some. We must create a desperate need in your town for a boys' band," he says, explaining his con of swindling parents of their money with the promise of training their wayward children in the wholesome art of the marching band. Every time Hill has collected their money, he skips town before anyone realizes he "doesn't know a bass drum from a pipe organ."

With a twinkle in his eye, Hill notices River City is just, at that very moment, getting its first pool table delivered, a relatively new gaming device the folks are unfamiliar with.

As he shimmies to the town square, Hill pulls a shopkeeper, a cyclist, and a mother with children his way, saying, "Either you are closing your eyes to a situation you do not wish to acknowledge, or you are not aware of the caliber of disaster indicated by the presence of a pool table in your community!"

The Music Man then launches into a litany of horrors that this new pool table is about to inflict on their wholesome little town: first, smoking, then cursing, then drinking, and before they know it, their daughters will become harlots and their sons hard-nosed gamblers, dancing to (gasp!) ragtime music!

Mothers in the crowd clutch their children tight at the thought of losing them to big-city sin.

"Ya surely got trouble!" Professor Hill shouts. "Trouble with a capital T!"

"Trouble!" the crowd gasps in return.

By the time I was born, hysteria about a pool table coming to town seemed laughably charming, allowing us to watch *The Music Man* without seeing ourselves in the allegory. But the trend of fast-talking grifters stirring up fear that big-city hedonists (or immigrants) would threaten the sober sanctity of Smalltown, U.S.A., was as alive as ever. Only instead of traveling salesmen it was politically charged televangelists, and instead of billiards it was drug dealers, welfare queens, crack babies, heavy metal, evolution, gay weddings, and Planned Parenthood.

One of my dad's favorite Bible verses is Ecclesiastes 1:9, which says, "What has been will be again, what has been done will be done again; there is nothing new under the sun."

This is certainly the case when it comes to the *Music Man* grifts of the Christian right.

The Satanic Panic I grew up with in the 1980s (the belief that preschools and day-care centers around the nation were ritualistically abusing, murdering, and eating children, using drugs and heavy metal as supernatural weapons of hypnosis and memory erasure) has returned today as the "QAnon conspiracy theory," the belief that Donald Trump is fighting a cabal of Satanic pedophiles that make up Democratic Party leadership (along with Tom Hanks, Bill Gates, and a few others) and control the world's economy. As absurd as this may sound to some, according to the nonpartisan Public Religion Research Institute it's a belief that was held by 26 percent of the Republican Party in 2022. The QAnon conspiracy was the primary motivating force for some of the January 6 insurrectionists, who believed they would be liberating captive children from the U.S. Capitol.

The last time I came to Iowa, in 2020, driving from Denver while listening to an evangelical talk-radio station (as I often do when traveling through the Bible Belt, keeping up with the latest trends in the Christian right), the host was answering questions about the COVID vaccine, and multiple callers asked some version of "Could this be the Mark of the Beast?"

For those unfamiliar, the Mark of the Beast is an integral part of the Armageddon story prophesied in the Bible. According to most evangelicals today (though this theology is disputed to varying degrees by other branches of Christianity), the book of Revelation says that one day God will release a horror of wars, famine, and disease across the globe in a seven-year period known as the Tribulation. Following this, the Antichrist will rise to power under the guise of peace, creating a one-world government with a singular, unified currency. All financial transactions will be conducted via the Mark of the Beast, tattooed on everyone's forehead or right hand.

This is, essentially, what has been used to fuel evangelical fears about communism, and government power in general.

As we drive out of Mason City and into Clear Lake, I see various groups of people decorating floats for the annual Fourth of July parade. One of them boasts a large black silhouette of a U.S. soldier, rifle in hand, kneeling at the foot of a Christian cross. You might think that this would contradict the distrust of government felt in these communities, but the blending of faith and patriotism is ubiquitous on Independence Day in Clear Lake. As long as that patriotism is viewed through the lens of Christianity.

Though we never used the phrase "Christian nationalism" growing up, we firmly believed that America was founded to be an exclusively Protestant Christian nation, and that it was our job to protect and defend its Christian identity at the ballot box, in the culture wars, and possibly, one day, in a literal holy war.

Watching the January 6 riots on TV in 2021, I couldn't help but notice a galaxy of Christian flags in the crowd, alongside signs reading "JESUS IS MY SAVIOR, TRUMP IS MY PRESIDENT," "MAKE AMERICA GODLY AGAIN," and "GOD GUNS & TRUMP." I was instantly transported back to the nineties, when nearly every day my friends and I were tasked with "reclaiming this nation for Christ."

As a teenager, I painted the slogan "God's Got an Army" across my bedroom wall in giant camouflage letters, an homage to the song of the same name by the evangelical pop star Carman. Watching the MAGA insurrectionists storming the Capitol on TV, I knew what it felt like to believe Satan was plotting a coup against America, to feel duty-bound to stop him, by deadly force if necessary.

The January 6 rioter William McCall Calhoun, Jr., who would later be convicted for his actions that day, had proudly posted on social media that he was a part of the group that had kicked in the door of Nancy Pelosi's office, claiming that the crowd would have torn her "into little pieces" had they found her there. He had also proclaimed that "God is on Trump's side. God is not on the Democrats' side. And if patriots have to kill 60 million of these communists, it is God's will. Think ethnic cleansing but it's anti-communist cleansing."

On fire for God!

One of the most enduring images of that day is of one of the leaders of the riot, the forty-one-year-old construction worker Doug Jensen of Des Moines, Iowa, sporting a QAnon T-shirt, arms spread in a "Come at me, bro" gesture aimed at a Black police officer, Eugene Goodman, whom he then chased through the building. Before he was sentenced to five years in prison, Jensen's attorney said his client felt "deceived, recognizing that he bought into a pack of lies . . . a victim of numerous conspiracy theories that were being fed to him over the internet by a number of very clever people, who were uniquely equipped with slight, if any, moral or social consciousness."*

This thread of Christian nationalism is stronger than ever in Iowa, with Republican Governor Kim Reynolds—bolstered by many evangelical state legislators—ushering in draconian bans on abortion and on transgender health care for children, signing a bill allowing teachers to carry guns in school, and also permitting censorship of library materials deemed "sexually explicit." Suggesting that certain reading material is a threat to children's purity has been a staple of manipulative conservatives for generations. In *The Music Man*, the mayor's wife is constantly harassing the local librarian for pushing "dirty books" by authors like Chaucer, Balzac, and Rabelais on her daughter. The threat of literature in Willson's satirical musical is still alive in 2023,

---

* Both Calhoun and Jensen were pardoned when Trump took office in January 2025.

with Iowa diverting its public-education funding to private Christian schools, many of which pledge allegiance to a Christian flag, punish queer youth, and teach the same young Earth creationism that made up my science education as a child.

Over the last decade, Iowa voters have swung harder to the right than those in any other state, going from a six-point win for Obama in 2012 to an eight-point win for Trump in 2020 (which would then increase to a thirteen-point win for Trump in 2024). This is in part because Iowa has one of the worst "brain drains" in the nation, with 34 percent of young, educated professionals (who made up much of Iowa's Obama vote) leaving the state for metropolitan areas, while 75 percent of rural homeowners are of baby-boomer age. These aging Iowans are more likely to be evangelical and conservative, feel that America was better decades ago, and have an outsized influence on our federal government. Despite being only a fifth of the national population, states made up of rural voters get the same number of senators as states with far more citizens, leading to a greater number of presidential electors per capita.

This is how Republican presidential candidates have managed to lose the popular vote yet win the presidency (George W. Bush in 2000; Trump in 2016), by manipulating rural and small-town religious voters with whatever pool-table issue is animating them at the time.

A few months after my trip to Iowa, Donald Trump held a campaign rally at the North Iowa Events Center in Mason City, in the same building where I performed in my church's "Hell House" plays, playing a drug-addled teen dragged to Hell following an overdose. Speaking of undocumented immigrants, Trump roared, "They're sitting with your children in schools, and they don't even speak the language! They're occupying the hospital beds." Trump recently posted to his social-media site, Truth Social, "Under Crooked Joe Biden, Christians and Americans of faith are being persecuted like nothing this nation has ever seen before." And in nearby Sioux City, he warned in 2022 that the "Iowa way of life is under siege," by communism and the "indoctrination" of children with "twisted race and gender lunacy."

River City ain't in any trouble.

Then we'll have to create some.

Over the last few years, there have been several books, documentaries, and cable news specials about the sudden rise of Christian nationalism in America, with much head scratching about Donald Trump's role as pope of this revolution. But if this book is about anything, it's that the past is always prologue, that those fighting for an American theocracy today are merely the reboot of a tired franchise repeated in this country again and again throughout history.

There is nothing new under the sun.

"Thanks for the lift!" I say when my new friend drops me at the carnival downtown.

"God bless!" he replies, and speeds off in his Trumpmobile.

The smells of cotton candy and funnel cake fill my nose as I walk through the bright lights and Jock Jams of the Fourth of July carnival. I pass along another row of vendors selling Confederate flag wallets and "Trump Won!" beach blankets, before finally arriving at City Beach.

I take a seat in the sand, which is warm and packed with tourists.

Looking out at the water, I'm reminded of a presentation on Clear Lake history that captivated me in third grade, where we learned of the immigrants, trappers, and farmers who settled this land. There was an advertisement posted in national papers in the late 1850s in which pioneers wrote about the beauty of Clear Lake, attempting to draw people from the East Coast to come work this land, ignoring the pull of the California Gold Rush. "We leave to others more versed in sophistry the work of painting or writing fiction," the ad ran. "We only want first-class settlers in our village and county."

A local judge wrote a similar editorial at the time, in which he said, "This country is admirably adapted to all classes and communities, except for the profane loafer. To all but him we extend a cordial invitation to come and help settle up this fertile country."

Even in third grade, I knew they were talking about me, or at least a person like me. Despite being solidly working class, I've never fit the hypermasculine stereotype of the Midwestern laborer. Growing up, I often related to Bobby Hill, the chubby, weak, eccentric cartoon character from *King of the Hill*. Even though he was from Texas and

I was from Iowa, we were both outsiders in our own homes, unable to relate to the culture we were born into, and we often embarrassed anyone with the misfortune of being related to us.

Both of our worlds considered us "profane loafers" for our aversion to physical labor and preference for solitude, books, and creativity. Many of the pioneers who settled this town were in constant survival mode, a state their current counterparts would often return to in the economy of low-wage, disposable jobs.

No time for "profane loafers" interested in "painting or writing."

The culture I grew up in despised artists and academics, those who resided within their own minds, fueled by curiosity, gleefully pursuing new perspectives, new realities, disdainful of normality and established conventions.

In fact, we were taught to despise these people.

The "intellectual elites," as we called them, thought they were better than us—better than God, even—yet were empty of faith, and therefore useless at best (and evil at worst).

Looking back, I can't recall a single moment of accomplishment in my youth: no goals scored, no money earned, no good grades to celebrate. I think my parents longed to be proud of me; we just didn't live in a culture that valued anything I brought to the table.

Whether it was implied or directly said, I was taught from an early age that my authentic self (queer, creative, provocative) was unacceptable, that it was potentially evidence that Satan had taken possession of my little body. And though I've overcome a lot through therapy, rationality, and psychedelic drugs, the stains of religious trauma are very much with me. I suffer constant nightmares, sleepwalking, and a ubiquitous fear of the dark.

Still, I'm far happier today as an adult, having become everything they said I would if I left Iowa: an unmarried, childless, bisexual atheist with a vasectomy, hopped up on weed and the writings of Noam Chomsky, coming for *your* sons and daughters with my shameless ideas about unions, cooperative housing, and universal mental-health care.

·   ·   ·

"Hello, son," I hear a familiar voice say, and turn around to see my dad.

He's smiling in a way that warms my heart, standing over me on the beach with a menthol cigarette burning between his fingers.

My arms almost don't quite fit around him as we hug, and I'm surprised he got out of his car to come meet me on the beach. Dad had his fourth heart attack last spring, followed by quadruple bypass surgery. (He has so many stents in his heart, I often imagine it looking like a pincushion.) Between that and a knee replacement surgery the year before (along with diabetes, neuropathic pain, and high blood pressure), he's been even more sedentary than usual.

It's unsettling how heavy he's become. I typically come stay with him for a couple weeks whenever he has these surgeries, and I've become a bit of a nag, forcing him to get out of the house (or just his chair) and exercise his body a little each day, perhaps even eating some fresh fruits and vegetables. I often feel like the obnoxious, condescending liberal in these moments, as I do when disagreeing with his "mainstream media" conspiracy theories or dismissal of COVID as "just another strain of the flu." So I bite my tongue and try to enjoy this moment with my dad, knowing I may not have many more of them left.

"I have something for you," I tell him as we both get into the car.

"What do I owe you?" he says, cranking up the AC.

He thinks I'm talking about the cannabis products I've brought him from the legalized state of Colorado. But along with them I hand him a copy of my latest book, *Runner's High: How a Movement of Cannabis-Fueled Athletes Is Changing the Science of Sports.*[*] His eyes light up, and he squeezes my shoulder, telling me he's proud of me. "I saw you on ABC News," he says excitedly. "You looked so intelligent!"

"Look here," I say, reaching over and flipping to the dedication page.

"'To my father, Henry, who taught me to question everything,'" my dad recites, his voice breaking and eyes tearing. After lighting a joint,

---

[*] Even though I hated physical activity of any kind while living in Iowa, my life is now centered on running marathons along the trails of the Colorado Rockies.

he sets the book down in his lap, sighs, and looks out at the lake. "You know, some people see me as a failure because I never became rich like I said I would. And I'm still poor as shit, but I look at my children, and I feel like my life has been a success."

People are often surprised when they learn my dad is an evangelical conservative who smokes weed, because marijuana was often the pool-table issue of the nineties. Honestly, I forget that this is even shocking, having known *so many* believers with secret vices, who often find themselves in a room full of others with dark secrets of their own, while everyone thinks they're the only sinner in existence.

People often have the misconception that it was my parents who forced evangelical Christianity upon me. Though they were certainly devout believers in their teens and early twenties, their feverish idealism waned with age, just as I was becoming a teenage zealot. They retained their faith, but no longer centered their lives on the coming Apocalypse.

It's been well over a decade since my dad regularly attended church, and even longer since he's given a fuck what people think about his indulgences in sex, drugs, and food. In this way, he's like a cheery Roman at a Saturnalia fest, gleefully lapping up all the pleasures of life, perfectly aware of how little time he has left and perfectly fine with the choices he's made.

In so many other ways, though, he's still the partisan Rush Limbaugh fan he's always been.

"So—what is it you're looking for with these interviews you're doing here? Is this book just you looking for revenge against the church?"

"Absolutely not!" I say, taking a hit off the smoldering joint before handing it back to him. "I want this book to be like a Rorschach test, where everyone sees something different based on their perspective. I know what it's about, and I'm passionate about that, but I don't want to tell anyone what to think. Leonard Bernstein once said, 'A work of art does not answer questions, it provokes them; and its essential meaning is in the tension between the contradictory answers.'"

Though hearing myself quote a long-dead bisexual Jewish composer to make a point about journalism as art between tokes off a joint makes me wonder if I really am just a liberal caricature, and whether

I truly can set my emotional ego aside and achieve sincere objectivity when reporting on the Christian right.

My dad gives me a look that tells me he's thinking the same thing, and we both laugh. When I ask him where we should go to lunch, he says nothing's open because "no one wants to work anymore." This is the first of about eighteen thousand times I'll hear this phrase while visiting Iowa. I get an earful from him, and so many others, about how Biden's stimulus checks ruined our economy and made everyone lazy. Rarely do I hear anyone point out that the minimum-wage jobs at these establishments aren't enough to keep people in small-town Iowa—which is why the population has been steadily shrinking since I was a kid.

I want to point out to my dad that he's on disability and hasn't worked in years, and that if it weren't for Obamacare he would be looking at a health-care bill the size of Italy's GDP for all the lifesaving procedures he's had over the years.

Many of the same working-class conservatives who screamed about Obamacare being a microchip program, beta testing the Mark of the Beast, eventually enrolled, just as the libertarian icon Ayn Rand filed for Social Security—a program she'd railed against—in her golden years.

But I keep my mouth shut, just nod and listen. Partly because I don't want to prove him right that I'm a liberal journalist who parrots everything Rachel Maddow and Nancy Pelosi tell me to say . . . but also because he's my dad, and I love him.

I spent most of my childhood terrified of this man, and looking back, I know he made a lot of selfish decisions that caused a lot of pain to people who trusted him, but I can relate and connect with him on a level I've never neared with the rest of my family (and, similarly, I am one of the few people he's ever connected with in his life).

We smile at each other, and I feel my heart softening.

Suddenly I am confident that I can navigate the interviews ahead of me. I have the empathy, the curiosity, and the journalistic skills to understand (without judgment or cynicism) why my people behave the way they do. If I can go back far enough, I can trace the steps of how a community of poor farmers and laborers were dazzled by gen-

erations of Music Men, trading what little they had for the promise of
unending riches on Earth, the admiration of their peers and children,
a reclamation of the American government for Christ, and existential
bliss in Heaven.

I am grateful for growing up in a land of fireflies and cornfields,
instilling in me the principles of hard work and self-reliance, without
which I never would've been able to build a successful career in journalism, lacking as I was in education, money, or connections in the
industry. When I look at my dad, I think of him as a frightened child,
an overwhelmed father, a conflicted human, and I feel a deeper connection to my roots than I ever have as an adult.

But then, staring out at the lake, he says something that strikes fear
into my bones, shaking my newfound confidence that I am up to this
task:

"You know, with all of this socialism taking over America, I'm more
convinced than ever that we're living in end times. I believe we're on
the cusp of the wars of Tribulation, the period of a one-world government, and the Mark of the Beast. It's all coming, son, I'm more
convinced than ever."

My blood runs cold, and suddenly I'm five years old again, listening
to Dad tell us that we may soon have to abandon our house and live
in the wilderness, foraging for our food and building our own shelter.
The armies of the Antichrist will be hunting all remaining Christians,
forcing us to get "the Mark" or suffer torture and execution—but if we
accept the Mark of the Beast, God will eventually throw us into the
lake of fire for all eternity.

You will never escape this, because you don't deserve to, Caldonia says,
still speaking to me despite my two decades as an atheist.

At this moment, I am a terrified child, then an angry adult.

And, for the briefest second, I truly hate this man, this town, and
wish my mother had gotten an abortion.

Ya got trouble, my friend.

CHAPTER ONE

Turn and Face the Strange

2023

The right-wing icon William F. Buckley once said, "A conservative is someone who stands athwart history, yelling Stop."

Speaking as a liberal, I couldn't agree more.

I've been in Iowa for about a week now, spending most of my time in the windowless archives-room at the Mason City Public Library, sporting a jeweler's magnifying headband to read stacks of yellowing newspaper clippings. After the years I've spent reporting on the machinations of the Christian right today, it's easy to see the old adage "There is nothing new under the sun" come to life in the history of North Iowa.

Again and again, with every new advancement in society—be it technology, culture, science, geopolitics, or the empowerment of a repressed minority—there has always been some conservative organization yelling "Stop!"

It's a gorgeous summer afternoon, and I've taken a break from the library archives to ride my bike through downtown Mason City, which has retained its early-twentieth-century, *Music Man*–era charm, with antique lampposts, footbridges, and several homes and a hotel designed by Frank Lloyd Wright. After riding past a bank once robbed by John Dillinger, I turn onto Federal Avenue, a street that in 1925 hosted a parade of six hundred robed members of the Ku Klux Klan— led by the city commissioner—who were headed toward the "immigrant ghettos" on the north end of town.

The Klan visited Mason City regularly throughout the 1920s, hosting Fourth of July carnivals at the local fairgrounds, with clowns, contortionists, fireworks, a high-wire act, and a "Klan baby contest."

Of all the changes conservatives have been fighting against throughout American history, threats to the exclusive power of rich white Protestant men has been the most consistent. The Klan members of the 1920s were much more media-savvy than their nineteenth-century forebears, attacking jazz music, drug dealers, and women in makeup as threats to "Christian, family values" and "Americanism." Like the Klan before and after, they fought for white supremacy, though they packaged their message a bit more tactfully, recruiting not just racists but anyone concerned with the moral direction of the country when it came to booze, dancing, sexuality, and the secularizing of public schools.

Mason City was experiencing an economic boom at this time. Cement plants on the north end of town were outperforming any in the world, and the demand for labor was drawing thousands of Black Americans from the South, as well as immigrants from Mexico, Ireland, Greece, and as far away as India and Iceland, all of whom had set up their own little communities on the north end of town.

Just as Donald Trump would a century later, the Klan recruiters— dispatched to the Midwest to sniff out problems and offer themselves as a solution—convinced white laborers that these immigrants were a threat to their livelihood (and their women).

River City ain't in any trouble.

Then we'll have to create some.

Like Trump, they would tap into a nostalgia for the wholesomeness of the past, using the song "Old Time Religion" as their rallying cry. And, like Trump, they tapped into the ubiquitous fear of humiliation among working-class white men, who are so easily manipulated by the phrase "They're laughing at us."

In 1925, the biggest threat to the pride of white Christian nationalism was evolution.

The state of Tennessee had just enacted a ban against both the teaching of Darwin's theory and the disparagement of creationism in public schools, leading to one of America's most heavily publicized trials when the high-school science teacher John Scopes found himself jailed for his lesson plan. Journalists swarmed the city of Dayton, mocking the prosecution for claiming that the book of Genesis was a literal, scientific account of the Earth's creation. The newspapers branded it "The Scopes Monkey Trial": *Time* magazine called it "a cross between a circus and a holy war." Radio broadcasters cracked jokes, cartoonists mocked fundamentalists, and a trained monkey was set on the courthouse lawn to dance. The journalist H. L. Mencken was perhaps the most overtly cruel, calling defenders of the law "morons," "yokels," "primates," and "hillbillies."

These widely publicized attacks against rural Christians by liberal, atheist intellectuals from the big city were a neatly wrapped gift to Klansmen seeking recruits in the Midwest. They joined forces with prominent evangelists like Billy Sunday and Bob Jones, Sr., in decrying evolution as an existential threat to American morality.

A backlash ensued against the media, intellectuals, and the ACLU for providing Scopes's attorney, Clarence Darrow. They all became iconic villains in the eyes of evangelicals, and the backlash led to greater church attendance for the evangelists and more recruits for the KKK. As with Harold Hill's band uniforms, the Klan charged each new member sixteen dollars for a robe and a hood, giving the organization millions in revenue.

According to newspaper reports of the Klan's Mason City rallies, recruits were called to be "living sacrifices to God" in their efforts to protect white Christian power; to sing "Onward, Christian Soldiers" as they marched into the streets; set up burning crosses on lawns; harass Black-owned businesses; set off bombs; and kidnap the socialist speaker Ida Crouch-Hazlett, who was in town attempting to unionize workers on the north end.

As I'm riding my bike through Mason City in 2023, my heart breaks for the immigrants terrorized by the Klan in the name of Jesus. At the same time, I am filled with rage when I think of all the young men manipulated by the KKK into believing it was their Christian duty to don those white robes. Just as my heart breaks for the young men today whose low wages, mental-health issues, and bleak prospects have been exploited by Trump's MAGA movement to push them into harassing trans people or Black Lives Matter protesters.

And as I ride my bike up to a small, abandoned TV station in downtown Mason City, my mind takes me to the 2000 presidential election, back when I was one of these reactionary young men.

The logo for KIMT News 3 still hangs above the doors of this single-story building, even though the TV station moved to Rochester several years ago. I was a camera operator for the KIMT studio in the fall of 2000 (one of forty-five low-wage jobs I held in my teens and twenties), and just before showing up for work, I'd voted in my first presidential election—for George W. Bush. Standing on the sidewalk today, I can easily recall my feeling of righteous arrogance when I stood in the KIMT studio that election night, viewing my ballot for Bush as an exercise of my Christian faith, protecting America from the threat of sex-crazed liberals like Bill Clinton (whose vice-president, Al Gore, was actually the Democratic candidate, but our ire was for Slick Willy).

During his presidency, Bush would put a halt on stem-cell research, attempt to get creationism taught in public schools, inadvertently launch a holy war against Muslims, and convince America that gay marriage was an existential threat to Christianity.

There is nothing new under the sun.

As I will many times during the course of researching this book, I mourn the loss of my youth, spent as a political soldier awaiting the coming wars of the Apocalypse, manipulated by those who taught me to fear science, art, my own body, and anyone who didn't fit the mold of the white Protestant American, never realizing I was a disposable pawn in someone else's game.

I've ridden my bike to this former TV studio not to indulge in self-pity, however, but because, in the course of my research today, I discovered a fascinating story behind the construction of this building eighty-five years ago, a tale of *Music Man* grifts tapping into the existential anxieties of small-town puritans to pick their meager pockets.

It was built as a church.

Not a Catholic or mainline Protestant church, but a precursor to the evangelical megachurch, a nondenominational tourist attraction with breathtaking showmanship, state-of-the-art technology, and modern interior design. Though it may seem contradictory, conservative hucksters are just as likely to manipulate their flocks with the fear of falling behind in the modern world—to be dismissed as hillbillies or rednecks—as they are to prey on their fears of change.

Either way, they utilize the dread of humiliation.

The hypervigilance to combat change, or stay ahead of it.

And, just like the Klan or Professor Harold Hill, the traveling preacher behind this church rolled into Mason City with a message of fear and the promise of salvation, then parasitically drained this boom town of its economic momentum, stuffed his pockets with all he could carry, and headed off into the sunset.

1937

"The signs are everywhere, the day of the Lord is upon us!" Doctor of Divinity Burroughs Waltrip shouted to a packed crowd of Iowans at his tent revival, sweat dripping from his forehead as he brandished a worn Bible high in the air. "And how will you, good people of Mason City, greet the Lord on the day of his return? Will you be a sheep in his flock, or *a goat from Hell*?!"

"Amen!" replied one farmer.

"Preach it!" exclaimed another.

It was a sweltering August night under this white canvas tent. Crickets and cicadas harmonized in the dewy fields surrounding them, as fireflies lazily breathed their fluorescent glow in and out. The people crowded together on wooden benches under a string of lights, fanning themselves with the *End Is Near!* pamphlets they'd been handed when they walked in. The recently paved streets of Mason City had been getting busier every year, as the town began its journey from a quiet outpost for farmers to an urban destination. As the Great Depression gutted agriculture, downtown Mason City diversified its economy, drawing influence from the nearby metropolises of Chicago and Minneapolis, with jazz concerts, movie houses, bootleggers, theaters, and motels that rented by the hour. The Mason City resident Orville K. Snav was a pioneer of conceptual art, selling novelty products with no purpose beyond the satirical humor of their marketing (a precursor to postmodern consumerism like the "Pet Rock"). In 1935, the drag queen Miss Tillie Yensen was a downtown celebrity, getting paid to show up at parties and take pictures with local politicians (seventy years before Paris Hilton made a career of it).

Plenty of newcomers loved the hedonism that came with their new jobs at the quarries, while just as many farmers (a lot of them descendants of pioneers) resented the indecency and intellectualism that came with this economic boon.

The typically raucous downtown was conspicuously quiet that night, as all the energy of the city was drawn toward the tent revival that had been gaining steam all summer. Two good-looking young preachers had been shaking hands on the street corners all afternoon, promising faith healings and the light heart of a child to all who attended their services that night.

A flop of hair swung back and forth across Waltrip's sweaty brow like the pendulum of a clock as he proclaimed, "The agents of Satan are among us! One of the Devil's most effective ways of dealing with Christians is to use the shadow of doubt like a cloak to hide the wondrous jewels of God's mercy! That's the aim of the intellectuals, to hide God's miracles behind a shadow of science!"*

Behind Waltrip sat a captivating woman in a long white dress. Her hands rested primly across her lap, and her posture was tall, her downhome smile nurturing, yet Kathryn Kuhlman nonetheless radiated a primal magnetism that was slowly driving the crowd into a frenzy before she even said a word.

When Burroughs Waltrip suddenly broke into song—"Onward, Christian soldiers, marching as to war!"—this tent-full of typically stoic Midwesterners marched in place with comic abandon, swaying from side to side as they sang along loudly enough to be heard in the cornfields. With each stomp of Waltrip's foot, each seductive pronunciation of the words "Sanctified!" "Purified!" and "Come into

---

* Reports suggest that Burroughs Waltrip ran tent revivals for six weeks in Mason City in the summer of 1937, at the corner of Pennsylvania Avenue and 2nd Street. The quotes from Waltrip's sermons here are taken from his notes, the tracts from his ministry, and interviews with his family, all provided by the Mason City Public Library. Quotes later in the story are taken from the Mason City *Globe Gazette*.

me, Jesus!," they raised their hands, closed their eyes, and shouted, "Yes Lord!" "I am yours!" "Forgive my disobedience!"

Shooting an index finger at the crowd, the preacher warned, "Theology won't save you! Science won't save you! Only the redeeming blood of Jesus can cleanse the filth of sin!"

Though I can't be sure that my great-grandparents attended Waltrip's services, I do know that all branches of my family tree in the 1930s attended such tent revivals when they came through town. And I also know—thanks to their writings, and conversations I've had with those who knew them—that my maternal great-grandparents, Nora and Oskar, and my paternal great-grandparents, Giles and Rose, would have held opposing views of Burroughs Waltrip and Kathryn Kuhlman.

Nora and Oskar were quiet, hardworking Methodists who supported FDR's New Deal and pushed their children to work as hard at school as they did on the family farm. They were as prudent with their faith as with their finances, and wouldn't be easily seduced by the histrionics of Burroughs Waltrip—particularly his attacks on education.[*]

Universities were a common whipping boy for preachers like Waltrip.

Throughout the 1930s, evangelists unaffiliated with any larger church organization set up their own DIY touring revivals known as the "sawdust trail." They were like a religious circus, with loud, animated orators blending comedy, song and dance, and the drama of sin and death. In addition to spouting the typical end-times rhetoric and denouncing the communism of unionized labor, they were almost all "fundamentalists."

Essentially, a fundamentalist believes that the Bible is infallible from cover to cover, that every one of its 783,000(ish) words is the unimpeachable truth of God, and any confusion readers encounter is due to their shortcomings, not the Bible's.

---

[*] When their daughter, my grandma Marilyn, was seventeen, she took a forty-eight-hour train ride to Chicago, where she enrolled in Kendall College, even though she didn't know a soul there, practically unheard-of for a farmer's daughter in 1947 Iowa.

The "fundamentalist" moniker arose when Christian theologians teaching in seminaries at colleges and universities like Oberlin, Harvard, and Yale began taking a modernist view of the Bible, considering it through a historical lens, as they would any other ancient document. Though the seminaries championed the Bible's wisdom, and even its divinity, they also recognized its many contradictions, historical inaccuracies, and questionable authorship.

To pull on the thread of Biblical history—to acknowledge the absence of original texts, the endless revisions and translations, the differing textual interpretations resulting from the historical context for scripture—was felt by some as a challenge to their Christian identity, creating the necessity for the "fundamentalist" label. But for many progressive Christians, like Nora and Oskar, their relationship with God was defined by faith, and that faith was practiced by caring for humanity, not by clinging to the historical infallibility of scripture.

Since they weren't threatened by women's rights, or unions, or science, they weren't as susceptible to the perceived humiliation of being a Christian in the modern world.

My fraternal great-grandfather, Giles Hesse, was another matter.

When a red-faced Burroughs Waltrip leapt into the audience, pointed a finger eastward, and said, "*Those* learned men at universities, and *those* rebellious, doubting preachers who *mock* God's word, will surely meet a horrible end in the *flames of Hell*!," I imagine Giles would have nodded and smiled, pleasantly satisfied by the image of those arrogant know-it-alls getting what was coming to 'em.

By all accounts, Giles was not a man who smiled very often.

A stiff, hulking German, Giles spent his days working at the quarry and his nights getting drunk at the north-end roadhouses, often waking up in jail after a night of brawling. It didn't take much—a joke at his expense, a word he didn't understand, a less-than-patriotic quip about America—and he was off, swinging his fists like a pumping hay-baler.

But Giles saved the worst of it for his meek and doting wife, Rose, who would be hospitalized at the hands of her husband on more than one occasion. It wasn't uncommon for the doctors at Mercy Hospital to insist she stay longer than officially necessary, just to give her a safe space to heal.

My grandmother Doris remembers her father-in-law as a sadistic drunk with a noxious body odor, who was constantly trying to get her into bed. The only times she can recall him smiling were when he was inflicting pain, particularly on children. She says that he would often sneak up behind his grandson—my father, Henry—when he was a toddler and shout in his ear, throw dirt in his face, or pinch and twist the skin on his neck.

My dad would jump with terror or cry in pain, and Giles would laugh like an evil Santa Claus.

Despite his debauchery and ruthlessness, Giles took great pride in his Christianity, and was happy to debate any atheist with his fists (same for any pinko disrespecting Old Glory). While he had no love for overeducated scientists, Giles was enthralled with modern technology, particularly engineering. He subscribed to *Popular Mechanics*, worked as a welder in a tractor factory, and—with the help of his son, my grandpa Hank—built a steam-powered vehicle with multiple circular saws on the rear, able to travel to various construction sites.

That apparatus was assembled completely from scraps found at the local dump, but the *Globe Gazette* pronounced it "fully functional." Despite his best efforts, however, the Hesse & Son invention was never patented, or even put to much use as a local service. Giles rode it every year in the Fourth of July parade, with a large sign across the side reading "America Needs the Old Time Religion."

Like most of America, Giles was glued to the newspapers throughout the Scopes Monkey Trial in the summer of 1925, fuming when good Christian Americans were characterized as "Neanderthals" who were a few centuries behind the times. Much of the animosity between fundamentalists and "educated folks" during the trial was an extension of the eternal rift between North and South in America, with the relatively young Midwest still up for grabs.

Fortunately, preachers like Burroughs Waltrip had come to show them the way, to usher them into the modern era without their having to sacrifice their Christian faith.

"Do not be deceived!" Waltrip shouted to the crowd as the crippling summer sun began to sink, mercifully, into the horizon. "Those who practice evil companionship, they are chaff blown by the winds of the world and will meet a horrible end. Will you let the winds of the world control *you*?"

"No!" the crowd roared back.

"Are we going to let scientists or politicians replace God?"

"No!"

"Can we build an ark for those seeking righteousness before it's too late?"

"Yes!"

As gripping as Waltrip's Pentecostal showmanship was (leaping about, speaking in tongues, trembling when speaking of "the fires of Hell"), everyone left in their seats focused on the woman seated at the back of the stage, a calm eye at the center of the storm of this Holy Ghost revival. The piercing yet tender eyes, bright-red hair, and movie-star dimples of Kathryn Kuhlman had captivated audiences around the nation, starting in Denver, Colorado, where she'd built a church of her own with a large congregation before teaming up with Waltrip on the sawdust trail.

Kuhlman understood that her silence could be just as powerful as her words. Simply nodding along, and occasionally waving her arms in the air, she had the people of Mason City under her spell before she spoke a word. Waltrip smiled, letting a dramatic pause hang in the air before continuing.

"How many of you here tonight believe that the miracle heal-ings of the Bible are as available to us today just as they were back then, amen?"

"Amen!"

"Sister Kuhlman and I have seen God perform a lot of miracles, haven't we? Miracles that would make H. L. Mencken's wig spin!"

Kathryn Kuhlman nodded demurely, an amused smile curling up one side of her mouth.

"The educated men would tell you that miracles, that faith healings, are impossible. But God is as active in the lives of men today as he was in the time of Christ!"

"Amen!"

"Why, it was only two weeks ago, when I was preaching in Sister Kathryn Kuhlman's church in Denver, Colorado, that the Lord spoke to me, telling me, 'Burroughs Waltrip, I need you to go to Mason City, Iowa!' Now, I'd never even heard of Mason City, never even been to Iowa, but God told me 'Go, *go*, my son, protect these, my chosen people, keep their town pure, give them a sanctuary to worship me in, free from the sin of alcohol, evolution, and a corrupt government.' God told me to build a non-denominational worship center called The Radio Chapel, as smart as tomorrow's sunrise, that will bring people from miles around to marvel at its beauty, its grandeur, its purity. And its . . . air conditioning!"

The crowd got to their feet and cheered at this, having only recently learned of the new technology that could save them from the brutally humid Iowa summers.

"They call you yokels, rednecks, holy rollers!" Waltrip said, stumbling back on his heels in a way that made the crowd laugh. "But with this state-of-the-art sanctuary, you will see visitors from far and wide travel to your community, bringing money to spend in your restaurants, your markets, your local retailers, reviving North Iowa to the glory God intended!"

Having ended on this high note, Waltrip handed the reins over to Kathryn Kuhlman.

Standing tall, in a pleated white dress reaching down to her ankles, snug around the waist and chest, with the wind blowing through her red hair and flared sleeves like a Pentecostal Stevie Nicks, Kuhlman shone a beatific smile at the crowd, saying in a loud yet graceful voice, "Good people of Mason City, I know you and your families work hard, and your lives are not easy. Your bodies are full of pain, disease, degeneration, all of which come from the *pit . . . of . . . Hell!*"

Kuhlman stabbed the air with her Bible while pronouncing those last three words.

"In the Bible, Jesus healed the lepers, brought Lazarus back to life, and cast out demons that tortured the minds of the innocent, and I am here to tell you his power is *just as available today* as it was then! Satan has no real power over you, disease has no power over you, if you believe in the deepest regions of your heart that God is *real,* and make him your master!"

"Glory!"

In addition to evolution, modern medicine had become a theological conundrum for many fundamentalists in the early twentieth century. Part of God's curse against Eve for eating the forbidden fruit was
the pain of childbirth. The necessity of suffering is a constant theme
throughout the Bible, as is God cursing humans with disease, pain, and
death. But now, with morphine, vaccines, X-rays, anesthesia, and so
much more, humans seemed to be flouting God's prescription of pain.

For some, like the Christian Scientists and many fundamentalists,
all medical ailments were matters of the spirit realm, and even to visit
a hospital was a sign of weak faith. Instead, many sought miraculous
healings from the traveling preachers of the sawdust trail, who told
them they would only experience a miracle if their faith was sufficiently
strong. (And if no miracle arrived, there was likely a good reason.)

The line to get to Kathryn Kuhlman snaked around the inside of the
tent and out into the nearby field. Farmers with burns, broken bones,
and chronic back pain; housewives with arthritis, inflamed knees,
and migraines; children with infected cuts or impacted teeth; cancer
patients; polio sufferers; veterans ravaged by mustard gas—all awaited
the touch of Sister Kuhlman. Just before she began to pray over these
tortured bodies, Burroughs Waltrip approached the front of the stage
with three large apple-picking baskets in his hands. "I would like to
take this opportunity, before Sister Kuhlman begins the laying on of
hands, to give us all the chance to show our gratitude and obedience
to the Lord with a special offering, one that will raise the necessary
funds to build Radio Chapel. God's promises are given upon condition; there are conditions to healing, to salvation."

"That's right," Kuhlman said, "you must have faith to be healed."

Over the course of Kathryn Kuhlman's life, more than two million
people would claim to have experienced miracles by her hand.

However, several investigations failed to show evidence of even a
single verified miracle, and many cases had resulted in catastrophe.
One elderly woman with spinal cancer was told by Kuhlman to throw
away her cane and dance across the stage, only to have her spine collapse the next day, resulting in her death months later.

Kuhlman is reported to have rented hundreds of wheelchairs before
each of her revival services, a move that would later become standard

for faith-healing preachers. The justification for this was the epically long lines people would have to stand in before coming onstage: allowing those in pain to rest while they waited. When these believers were wheeled onto the stage, then leapt out of a wheelchair following the touch of Kuhlman's holy hands, it appeared to the audience that the lame were made to walk. Given the baskets circulating throughout the crowd—some tossing in nickels and dimes, others dropping whole money-clips, which landed heavily enough to be heard across the room—I can imagine my great-grandparents Nora and Oskar getting up and leaving the tent revival. Not because they didn't believe in the healing power of faith, but because they would have rejected Waltrip's implication that the more money these desperate people gave to his ministry, the more likely it was that God would heal them. I imagine that my great-grandmother Rose could have used some healing—the kind she was never afforded at home—but that Giles wouldn't have cared much for the idea of his wife being relieved of the pain he'd inflicted upon her.

I can imagine both couples leaving the service at the same time, Giles and Rose headed back to their home on the north end of Mason City, and Oskar and Nora to drive back to their farm thirty miles outside of town. Though they would not have realized it then, they represented a split that occurred in American Christianity in the twentieth century—the working-class, anti-communist fundamentalists versus the educated, progressive, mainline Protestants—a split that would have far-reaching consequences for generations to come.

I haven't encountered any evidence that Meredith Willson was inspired by the story of Burroughs Waltrip when he wrote *The Music Man* (by 1937, Willson had left Mason City for Hollywood, where he would write the score for Charlie Chaplin's Nazi satire, *The Great Dictator*). Still, it's impossible to overlook the similarities between the traveling preacher and the traveling salesman.

For starters, they were both complete frauds.

Just as Professor Hill would proudly present his boys' marching band, splendid in their uniforms with no idea how to play their instruments, Waltrip would wow the people of Mason City with the grand opening of Radio Chapel, though he didn't know the first thing about overcoming sin. Despite their railing against dancing, flirtation, immodest dress, and the sexual cauldron that was the back seat of an automobile, Waltrip and Kuhlman had been engaged in an extramarital affair for two years before they even arrived in Mason City.

Waltrip's affair with Kuhlman was an open secret to the rest of their ministry team—their separate rooms at the Hanford Hotel were, in fact, adjoining—and though this behavior was certainly frowned upon, their revivals were such a success that no one wanted to be responsible for launching a scandal that could bring down a house of God.

It would be another year before reporters at the Mason City *Globe Gazette* discovered that Waltrip was already married to a woman in Houston, Texas, and had abandoned her and their two sons five years earlier, skirting the court-ordered child-support payments owed to them and winding up in Denver, Colorado, where he met a beautiful woman captivating a packed church.

On the night of Radio Chapel's grand opening, Burroughs Waltrip stopped in the hallway outside his room at the Hanford Hotel, adjusting the tie of his wool herringbone suit. Seeing reporters from the *Globe Gazette* calling his name from down the hall, Waltrip growled to himself, then smiled brightly.

All five of the reporters had recently spoken with different people— both donors and church leaders—who had raised serious concerns about Radio Chapel's finances. The church itself was forty-five thousand dollars in debt. There were numerous unpaid bills to local contractors. And the family of an elderly man declared of unsound mind—Andrew Kaduce—had just filed suit against Waltrip for the two-thousand-dollar donation Waltrip had accepted from him.

Doctor of Divinity Waltrip slammed his fist into the antique desk in the hallway.

" 'Then they will deliver you to *Tribulation*, and will *kill* you, and you will be hated by all nations because of My name!,' " he said, according to the *Globe Gazette*, quoting the Gospel of Matthew, before storming out of the hotel and driving to the grand opening in his new Buick.

Every one of the seven hundred seats of Radio Chapel was filled, along with a small army of reporters standing in the back. A giant neon cross in the ceiling gave the sanctuary a celestial glow, while the silver-and-dark-blue drapes and mahogany opera chairs upholstered with silver leather filled the air with the smell of freshly minted success.

Backstage, a technician adjusted dials and cords, broadcasting Radio Chapel's debut sermon to audiences around the nation (hence the name of the church; radio broadcasts of preachers, once thought to be sacrilege, were becoming mainstream on the coasts).

Kathryn Kuhlman's trademark white dress with the billowing sleeves matched the ivory Steinway piano she played onstage next to a collection of white leather furniture, as she led the congregation in "Satan, Your Kingdom Must Come Down."

Multiple reports of the event stated that Kuhlman could be seen weeping throughout the service, desperate to keep her face turned away from the crowd, though few at the time knew she'd recently learned about Waltrip's secret family in Houston.

The full house sang along with Kuhlman, their voices amplified by the acoustics of the arched ceiling and the rich, powerful sound of the new piano. There wasn't a hymnal book in sight: the words were projected onto a screen that was hydraulically lowered from the ceiling. Everyone gasped when the curtains behind Kuhlman drew apart, revealing a baptismal pool with a mural of the Jordan River behind it.

More curtains parted, and a balcony appeared above the stage, holding a choir of forty singers dressed in pure white robes, who joined Kuhlman in "Old Time Religion."

The crowd laughed, applauded, and wiped away tears.

Just when they thought they'd seen it all, a head rose, emerging in the middle of the stage.

It was Burroughs Waltrip, seated before a glowing white electric Hammond organ, magically rising out of the stage floor on an unseen hydraulic elevator.

Waltrip stood to greet the crowd, waved and smiled, then suddenly collapsed to the ground and banged his head on the leg of Kuhlman's piano.

The music stopped, and Kathryn rushed to his side. When she had pulled him to his feet, she turned to the audience, shouting, "He's been fasting for *three days* in the hopes that this act of faith will bring the remaining ten thousand dollars we need for Radio Chapel!"

Two men approached Waltrip with a wheelchair and rolled him to the front of the stage, where he rebuked "the spirit of doubt in this house tonight!"

The room exploded, as if their baseball team had just scored a grand slam.

After detailing the attacks he and the good Christians of Mason City had endured at the hands of the godless media, and the ten thousand dollars Radio Chapel would soon need in order to survive, Waltrip pleaded for the audience to "give to the Lord tonight in the measure of your faith, which is your salvation."

Heavy bronze offering plates circulated through the crowd.

When Burroughs Waltrip and Kathryn Kuhlman left town in 1939 (Waltrip in his Buick Roadmaster, Kuhlman in a new Oldsmobile Coupe), they explained to their congregation that they'd be out raising funds for the Radio Chapel, returning as soon as they'd earned enough to cover the debt the church had incurred.

The audience was considerably slimmer than it had been during the grand opening six months earlier. The *Globe Gazette* and other papers had been relentless in their pursuit of dirt on Waltrip, which didn't require much digging.

In addition to the news of his family in Houston, it was also uncovered that Waltrip wasn't even a doctor of divinity (despite placing the "D.D." at the front of his name), just as *The Music Man*'s Professor Harold Hill had never attended that university in Gary, Indiana, he was always singing about.

Right before leaving, Waltrip took ownership of Radio Chapel out of his name, placing the property, and debt, into a corporation, and naming a local tire repairman as the new head of the church. Radio Chapel filed for bankruptcy soon after, and many businesses that had provided labor and materials to the operation, on credit, were never paid.

Several months after his departure from Mason City, the *Globe*

Gazette reported that Waltrip was discovered to be captivating audiences in a small town in Georgia, pitching the idea of building a modern, state-of-the-art, nondenominational worship center and tourist attraction.

Kathryn Kuhlman would divorce Waltrip in 1948, and would, in the years ahead, refuse to speak about the matter (once even denying she had married him at all). Though the scandal she suffered in Mason City would put her out of commission for a few years, by the 1960s Kuhlman had become the most famous female evangelist in America, building a multimedia empire around her "faith healing" ministry, which included the talk show *I Believe in Miracles*. The program aired on CBS every Sunday for a decade.

After spinning a few more grifts around the nation—he was last spotted at "a storefront church, conning old women out of their pension money," according to his son—Burroughs Waltrip would disappear completely, never to be heard from again. This was no easy feat, considering the number of people looking for their money back, their dreams to be fulfilled, or revenge to be tasted. To this day, there has never been a death certificate, or gravestone, for D. D. Burroughs Waltrip.

CHAPTER TWO

Unfortunate Son

1963

As my grandfather leaned over and opened the passenger door—
attempting to kick my six-year-old father, Henry, and my pregnant
grandmother out of the speeding pickup truck—the voice of Billy
Graham thundered from the radio, asking: "What is wrong with this
world?"

The truck was moving at sixty miles an hour down a deserted
Mason City farm road, and Henry could see the frozen gravel rushing
by inches beneath them. February winds blew gusts of snow into the
car as Grandma Doris gripped her son's little arm so tight his hand
turned numb.[*]

"The race problem, crime, a possible war in the Far East are all
symptoms, but what is the cause?" Graham—the most popular and
powerful evangelist in the nation—asked from the radio speakers.
"Well, the Bible says man's nature has a disease, and it's called sin."

Henry wondered what sins he'd committed to make his father not
want him anymore.

---

[*] My grandmother does not remember that Henry was in the car during this.
My dad, however, does recall being there, and multiple other sources at the
time recall hearing that he was in the car. The Billy Graham quotes are from a
sermon he preached that was broadcast on the radio at the time. Its appearance
in this scene is, admittedly, a storytelling embellishment, yet only a small one,
because Graham's sermons were often played in my grandparents' car.

Hank Hesse hadn't appeared to have any of his father Giles's sadistic impulses when Doris first met him when she was seventeen. Too young for World War II, Hank was an air-force pilot stationed in Greenland until 1957, when he returned home to Iowa to work in the John Deere factory.

Grandma Doris was working at Mercy Hospital when Hank came in following an accident at the factory. Though he was shy and insecure, he charmed her with stories of the glaciers, icebergs, mountains, and northern lights of Greenland. Doris had never left the state of Iowa, and had known little more than her parents' farm and a country schoolhouse until she was fifteen. When her parents moved into town, Doris was intimidated by the enormous public school and took the quite common route for many young women at the time, dropping out of school and becoming a nurse's aide.

After a courtship of only a few weeks, Doris and Hank were married in late 1957; a child (my father, Henry) was on the way almost immediately.

And that's when everything changed.

Hank worked long hours at the factory, then weekends at his uncle's farm. Afterward, he'd wet his whistle at one of his favorite taverns and rustle up some kind of adventure. Grandma Doris was no teetotaler, but had she known when nursing him at the hospital about Hank's proclivity for getting cross-eyed, she would've kept a professional distance.

Doris had spent her entire life surrounded by pathetic, drunken men.

Her grandfather died of liver cancer at a young age, and her father spent most of his time guzzling moonshine with a vagrant woman who lived at the dump. She once saw them together, swapping stories and singing songs, and felt resentful that he'd never been so free and jolly with his own family.

"My teenage brother would come home snot-licking drunk every night and pass out on the living-room floor," Grandma Doris recalled. "I'd get up to go to the bathroom and trip over him, scarin' the life out of me. Happened all the time."

At seventeen, she was lifting patients in and out of hospital beds all day, and would then care for a disabled aunt and haul drunken men off to bed every night. Hearing Hank's stories of adventure, Doris had hoped that marrying him would offer her a different life, one in which she wasn't so exhausted and silently infuriated all the time. Though she found a sense of purpose in caring for people in need, she hated the emotional repression it sometimes required.

I am told that my father was a profoundly fussy baby; his incessant, inconsolable screaming kept her awake around the clock. Meanwhile, Hank would sometimes not come home at all for days on end. When Doris called him at one of the taverns he frequented, a tipsy Hank would invite her and the baby down to the bar; he never understood her objection to the idea.

Years passed, and the two of them grew apart, yet the pregnancies continued, one after another. In addition to her four children, and numerous aging relatives depending on her, Doris also agreed to take in Hank's nephew, who'd been abandoned by his brother.

Hank was moody and defensive about his drinking, resenting Doris's pleas that he give up the booze and start attending AA meetings. He was just as unsatisfied with the promises of marriage and the American Dream as Doris, and during the year he'd been home from the air force had been on a quest to find the good life he had been sure awaited him.

Earlier that afternoon, before they had hopped into the truck to go to town, Doris had taken a phone call from a woman asking for Hank. The woman said she was Hank's fiancée and, after a little more conversation, revealed she was eight months pregnant with his baby.

After the call, the three of them had ridden in silence down the gravel road for half an hour before Doris turned to her husband and asked, "Are you starting another family across town?"

"What the hell are you talking about?" Hank snapped.

She calmly explained the phone call she'd just received. Suddenly the truck's accelerator was pressed to the floor, knocking all three of them against the seatbacks.

Without warning, Hank leaned over the two of them, opened the pickup's heavy, rusted door, and tried, literally, to kick his family out of his life.

His manure-stained boots smacked repeatedly at them both, but Doris clutched the handle of the open door with one hand, her six-year-old son in the other, while desperately anchoring her legs to the truck floor.

"God hates sin and will judge sin with the fierceness of his wrath!" Graham explained on the radio.

It was Doris who had tuned the radio to Graham's sermon when they first got into the truck. She was often trying to get Hank to listen to Billy Graham, a passive-aggressive move that filled him with an unspoken rage he could only repress for so long. At any given time, there were multiple stations across the dial broadcasting religious programming, Graham's being far and away the most popular and influential.

By 1963, Billy Graham was bigger than Jesus.

His revivals were selling out stadiums around the world, presidential candidates hungered for his endorsement, and he would go on to set a Gallup poll record for making the top-ten list of the "Most Admired Men in America" sixty-one times.

Grandma Doris was captivated by Graham's booming voice, his wavy blond hair, strong chin, and fierce blue eyes whenever his revivals appeared on television; she always wished her husband were home to watch the program and possibly become saved, from the bottle and from Hell. (Or, better yet, she wished she had a man like Graham—wholesome, charming, disciplined, and oh so confident—as her own husband.)

Like many Americans at the time, Hank had no trouble calling himself a Christian, even though he rarely attended church or made the practice the center of his life, and certainly never described himself in terms like "saved" or "born again." But the religious malaise in America was all about to change, in large part thanks to Billy Graham.

Before the Cold War, Graham was one of thousands of failed tent-revival preachers working the sawdust trail. But, as luck would have it, just before Graham launched an ambitious revival in Los Angeles, news broke that the Soviet Union had detonated its first nuclear weapon, and this was followed soon after by China's fall to Mao

Zedong's communist revolution. Never an intellectual or theologian, Graham had instead developed a message of patriotic optimism and vivid anti-communist rhetoric. Just as the nation was suffering collective apocalyptic anxiety, Graham was making headlines with his eloquent, comforting message about God's plan for our lives, the peace and hope of the born-again experience, and the clear binary of America's righteous capitalist system versus the atheistic communism of the USSR. The newspaper tycoon William Randolph Hearst was so taken with the preacher that he sent out a telegram to all his editors demanding that they "puff Graham."

The L.A. revival was scheduled to last three weeks. It went on for eight.

Almost overnight, Billy Graham was a household name, interviewed on Edward R. Murrow's celebrity program, *Person to Person,* and consulted on political shows like *Meet the Press.*

He soon partnered with President Eisenhower on a campaign to promote America as the most Christian nation in history, leading the president to sign legislation mandating that "In God We Trust" appear on all U.S. currency, and that "Under God" be added to the Pledge of Allegiance. The two helped turn the National Prayer Breakfast into a Washington institution, which eventually grew into one of the premier political rallies of the Christian right.

In the nineteenth century, the term "evangelical" was often synonymous with "liberal"—the "social gospel" of charity and social justice driving the abolitionist and women's suffrage movements—but in the twentieth century, evangelicals found themselves courted by industrialists of the hard right, aiming to undo the progressive gains of the FDR era.

The oil executive J. Howard Pew (the man behind Sunoco) teamed up with Billy Graham and Graham's father-in-law, L. Nelson Bell, to launch *Christianity Today,* a magazine that would grow to be a staple of every evangelical household in America. Both Pew and Bell despised FDR and saw the New Deal as a socialist takeover of America. The National Association of Evangelicals was formed as a counterpoint to progressive Christian organizations (and was similarly funded by wealthy industrialists), opposing civil-rights laws, national health care, and public education, while advocating for a "Christian amendment" to the Constitution stating "Jesus Is Lord" of all Americans.

By linking social issues with sin, and capitalism with Christianity, Graham reinforced the notion of the Protestant work ethic, a Calvinist belief that the economically prosperous had been blessed by God for their virtuous living and should be elevated to a place of righteous adoration by society.

At a time when postwar America was grappling not only with nuclear war but also with rock and roll, birth control, and *Playboy* magazine, Graham's ability to shape a moral narrative—and a corresponding political solution—was a welcome tranquilizer for a nation that no longer recognized itself.

Right and wrong, good and evil, were just as clear as black and white.

"I believe today that the battle is between communism and Christianity," Graham said in a 1952 speech. "And I believe the only way that we're going to win that battle is for America to turn back to God and back to Christ and back to the Bible at this hour! We need a revival!"

Following Graham's efforts, church attendance went from a record low of 49 percent in 1940 to 65 percent by 1960.

"When communism conquers a nation, it makes every man a slave. When Christianity conquers a nation, it makes every man a king," Graham preached through the radio, as Hank Hesse shouted "You lyin' bitch" at his wife and Henry was pulled back into the truck by his mother.

They never made it into town, and no one spoke on the drive home.

Henry and his mother got out of the car, but Hank remained behind the wheel, engine idling. A hot bolt of anxiety shot through Henry's stomach as he watched his father's pickup disappear into the sunset; it would never be seen again.

Henry forced a smile onto his face, and the two of them went inside, where his siblings and several neighbor kids were playing hide-and-seek in the tiny house. Later, Henry and his mother ate ice cream and watched *The Fugitive,* acting as if nothing had happened.

When I speak with those who knew him as a kid, my dad is often described as having been "a mama's boy," constantly clinging to his mother's leg everywhere they went. Following Hank's abandonment of his family, Henry was often reprimanded for wearing his heart on his sleeve, because he was "the man of the house now."

At six, he was considered a greater authority figure than his twenty-three-year-old mother. There was a lot of sewing-circle gossip about Doris, who was often called selfish for divorcing her husband. It wasn't Christian, it wasn't American, it just wasn't done, no matter the abuse or neglect a woman suffered. Following the publication of Betty Friedan's *The Feminine Mystique*—released the year of my grandparents' divorce—many reactionaries viewed a woman who divorced her husband as a wanton harlot, a gold digger, a man eater, possibly even a lesbian.

Doris gave up her rights to everything in that divorce, apart from her children.

They crashed on the floors and spare rooms of family members for a number of years throughout the 1960s, before eventually landing in their own small house on the south side of Mason City. In addition to Doris's work as a secretary and seamstress, she was paid by the state to foster unwanted children, most of whom had endured unspeakable trauma before entering my grandma's home. She was licensed to care for only one child at a time, but she never had fewer than three or four, and once cared for twelve in the two-bedroom house.

Just when it seemed the madness of their lives had begun to subside, a car accident hurled Doris's three-month-old son, my uncle John, into the windshield at fifty miles an hour. The accident led to a severe case of hydrocephalus, requiring regular draining of the fluid in his brain. Midnight trips to the emergency room became a common routine, and John's needs only intensified with time. At the age of three, he developed a fever of 107 degrees, leading to brain damage so severe that he would never be able to speak, walk, or even move enough to feed himself or communicate.

Doris knew he was still in there and loved him the same as any of her children.

As the eldest, my dad took on a great deal of John's care, changing his diapers, dressing him, and moving him every ten to fifteen minutes to prevent bedsores. He learned quickly that if you fed John too large a spoonful of his baby food, he could easily choke. My dad was warned that his brother could die at any time, for any reason, and every time he opened John's bedroom door, he half expected to confront his brother as a pale corpse with black lips, knowing it would have been his fault. Henry slept poorly most nights, nodding off in school the next day. So many dramatic life changes so quickly gave him a hypervigilance about safety, thinking of little else but money, keeping his brother alive and his mother happy, and getting through each night. (For whatever reason, my dad recalls being convinced that a man was living under his bed and would, at any moment, leap out and strangle him. So, each night, he slept with his hands on his neck.)

When she was married to an air-force veteran with a stable job at the John Deere factory, Doris had had the security that she could maintain a comfortable life for her family, perhaps even raise them to live better than she had. But with Hank nowhere to be found, having fled the state to avoid paying court-mandated child support, she was on her own with very few options.

The American economy was at its strongest during the 1960s, but many of the working-class victories of the progressive era were given to men with union jobs, who would, presumably, pass those benefits along to their families. Jobs performed by women and minorities (restaurant services, housekeepers, field workers), on the other hand, were exempt from these benefits.

In an age where a woman needed a husband to get a bank account, a home loan, a credit card, or even an apartment, a father's abandonment of his family meant more than just the absence of a strong male role model. It meant being left behind economically, labeled with the most scandalous of scarlet letters: a single mother on welfare.

"Nobody wants to work anymore," Henry often overheard retired farmers say at the grocery store, eyeing his mother as she paid with food stamps, even though many of those men were the recipients of government aid in a variety of forms. Only a few generations earlier, their (and my) European ancestors were given large swaths of farmland— along with tools, low-interest loans, and education in farming—across the Midwest via the Homestead Act, a government program to build "America's Breadbasket." Throughout the Great Depression, farmers were given exceptional lines of credit, massive infrastructure projects, and enormous subsidies (many of which continue to this day); at times, they were even paid *not to farm* (with the aim of stabilizing the price of food).

The white working class had loved FDR and his New Deal. They were delighted by government programs to feed the hungry, educate children, hire out-of-work men to build up American infrastructure, and create public services like parks, public amphitheaters, and swimming pools. That is, until people of color wanted in on the deal. Then, all of a sudden, it was "un-American," defying the rugged individualism that made this country great.

The Civil Rights Movement—which, on the whole, was seeking access for people of color to the same economic and social opportunities as white people—was accused of being a communist plot almost from the beginning. These were not "real Americans," but "outside agitators," who were ungrateful for all the opportunities for work and prosperity that surrounded them.

People of color ascending the socioeconomic ladder were viewed as a threat to white people in power for many reasons, one of them being they undercut the message to working-class white people that they were doing better than those Black families down the road, and shouldn't complain about their wages or working conditions.

From then on, low-income white people in need of government assistance were viewed as lazy and trashy. This sentiment even bled into the lyrics of country music songs, a medium that, though built on the progressive movement of workers' rights in the 1930s, had since been consumed by the uber-patriotic messaging of the hard right. On Henry's twelfth birthday, in 1970, two of the most popular songs in his neighborhood were Merle Haggard's "Workin' Man Blues" and Guy Drake's "Welfare Cadillac." The former is the tale of a man with "nine kids and a wife" that champions the virtues of grueling labor, proudly declaring, "I ain't never been on welfare, and that's one place I won't be, / 'Cause I'll be *working*."

"Welfare Cadillac" ups the ante on this narrative, which is told from the perspective of a man living in a dilapidated shack with *ten* kids. Only, instead of working hard, like Merle Haggard, this fictional character boasts that his rent and his children's lunches are paid for by the government, which is also raining so much cash down on him that he's bought a Cadillac for himself and one for his wife. So why should he work?

It was the birth of the trailer-trash trope, the hillbilly seeking a handout, nothing like the rugged individualist heroes, such as Gary Cooper or Ronald Reagan, in the Westerns my dad watched at the drive-in theater, bathing himself in the myth of the lone rider making his fortune on the prairie, an archetype that would one day morph into the fantasy of the American Dream.*

In working-class memoirs, people often say something like "We didn't know we were poor, because everyone else was." That was not the case with Henry. Mason City was full of tycoons who ran the meatpacking plants, factories, and construction crews. Just next door in Clear Lake, millionaires had summer homes on the water (Clark Gable even vacationed there shortly after filming *Gone with the Wind*), leading to the colloquial slogan "Clear Lake: The Hamptons of Mason City."

Brand-new cars filled the streets, teenagers crowded the record shops, and everyone's clothes seemed recently purchased from one of the department stores downtown—unlike Henry's, which were sewn by his mother.

My father's handmade clothing, bad haircut, and government-issued lunch card (a bright blue, contrasted with the red ones given to the children of hardworking parents who paid for their lunches with actual money) made him a target for other kids in school. Once, while being chased home by a group of older teenage boys—who were chucking clumps of mud at his head, chanting, "Henry Handout! Henry Handout! Why'd yer daddy leave ya, Henry Handout?"—the twelve-year-old suddenly stopped a block away from home, unable to soothe the pressure cooker of rage boiling within him. Henry has no memory of what happened after that, but was told later that he lunged

* The true story of how the West was established—via Chinese immigrants who would work and die without recognition as they built the railroads that linked the nation's commerce—inspired far less patriotism.

at one of the older boys like a rabid mountain lion and punched him relentlessly until he was pulled away, bucking and grunting wildly.

Later that winter, Henry contracted mono and spent six weeks in crippling exhaustion on the couch, absorbing hours of television while eating ice cream in his pajamas. He watched game shows each morning—and lottery winners each evening—with relentless wonder, fantasizing about winning his family a washer and dryer, a new car, an exotic vacation, or a treasure chest brimming with cash.

Then maybe his father would come back.

And his mother would smile again.

For years Henry had dutifully watched *The Adventures of Ozzie and Harriet,* and he often longed to crawl through the TV screen, into a world of nuclear-family abundance, where Ozzie instructed Ricky Nelson on how to be a strong, hardworking man, and Harriet comforted him through each confusing passage of adolescence.

Everything made sense on the other side of that TV screen. The distinction between right and wrong, poverty and prosperity, was clearly understood, like a fork in the road, and it was only a simple matter of choosing one over the other.

After watching too much TV, he chastised himself for being lazy and went back to the work of caring for his disabled brother, his two younger siblings, his mother, and a revolving door of foster children. When this work left him unable to think or feel, he'd return to the television with a bowl of ice cream, teetering between self-loathing and dissociation.

Henry found a new, considerably more insidious form of escapism when a foster boy five years his senior instructed him on the pleasures his body was capable of with proper stimulation. The seventeen-year-old boy demonstrated this for Henry first on himself, then on him, with multiple variations of hand and mouth application. The older boy threatened him with violence if he ever told, forever associating this primal craving with shame and secrecy. Henry engaged in this practice multiple times a day, hating himself all the more each time and vowing that he'd never succumb to the sinful act again. But the larger his shame and self-loathing grew, the more essential, and downright addictive, the practice became.

God hates sin and will judge sin with the fierceness of his wrath!

You're a disgusting, poor, filthy loser, a growing voice inside of Henry told him, the same bully of self-loathing he'd one day pass along to his son. *No one else does this. They save it for marriage. It's no wonder your father left and you have no friends at school.*

Henry was confused.

Henry yearned to be an adult.

He wanted to understand what it meant to be "the man of the house."

He wanted to get a job so he would no longer be a lazy commie on welfare. He wanted to have a family of his own, one that would never leave the way his father had left him.

1976

When Henry graduated from high school at seventeen—wearing a corduroy suit stitched by his mother—there was never any conversation about his going to college. In the late 1970s, North Iowa was chock-full of labor jobs that paid enough to provide for an entire family.

After working as a farmhand for the summer—during which he was introduced to marijuana by a co-worker, then remained constantly stoned for the next two years—Henry got a job at the local Winnebago factory. On his eighteenth birthday, he moved into the first house of his own, a rental on the north end, practically hyperventilating with joy the closer he came to building a family that could soothe his anxious spirit.

Like most working-class men, Henry didn't often reflect on his feelings.

So, when the crippling loneliness of living alone, disconnected from the soothing voice of his mother, created an intolerable rumble of panic in his gut, Henry just lit another joint and asked for overtime hours at work. At home, he played his stoner-rock albums at full volume—Alice Cooper, Led Zeppelin, Foghat—to push away the dreadful silence, the sense that he could die in this house and no one would know.

He grew his hair long and shaggy, letting his bangs hang down over his eyes like John Fogerty of Creedence Clearwater Revival (who, with his freckles and gap in his front teeth, my dad could have played in a CCR cover band), and wore the same jean jacket and stained bell-bottoms like a uniform. He dabbled with cocaine, speed, and acid (though he hated alcohol, because it reminded him of his estranged father), but cannabis was the best salve for his frayed nerves.

When he landed his first girlfriend, a Mexican immigrant who also worked at the factory, all of his childhood neurosis—the terror of abandonment, the desperate craving for validation—was poured into her lap. He was intimidated by her family, who mocked his neediness and awkward stoner vibe, and one night, while they were drinking at a bar after their shift was over, she ended things, as delicately as possible.

Henry humiliated himself with desperate sobbing and pleading; he felt his whole world crumbling, just like the day his dad left.

When he left the bar, Henry lit a joint and walked through downtown Mason City. A drizzle of rain began to fall, and he pulled the collar of his jean jacket up around his joint. It was a Friday night, and downtown was packed full of laborers eager to blow their paychecks. He passed an old warehouse and heard the muffled sounds of a live band playing a cover of George Harrison's "My Sweet Lord." Standing there for a moment, he saw a handwritten sign in a window on the building's second floor that read "Good News Center."

As he walked up the steps along the side of the building—taking one last hit of his joint before stubbing it out on the railing—he noticed the singer had changed the lyrics of Harrison's song from "Hare Krishna" to "Jesus Christ," and "Hare Rama" to "Holy Spirit."

It was cold in the giant warehouse space, and Henry shook the rain off his jacket as he took a look around. The room was full of teenage kids dressed like they were headed for a Doobie Brothers concert, most of them sitting or lying casually across the dusty floor, except for the handful of musicians standing on a makeshift stage.

Speaking of, they sounded *really* good.

He assumed that this was some kind of squat, that he could probably find some heroin here if he was interested. But then he saw tables with coffee, water, sandwiches, and fruit, a large "FREE" sign next to them.

Another table was loaded with pamphlets, books, and vinyl records for bands he'd never heard of: Larry Norman? 2nd Chapter of Acts? Keith Green? Children of the Day? Who the hell were these people?

Henry had spent a great deal of time in record stores the last few years, but had never heard of a single band in this LP collection.

The scene looked familiar in so many ways, reminding him of parties and concerts he'd been to; the music was loud; everyone looked playful and un-self-conscious; some were dancing, some grooving, and everyone smiling. But there wasn't a bottle, bong, or bag of pills in sight. It slowly dawned on Henry that these counterculture teenagers were all stone-cold sober.

A pale kid around his age sporting a ginger Afro the size of a beach ball approached Henry, saying "Welcome, brother!" and gave him a strong hug. Typically, Henry flinched when touched, but for whatever reason, he embraced this stranger right back, even held him tighter, and was unable to stop himself from weeping.

"Hey, man, that's okay," the pale kid said. "We all know how you feel."

With that, Henry pulled the boy closer and cried even louder, attracting two girls and another guy his way. They all wrapped their arms around him, whispering something Henry couldn't understand, something that almost sounded like a different language. But he didn't care, as long as they kept holding him, kept seeing him.

He didn't know if this embrace lasted a few seconds or a few minutes, but when they pulled away—much to Henry's reluctance—he saw they were all crying, too. But they were smiling, crying tears of joy.

Grasping his shoulders tightly, looking deep into his eyes without blinking, the man with the ginger Afro asked, "Tell me, brother, have you heard the Good News of Jesus Christ?"

CHAPTER THREE

Get Your Jesus Freak On

1977

As Janet Chastain sat with her parents, watching Jimmy Carter's inauguration on the living-room TV, she wanted to scream.

It wasn't that she was unhappy that Carter—America's first evangelical president—was being sworn in on his old family Bible. At sixteen, Janet was too young to vote for him, but she had volunteered on Carter's campaign, canvassing her neighborhood for the Democratic nominee. Her parents were old-school Democrats, raised on farms saved by FDR's Agricultural Adjustment Act, and were proud to now have a "social gospel" Christian in the White House. Which was part of the reason Janet (my future mother) had volunteered for him.

Otherwise, she felt invisible much of the time.

The result of an unplanned pregnancy, born several years after her three older siblings, Janet had always felt disconnected from the momentum of her family. They'd all grown up on the family farm, which meant a hard life of round-the-clock labor and no indoor plumbing. She was only an infant when her father sold the farm to his brother in 1960 and moved them into a house on the north end of Mason City.

While generations of Chastain families kept struggling as farmers, their new family business of selling farm machinery and repairing silos did very well. Midwestern agriculture played an increasing role in global trade and U.S. foreign policy, so small family farms were encouraged by Nixon's secretary of agriculture to "get big or get out" and "plant fence row to fence row." Farmers were up to the task, because the value of their land was skyrocketing, and many bankers encouraged them to take on large amounts of debt to increase the size of their operations (a move that would come back to haunt them during the farm crisis of the 1980s).

With her family business in high demand, Janet's middle-class childhood provided her with a level of comfort and security never known to her parents or older siblings. Consequently, she was dismissed as spoiled and undeserving of attention by her brothers and sister, who were entering high school, the army, and parenthood, respectively, before she'd reached adolescence. They often accused her of being "too much," of exhausting them with her incessant questions, her need to drill down into every subject, analyzing all sides of an issue until there was no room for a single, coherent perspective.

On the other hand, what made her an obnoxious little sister served her well in school.

Janet's mother, Marilyn, was deeply insecure about having never finished college herself, and—newly flush with cash—offered to pay for four years of her children's higher education (which cost, on average, $740 in the late 1970s). Marilyn had attended one year of a Methodist college in Chicago in 1947, and another year at Waldorf University in Iowa, but marriage, farming, and motherhood prevented her from finishing. And, one after another, her children followed the same path of completing one or two years of college before dropping out and launching families of their own.

She viewed Janet as her last chance for academic salvation and forbade her to engage in anything not related to school or church, and even gave her a hearty allowance so she wouldn't be distracted by a part-time job. Grateful to have, finally, a morsel of attention (even if it was anxiety-fueled discipline with little positive reinforcement), Janet plunged herself into academia, developing an insatiable hunger for a wide range of topics.

"She was into everything," her childhood best friend would tell me, years later. "Speech Club, Forensics League, Foreign Exchange Club, she was in plays, very social—just wicked smart. She picked up on things so quickly, much faster than anyone else."

On the debate team, Janet found deep satisfaction in being able to argue two sides of the same issue, bathing in the nuance of complex affairs like prison reform or a one-world government.

At fifteen, she learned fluent Spanish and traveled to Argentina for a three-month exchange program; her trip happened to coincide with the 1976 right-wing coup d'état that ousted Isabel Perón, which gave her a visceral lesson in the fragility of democracy, the threat of economic inflation, and the fine line between revolution and genocide. As challenging and treacherous as international politics could be, Janet didn't want to return to North Iowa. She dreamed of one day being a U.S. diplomat, traveling the world, negotiating peace treaties, and boosting foreign economies. Janet couldn't wait to finish high school and climb the ladder of higher education, narrowing her choices to either the liberal arts Macalester College in Minneapolis or the University of Chicago—both renowned for their international relations programs.

She expected a certain level of excitement and curiosity from her family when she came home from Argentina, but her grown siblings were still sucking up all the air. One brother was getting married; the other, traumatized by his stint in Vietnam, announced that God had told him to become a Mormon. Her sister, married to an Open Bible pastor, accused this brother of sacrilege, saying he would burn in Hell while they watched from Heaven.

The one thing all three of her siblings did have in common was a gravitation away from the Democratic Party of their parents; instead, they embraced the "new right" of conservatives like William F. Buckley, Bill Bright, and Ronald Reagan, who they believed would have been president if he hadn't lost the nomination to Gerald Ford.

In the years to come, my grandmother would repeatedly ask the world what she had done to wind up with four children who voted Republican. For her and so many working-class Christian families in America, there was no better manifestation of the teachings of Jesus in government than FDR's Second Bill of Rights speech in 1944, promising economic justice through adequate wages, Social Security, education, housing, medical care, and restrictions against monopolies.

They were part of a long legacy of politically active Christian liberals, who throughout history have been at the forefront of progressive movements like the abolition of slavery, child-labor laws, women's suffrage, and civil rights.

The election of Jimmy Carter was the apex of leftist Christianity in America.

There were forty to fifty million evangelicals in America at the time, but most political journalists were unfamiliar with the term before that Democratic candidate, who would often refer to his "born again" spiritual experience. "The most important thing in my life is Jesus Christ," Carter said in a campaign speech. Carter was a Sunday-school teacher in the Southern Baptist Convention, a denomination that had favored Republican candidates since 1948, but almost 60 percent of which went for Carter in the '76 election.

As a teenager with a hyper-analytic mind, Janet gorged on as much information and ideas as she could get her hands on; she felt pulled in several directions at once, since her worldview refused to solidify into any one, singular identity.

Feminism was a provocative label at the time, but it felt right to Janet. Looking at the framed pictures of weddings and newborn children of her siblings, which were hung with pride above the TV, she thought it was profoundly unfair that a woman's only measure of success was marriage, kids, and housecleaning. Which made her all the more humiliated after she tried, and failed, at that very endeavor.

The previous fall, desperate for validation from her family, Janet had accepted a marriage proposal from her boyfriend—the son of an Assemblies of God pastor—only to have him break it off months later and marry her (now former) best friend.

After this, Janet felt a sense of embarrassment everywhere she went, even around total strangers—as if they all knew about her getting dumped, and were whispering to one another about all the ways she was unlovable. She began obsessively criticizing her appearance in the mirror, hating her baby-fat cheeks, her short legs, her flat, brown hair—everything that, she believed, had caused her fiancé to call off their engagement.

Naturally, her mother was relieved at the breakup, not only because she was adamant that Janet get her four-year college degree before marriage, but because she hated the Assemblies of God Church. Hers was a Methodist, progressive family, and they all viewed the Pentecostal AG Church as politically conservative, as well as given to the bizarre rituals of speaking in tongues and falling to the floor. Also, for many young people in the late 1970s, Assemblies of God was usually the first church they'd attended that incorporated rock music, along with modern fashion and language, into their services.

While her classmates snuck out of the house to do drugs or have sex, Janet snuck out to attend the AG youth group. Even now—as Aretha Franklin sang "God Bless America" at the inauguration—Janet disguised a copy of *Time* magazine within her biology textbook, so her mother wouldn't see what she was reading. The cover image of the magazine looked like a poster from a Haight-Ashbury concert, full of clouds and psychedelic colors. "The Jesus Revolution," read the headline, above a picture of the man himself, neither white nor olive-skinned, but fluorescent pink. The story about a wave of California hippies who had renounced drugs and were getting high on Christ was five years old, but, like most trends that begin on the coasts and slowly work their way to the Midwest, the Jesus Revolution had finally come to Mason City, Iowa.

She'd been given the magazine by a friend from the AG youth group, who'd recently moved to Iowa from Los Angeles, where she'd attended Calvary Chapel, the Pentecostal church that was the epicenter of this new Christian-rock scene. In the last few months, Janet had been pressing her friends at AG for any information they had on the born-again hippies, obsessively writing down the names of books, bands, and lecturers for her to track down.

By the late 1960s, the counterculture generation spawned in California was becoming disillusioned with its own hedonism and in need of a reset. Between 1967 and 1971, over half a million young people left their homes to join experimental communities throughout California (captured in the melancholy Beatles song "She's Leaving Home" and Scott McKenzie's syrupy "San Francisco"). Many of them flourished, but others were hotbeds of drug addiction, poverty, disease, and the sexual abuse of young women. By 1971, Janis Joplin, Jim Morrison,

Jimi Hendrix, and Brian Jones had all died at the age of twenty-seven from drugs and alcohol. Charles Manson had turned the hippie identity into one of night-stalking terror. And at the Rolling Stones free concert outside San Francisco, the Hells Angels beat dozens of audience members with weighted pool cues before stabbing and beating one of them to death.

"So flower power didn't work," John Lennon said. "So what? We start again."

Whether it was Leonard Cohen and William Burroughs embracing Scientology, or Sammy Davis, Jr., and Jayne Mansfield joining the Church of Satan, there was a rich marketplace of spirituality for California bohemians. And, for many, the answer was Pentecostal Christianity.

Arguments abound as to who started what would come to be called "the Jesus Movement"—led by "Jesus People," or "Jesus Freaks" if you ask cynics like Hunter S. Thompson—but it can largely be traced back to two events: the recording of the song "I Wish We'd All Been Ready," and the acid trip of a gay, naked hippie who spoke to God.

Larry Norman was a struggling rock musician living in L.A., opening for A-list acts like The Who and Jimi Hendrix, when he struck upon an idea: Why not blend the feverish, apocalyptic messages of the Black Pentecostal Church he was raised in (despite being profoundly white, almost an albino) with modern rock music? After all, every rock-and-roll pioneer from the fifties—from Ray Charles and James Brown to Elvis Presley and Jerry Lee Lewis—stole his act from the wild Pentecostal services of his youth.

His debut album, *Upon This Rock,* didn't sell many copies and would lead to his getting dropped from Capitol Records in 1969, but would go down in history as the first Christian rock album. The album's macabre rapture anthem, "I Wish We'd All Been Ready," depicted the apocalypse of Revelation through a series of haunting vignettes set in the modern age. Not only would it become the "Blowin' in the Wind" of the Jesus Movement, but, decades later, the song would inspire a series of wildly successful Christian novels depicting the events of the Apocalypse, particularly the line "you've been left behind."

Janet had heard the song played almost every week at the AG youth group, and though she was as convinced as anyone that the end-times prophecies of Revelation were legitimate, she bristled when people would tie them to a specific date. Both in California and Iowa, many Jesus People were certain the events depicted in Larry Norman's song would occur in either 1981 or 1988. But, unlike most of them, Janet was a student of history, aware that every generation of Christians since the death of Jesus has had elaborate theories as to why his return was imminent.

In addition to Larry Norman, Janet had heard a lot of talk about Lonnie Frisbee, the handsome hippie prophet leading the Jesus Freaks of California into the promised land. Rumors of his sexual proclivities hadn't yet made the trip to Iowa.

Frisbee was a teenage runaway hiding out in San Francisco's flourishing gay scene, and it wasn't uncommon for him, high on LSD, to read aloud from the Bible to the men he'd just slept with. During a particularly rowdy acid trip, Frisbee wandered into the California desert, stripped naked, and demanded that God reveal himself. Frisbee recounts feeling bathed in warm light and then having had a vision of himself leading thousands of hippies into the Pacific Ocean to be baptized.

That prophecy materialized little more than a year later, as the street-preaching Frisbee launched the House of Miracles commune in Costa Mesa, alongside struggling preacher Chuck Smith of Calvary Chapel. Thanks to Frisbee, Smith's church went from a dozen retirees to thousands of barefoot believers. Calvary became the epicenter of the scene, launching Christian rock bands like Love Song and Children of the Day.

For years to come, Frisbee and Smith would baptize hundreds of converts every Sunday at Newport Beach.

"People tell me I look like Jesus," Frisbee said when appearing on Kathryn Kuhlman's TV show, *I Believe in Miracles*, referring to his long hair, the flowing fabrics and leather sandals he wore, and his beard, "and I can't think of anyone I'd rather look like."

This look wasn't relegated to the Jesus Movement scene. As any photo of John Lennon, Kenny Loggins, or Gregg Allman in the early seventies will attest, Jesus was one of the most influential forces in fashion at the time, as well as in pop culture.

Musicals like *Godspell* and *Jesus Christ Superstar* were dominating Broadway, and songs like The Doobie Brothers' "Jesus Is Just Alright" and Norman Greenbaum's "Spirit in the Sky" rebranded the stuffy, pious Jesus of their parents' generation into a groovy peace activist. The Christian hippies were even name-checked in the novelty country song, "Convoy," which spoke of "eleven long haired Friends of Jesus / In a Chartreuse microbus."

Frisbee's sexual behavior was somewhat of an open secret in the scene, but Calvary Chapel grew into an international organization (eventually blossoming into a network of eighteen hundred churches), and Frisbee was fired for being gay. He would die of AIDS in 1993, though initially the reported cause was a brain tumor.

The internal conflicts of the Jesus Movement weren't reported in the *Time* article Janet was reading, but in the second magazine she was given by her friend from California—an issue of *Life* magazine from 1972—the story of wealthy conservatives co-opting a movement of idealistic, DIY hippies was all there, if you read between the lines.

The cover read "The Great Jesus Rally in Dallas," and inside were pictures of a hundred thousand Christian hippies crowded into the Cotton Bowl Stadium. Many of them were holding their index fingers in the air, a popular gesture among Jesus People meaning "There's only one way to Heaven"—i.e., Jesus. (Fifty years later, it would become the salute of QAnon followers at political rallies.) Janet marveled at the size of the crowd in the pictures: the number of Jesus Freaks in Mason City could hardly fill a sanctuary. Though the event had taken place five years earlier, it felt more contemporary than anything in Janet's life.

The Explo '72 festival, a six-day conference of live music and lectures for young Christians, is known as the culmination of the Jesus Movement—even though they really had little to do with it. Acts like Children of the Day, Larry Norman, and Love Song would perform, but the event was organized by Billy Graham and Bill Bright's Campus Crusade for Christ, which preached the virtues of conservative Christianity to college students across the nation. Bright would go on to cofound the Alliance Defending Freedom, a right-wing legal advocacy group that would labor to end abortion access and LGBTQ rights.

"The Jesus Movement was certainly courted by conservatives, even though we didn't realize it at the time," remembers Marsha Stevens-Pino,* who performed at Explo '72 with her band, Children of the Day. (Stevens-Pino spoke with me over the phone in 2023.) "We were made to feel special, these kids who'd been disparaged by the media, and in our homes. We were outcasts, and now we were made to feel like we were on the inside of something. And Explo '72 was really a launching point for a lot of political people to cash in on us, because it was an election year and we were now of voting age."

Many conservative evangelists, like Jerry Falwell and Jimmy Swaggart, denounced Christian rock, but Billy Graham saw Explo '72 as an opportunity to evangelize to young people about the dangers of sex and drugs, and why America is the greatest country on Earth. He called it "a religious Woodstock," but many of the original Jesus Freaks refused to participate because of its affiliation with right-wing groups like Campus Crusade. Though the dissenters were in the minority, as this was the direction the movement was headed.

While it may seem like these Christian hippies should've gravitated toward the social gospel of Jimmy Carter, the doomsday prophecies and distrust of government preached by conservative fundamentalists jibed well with the Jesus Freaks.

"The Jesus People didn't leave counterculture behind; they thought that adopting fundamentalism was to swim upstream," says Brad Onishi, a religious scholar and the co-host of the *Straight White American Jesus* podcast. He also spoke with me over the phone in 2023. "Back then, mainline Protestant churches were seen as the establishment; they were the ones that helped give us the New Deal, helping build the Great Society. The Jesus People viewed them as 'The Man,'

---

* Like Frisbee, Pino would see her career end when she came out as a lesbian in 1980, despite her having been credited with writing the first Contemporary Christian Music song, "For Those Tears I Died," in 1969. She would go on to form Born Again Lesbian Ministries, a resource for LGBTQ Christians.

as they had the money and power, they were the ones who got invited to the White House."

This was what drew Janet away from the Methodist Church her parents had raised her in—with its pews, hymnals, and stained glass—and toward the Assemblies of God Church, with its young people playing electric guitars while sporting bell-bottoms and denim vests. AG leadership had denounced rock and roll throughout the fifties and sixties, only to embrace it by the late seventies, when it proved to be an effective recruiting tool for young people.

Though Jimmy Carter was technically an "evangelical," his brand of evangelizing—caring for the poor, showing compassion to your enemies, striving for world peace—would, in the years ahead, be replaced with a new kind, one that would forever alter the meaning of the word in the public consciousness.

Janet closed the issue of *Life* magazine and quietly slipped it into her backpack before her mother could notice she wasn't reading about biology. Her sneakiness was unnecessary, however: her parents' attention was still fixed on the TV, and they beamed with pride as Jimmy and Rosalynn Carter danced together at the inaugural ball.

Carter may have been known as the leader of "the New South" (promising an end to the racist terror of Dixie's past), but after Janet read about the Jesus Movement of California and reflected on the scene at the AG youth group, the Democratic Party that her parents had been championing for as long as she could remember suddenly felt very old.

She could relate to the hippies' feeling that they were dismissed by society, and was experiencing the same draw toward the new conservativism of Bill Bright and his Campus Crusade for Christ. That would certainly give her a bond with her older siblings, and give her mother something to worry about beyond her grades.

Suddenly academia didn't have the same shine for her it once had.

Janet no longer wanted to be a diplomat, and wasn't even sure about college.

A new scene had arrived in Iowa, and she was determined not to be left behind.

CHAPTER FOUR

Revelation Romance

1978

"This is it! Russia has initiated the war of Gog and Magog!"

Janet heard a boy shouting these nonsensical words as she walked down the stairs of her house, and her mind was conjuring a rebuttal before she even saw who'd uttered them. She'd been running late for Revelation Bible Study, the weekly event her mother let her host in their living room as long as it didn't interfere with her "studies."

She was familiar with the names Gog and Magog—depicted as agents of Satan in the end-times prophecies of Revelation—but felt confident that this boy, whoever he was, didn't know what he was talking about. Most likely, he'd picked up that phrase from *The Late Great Planet Earth,* the popcorn theology book that was recently adapted into a film narrated by Orson Welles, and would go on to be the best-selling nonfiction book of the 1970s, according to *The New York Times.*

Hal Lindsey's doomsday tome had captivated the Jesus Movement and beyond with a narrative that, like those of so many prophets before him, dramatically tied the world affairs of the modern age to the ancient prophecies of the Bible; he had concluded that the horrors of the Apocalypse would likely unfold in the year 1988.

"We all thought that Jesus was coming back on Thursday," Marsha Stevens-Pino recalls. "We were told that we were the chosen generation, the last generation."

It wasn't just that Janet found Lindsey's arguments a bit simplistic and his interpretation of scripture wildly misleading; she was also troubled that so many of her friends suddenly felt no need to plan for the future, refusing to do their homework or even apply for college. What was the point, if God would destroy the Earth in a few years? (Calvary Chapel's Chuck Smith disagreed with Lindsey, believing Christ's bloody return would begin in the year 1981.)

Janet was less invested in academic achievement than in previous years—angering her mother by falling a couple points short of the honor roll—but her hunger for Biblical knowledge had only increased. She would be attending Open Bible College in Des Moines next fall, a Christian college that many jokingly referred to as "Open Bridal," because many young women only attended long enough to find husbands. This ambition—and the desperate need for validation by her siblings that spawned it—was as strong as ever in Janet, even though she would never admit it publicly.

As she came down the stairs and into her living room, Janet was floored by the number of teens in her house. The walls were ready to burst with them, all feverishly taking notes and highlighting passages in their copies of *The Way: The Living Bible* (a paraphrasing of scripture that used contemporary language—and illustrations—to make the Bible accessible to young readers), intently listening to a shaggy-haired boy in a Keith Green T-shirt and denim jacket who pontificated, "The Soviets shooting down that airplane was foretold in Revelation, signaling that we are truly living in the last days!"

Janet rolled her eyes, feeling a rush of annoyance.

She'd never officially met this boy, but he kept popping up in her life.

She knew him as the stoner from her high school who often cut class and rarely participated when he did show up. Lately, however, she'd been seeing him at the Good News Center, a Christian hangout space some friends from the AG church had launched in a downtown warehouse two years earlier. They'd modeled it after the communes of the Jesus Movement, keeping it informal, DIY, and nondenominational. This kid had been eagerly volunteering for whatever the Good News Center needed—loading gear for traveling musicians, driving guest speakers to the venue, and staying late to clean up.

Weirdly enough, he'd also rented out the house next door to Janet's.

She had to admit, for a while she'd thought he was cute in a "bad boy" sort of way—with his messy hair, beard, and working-class gruffness—but now, hearing him spout "end times" nonsense in her living room, she found him terribly obnoxious.

It had only been twelve hours since a Korean Airlines commercial plane accidentally veered off course and, because it was thought to be a U.S. spy plane, was shot down by a Soviet fighter jet. Already, guys like this one standing in Janet's living room had convinced themselves the attack was the first of God's Apocalyptic chess moves from Heaven.

"And what makes you so certain this has anything to do with Bible prophecy?" Janet asked from the back of the room, still sitting on the stairs.

Everyone looked her way, a few friends smiling brightly at her.

The boy looked scared at first, then smiled and said, "It's prophesied, in Ezekiel 38."

"And you've read Ezekiel 38, have you? Or are you just plagiarizing Hal Lindsey?"

"I've read it," the boy, Henry Hesse, replied, but his cheeks turned a deep shade of red: the truth was, he'd skimmed it, but couldn't make heads or tails of the whole prophecy. This girl—whom he knew as Janet Chastain, the organizer of the Bible study—was right, he was just repeating what he'd read in *The Late Great Planet Earth*.

"It says that Israel will be attacked by a land from the North," Henry said, "which is obviously the Soviet Union."

"Yeah, but South Korea is hardly *Israel*," Janet said, leaning forward over the banister.

"They're pretty close."

"What are you, five years old?" she said, laughing derisively. "They're, like, five thousand miles apart!"

Henry's face was nearly purple by now.

Janet noticed and started to feel guilty, but she just couldn't stop herself. "And, besides, in Ezekiel the prophecies say that the war would be accompanied by earthquakes, hailstones, fire, and sulfur, and you'll have to forgive me if I missed that part of Walter Cronkite's report on the plane being shot down. The whole thing was just a big mistake, and the Russians are probably kicking themselves over it."

"Ah," Henry said, his tone improving, "but don't you think a big airplane being blasted to pieces in the sky would create a loud explosion, shaking the earth? And when it rained down in a torrent of flaming wreckage, wouldn't it look something like 'hailstones, fire, and sulfur'?"

Janet shook her head, sighing, holding the bridge of her nose.

"Yeah, sure, whatever," she said, exasperated. She kept admonishing herself to stop talking, let it go, leave this poor, dumb kid alone, but in that moment, she was so annoyed she just couldn't help herself. "Except for the fact that the plane didn't 'explode,'" she said, mimicking Henry with an idiotic voice while making air quotes. "They had an emergency landing in Finland. Only two people out of a hundred and nine died. Hardly Armageddon, wouldn't you say?"

"Maybe you're right," Henry mumbled, sheepishly; then someone changed the subject, wondering whether the Son of Sam murders had been the work of the Antichrist.

Janet sat quietly on the stairs during the rest of the Bible study.

When it was over, she stood and was ready to go back up to her bedroom when—*Oh Lord, no*—Henry Hesse pushed his way through the crowd and approached her. He was standing too close as he blurted, "You were totally right to call me out on that."

"It's okay," she said, taking a step back. "I was the one who was being rude."

"Not at all. You're obviously very smart, and I'm just learning all this stuff. I only got saved a year ago, at the Good News Center, but since then, I've been reading my Bible and anything I can get my hands on every day. Becoming born again has changed everything for me, and I'm eager to serve Christ any way I can."

Henry was definitely flirting—or at least attempting to—but he wasn't exaggerating about his newfound devotion to evangelical Christianity.

His born-again experience at the Good News Center had transformed him. "In that instant, I felt a peace in my heart like I'd never felt before," my dad would recall to me, years later. "The room was suddenly filled with light, and I felt Jesus come into my heart, filling me up with joy, telling me he was my Father, and I was his son, and since then I've never felt lonely a day in my life."

Henry related all of this to Janet, but didn't mention the daddy issues that had fueled his longing for a father figure; he still felt shame and personal responsibility for being abandoned (and nearly murdered) by his own dad when he was a boy.

"I'd been smoking weed constantly for years, but haven't touched the stuff since becoming born again," he said, unsure if Janet would judge him for his past, or be impressed with his testimony of transformation. "Don't need it anymore. Jesus is the best high in the world!"

Janet began to feel a bit guilty for bullying this kid in front of everyone. It was obvious that Henry was her intellectual inferior, but his enthusiasm—what some people might characterize as being a bit "too much"—was actually quite charming, at least enough so she could forgive him for his pompous sermon about Gog and Magog. And he did have the cutest freckles, and an adorable gap between his teeth. The two of them stood on the staircase for the next hour, discussing creationism, dispensationalism, and their favorite Christian songwriters. (Hers: Keith Green, Amy Grant, and Gary Chapman. His: Randy Stonehill, Larry Norman, and Petra.)

"This summer, I'm going to go to Chicago to volunteer with Jesus People USA," Henry said, referring to the largest Christian hippie commune in the nation. "Then I want to come back here and start my own church. And, of course, a family. A *big* family. I think the Lord has called me to do great things with my life."

It was obvious that Henry liked Janet, and, she had to admit, it was nice being pursued so aggressively after her humiliation with her former fiancé. She wondered what her older siblings would make of this shaggy convert.

Though he hid it well, Henry was overwhelmed with feelings of impostor syndrome (though he was unfamiliar with that exact term), knowing Janet was far too good for him. She was so popular, so intelligent, so pretty. He thought she looked like Lynda Carter, or Emmylou Harris (two pinups Janet would *never* have compared herself to). She came from a middle-class family, with parents who were still married. She had a kitchen full of food and a color TV. No brood of foster siblings zipping and screaming about, knocking things over and getting into fights; just well-adjusted, studious teenagers discussing the Bible.

It looked like the *Ozzie and Harriet* life Henry had always longed for, and he felt wildly intimidated. But Henry trusted that God was guiding him on his journey to start a family, and that gave him enough confidence at least to hide his insecurities.

"Hey, some of us are getting up early tomorrow to go to Pilot Knob and watch the sunrise," Henry said. "You wanna come?"

"Sure," Janet replied, surprising herself and Henry.

At five a.m. the next day, they all drove out to the old Civil War watchtower to see God's painting of the morning sky. On the drive home, Janet fell asleep with her head on Henry's shoulder, causing his whole body to tingle. When they got back, without thinking about it, Janet walked with Henry to his front door instead of her own; neither of them said a word about it. Inside, they cuddled some more on the couch, silently listening to a band called the Armageddon Experience. When the record finished, Henry nervously asked her to be his girlfriend, and Janet thought to herself: *Maybe we can be "too much" together?*

One Month Later

As Henry watched a guillotine blade rip through the back of a woman's neck—while another woman watched in horror with a blood-curdling scream, knowing she was going to be next—he thought to himself: *I really need to start a family soon.*

They were at the Good News Center, attending a screening of the new rapture film, *A Distant Thunder*. The movie was the first of three sequels to *A Thief in the Night*, a low-budget 1972 film that would spark a Christian cinema revolution, being translated into several languages and viewed by hundreds of millions of people the world over.

And it was filmed in Des Moines, Iowa, a short drive from Mason City.

Beyond *The Music Man,* Iowa isn't known for its game-changing contributions to popular culture, but it could be argued that *A Thief in the Night* had an even bigger impact on the world than Meredith Willson's musical. Utilizing horror-film techniques and a musical refrain from Larry Norman's "I Wish We'd All Been Ready" (spookily sung by a choir of children), *Thief* opens with a teenage girl, Patty, hearing on the radio that millions of people had suddenly vanished from the Earth. Patty eventually recognizes she's been "left behind" in the rapture, and in a state of panic, she becomes a born-again Christian. For this, she is arrested by the newly minted armies of the Antichrist, who are rounding up all believers into prison camps.

Following the worldwide success of *Thief*, its sequel was given a larger budget, and upped the ante on the "scaring the literal Hell out of you" approach to Christian evangelizing. *A Distant Thunder* continues where its predecessor left off, with Patty sitting in prison alongside hundreds of other recent converts, who dialogue about their collective conundrum throughout the film: either renounce Christ and receive the Mark of the Beast, or be put to death.

Janet was only mildly curious about the possibility of the coming rapture—"I know I am saved," she often said, "that God loves me and will take care of me, so I really have nothing to worry about"—but Henry agonized over the subject day and night.

The phrase "left behind" put an electric sizzle through the marrow of Henry's bones, viscerally reminding him of his father driving his pickup into the sunset. Though this was often more of a groundless, anxious sensation in his belly rather than a rational thought.

There are two schools of thought when it comes to the timeline of the Christian Apocalypse. Well, there are actually *thousands* of different interpretations of the prophecy, but the two major ones are the belief in a "pre-Tribulation rapture" or a "post-Tribulation rapture." Will God test *all* Christians with the horror show of the Antichrist and the Four Horsemen? Or will He first rapture all Christians to Heaven, and only those who are left behind will have to convert and prove their worthiness through years of profound hardship?

This question was on the lips of many in the Jesus Movement, including their hippie godfather Bob Dylan, who became born again in 1978 and would go on to record three Christian rock albums. "Are you ready for the judgment?" Dylan preached from the stage (often to as many boos as when he "went electric" in 1965). "Are you ready for the terrible swift sword? Are you ready for Armageddon? Are you ready for the day of the Lord?"

A few months after his conversion, Henry spoke to his uncle about what he'd been reading in *The Late Great Planet Earth*, worried that he would have to suffer through the Tribulation. His uncle was only mildly interested at the time, but at three a.m. that same night, he was banging on Henry's door, telling him God had given him a prophecy in the form of a dream.

"We will all suffer horribly in the Tribulation, *all* of us," he'd said, sweaty and disoriented, standing in Henry's doorway. "Long before we are raptured, winged demons will descend from the sky, ripping the flesh from our bodies. We will be burned alive, dragged by semi trucks across roads of broken glass, slowly eaten by armies of insects with teeth like razors!"

Henry took the prophecy seriously, but this didn't deter his desperate need to start a family as soon as possible. He was confident that he could hide his family in the wilderness when the time came, live off the grid, evade the Antichrist and his Mark of the Beast, until the Father called them home. He would need to earn a great deal of money before then, to prepare for the harsh life ahead.

According to *The Late Great Planet Earth*, the Apocalypse was set to occur in 1988; so there was only one decade of peace on Earth remaining, one decade for my dad to paint his domestic masterpiece.

A great deal of planning was churning behind Henry's eyes as he watched one Christian after another be executed in the name of Jesus on the movie screen.

As the credits for *A Distant Thunder* rolled across the screen of the Good News Center, Henry turned to Janet and asked, "Will you marry me?"

"Yes!" she said, without hesitation, and kissed him aggressively as "I Wish We'd All Been Ready" played in the background.

My grandma Marilyn insisted her daughter complete at least one semester at Open Bible College before getting married, hoping this engagement would fizzle out as quickly as the last one had. Janet agreed, and Henry went to volunteer at Jesus People USA in Chicago while he waited for his bride to return.

My grandma's plan failed, and the two were wed the following summer.

Collectively, these teenagers had spent a total of six months in each other's presence before committing to spend the rest of their lives together.

Neither of them knew what a recipe for disaster their union was.

A double-rebound with unrealistic optimism.

It was a time before words like "codependency," "sex addiction," "anger management," "anxiety disorder," "hoarding," and "dissociation" had entered the mainstream lexicon. (Though by the end of the 1980s, both of my parents would be very familiar with these terms after attending a great deal of couples counseling, individual therapy, and, in my dad's case, addiction treatment.)

When he proposed marriage, my dad didn't know that, deep down, my mom really just wanted the recognition from her siblings that could only come if she had a wedding, a home, and a family. And my mom had no idea about Dad's unconscious need to heal the buried wounds of his own childhood trauma and taste just a few years of the domestic bliss he'd witnessed on television before God destroyed the Earth. Nor did she know that his addictions to cigarettes and marijuana, which he'd mentioned to her (along with his compulsion for reckless sexual behavior—extending from his sexual abuse from the foster boy when he was twelve—which he hadn't disclosed to her), were never cured by being born again.

Nearly a half-century later, I am sitting with my mother at a picnic table in Mason City's East Park—near the wooden footbridge featured in *The Music Man*—the two of us leaning over a 1970s wedding photo album.

We look at pictures of her in her wedding dress, radiating with joy, surrounded by her parents and siblings, finally bathed in the validating glow of the family spotlight.

"I was so happy that day," she recalls, looking deep in thought, her mouth flickering between a smile and a frown. "I really wish you kids could've known your dad back then, when he was so full of energy and confidence, so gregarious and embedded in a community, before he changed into someone I no longer recognized. We had support from so many friends and family at the wedding; it was all so beautiful. But I look at that girl and I think, *You poor thing, you have no idea what you're getting yourself into.*"

CHAPTER FIVE

The Camel and the Needle's Eye

It's difficult for some people to wrap their heads around how the hippies created the Christian right. That may be a bit of an oversimplification of what happened, but it's really not so inconceivable, when you stop and think about it.

The line "If you're not a liberal at twenty-five you have no heart; if you're not a conservative by thirty-five, you have no brain" is erroneously attributed to Winston Churchill (there's no record that he actually said this), but the confused provenance aside, this adage certainly applies to the counterculture of the 1960s as it moved into the 1980s.

Jerry Rubin was one of the most radical, left-wing activists of the 1960s, but by the 1980s he was making millions as a broker on Wall Street, the ultimate embodiment of the "yuppie" caricature. The shock rocker Alice Cooper became a sober soldier in Christ's army and—along with Gene Simmons, Ted Nugent, and Johnny Ramone—started voting Republican.

This was equally true with the Jesus Movement: that counterculture scene of idealists gathering in basements, coffeehouses, and public beaches morphed into a faction of clean-cut grown-ups running multimillion-dollar megachurches functioning as thinly veiled campaign centers for the Republican Party.

In the *Encyclopedia of Contemporary Christian Music,* Mark Allan Powell writes that, by the 1980s, "The Jesus Movement revival was over: some say it morphed into the Religious Right; others (including this author) contend that it was devoured (destroyed) by that aggressor."

My parents and their scene at the Good News Center went through a similar transition. Shortly after they were married, they moved from downtown Mason City to a small house in the up-and-coming tourist town of Clear Lake. Across the nation, many white families were fleeing city life and moving to the suburbs at this time, wanting the peace and isolation of the country, but not the filth and labor of farm life. They wanted the clothes, technology, and entertainment of the big city, but not the crime, the diversity, or what they saw as liberal indoctrination.

Many followed them, and soon the Good News Center closed, to be replaced with a new church in Clear Lake, one that would reflect the greed, materialism, and "me first" ethos of the 1980s. Turning the hippies into yuppies was relatively easy, as they were now grown-ups with kids, mortgages, and careers; they were bored with drugs and the struggle of living with principles, happy to trade it all in for a bit of security and some name-brand goods. Mobilizing evangelicals into a cohesive voting bloc was actually a far more challenging task, one that took decades of slow, methodical strategizing on the part of GOP political operatives.

Ever since the Scopes Trial in 1925, evangelicals had been wary of political activism, still reeling from the public humiliation they'd been put through at the hands of scientists and journalists. When the Christian left was spearheading the Civil Rights Movement of the 1960s, fundamentalist preachers like Jerry Falwell called them "civil wrongs," denouncing the Reverend Martin Luther King as "a communist."

"Preachers are not called to be politicians" was Falwell's stance at the time; he denounced Christians' meddling in worldly affairs.

And the feeling was mutual. The libertarian icon—and failed 1964 GOP presidential candidate—Barry Goldwater famously despised evangelicals: "If and when these preachers get control of the [Republican] party . . . it's going to be a terrible damn problem."* But Billy Graham had never shied away from politics, playing a large role in both

---

* Living up to the libertarian ethos of keeping government out of the private lives of citizens, Goldwater would remain staunchly pro-choice and supportive of gay marriage for the rest of his life.

the Eisenhower and Nixon administrations. This inspired the political strategist Paul Weyrich—part of the "new right" of conservatives like William F. Buckley—to view evangelicals as an untapped resource of political power.

Though the evangelicals that *did* vote often leaned Republican, a significant portion of them were also Democrats, and before the 1980s, few were motivated by conservative issues like cutting taxes, dismantling the New Deal, or abolishing antitrust regulations. Thanks to Paul Weyrich, that was all about to change.

After launching The Heritage Foundation (which would grow into the most influential conservative think-tank in America) with Joseph Coors, Weyrich began traveling the country, interviewing evangelicals of all walks of life—pastors, waitresses, congregants, farmers, and truckers—searching for insights that would help him shepherd them into becoming right-wing voters. He tried to mobilize them with issues like prayer in school, the rise of pornography, and feminism.

River City ain't in any trouble.

Then we'll have to create some.

But none of these seemed to get their goat enough to make them enlist in Weyrich's political army.

Jimmy Carter's support for the Equal Rights Amendment, gay rights, and marijuana legalization made him an enemy of many evangelical preachers, and this led Weyrich to adopt a top-down strategy in pursuit of his elusive political base, finding it easier to influence the shepherd than the sheep.

Thanks to their presence on radio and television, evangelists like Jerry Falwell, Oral Roberts, and Pat Robertson wielded tremendous influence over millions of potential voters. And when the fundamentalist Christian college Bob Jones University had its tax-exempt status revoked by the IRS in 1976 (backdated to 1970) because of its violation of the Civil Rights Act, these televangelists' stance on political neutrality was re-evaluated.

Following the *Brown v. Board of Education* ruling that integrated U.S. schools, there was an explosion of private Christian schools— pejoratively known as "segregationist academies"—across America. It was actually the Nixon administration that ordered the IRS to deny tax-exempt status to any segregated school, but Weyrich was able to tie it to Jimmy Carter's new Department of Education, creating the narrative that this expanding liberal government was persecuting Christian churches.

This was enough to mobilize evangelists like Falwell (who had a segregationist academy of his own, Lynchburg Christian Academy) to the Republican cause, but by the late seventies, the integration of public schools wasn't the pool-table controversy it had been decades earlier.

Then, during a trip to Iowa in 1978, Weyrich stumbled upon the "trouble" he'd been looking for, a divisive political issue that would not only achieve his goal of mobilizing a Christian right voting bloc, but would fundamentally transform American politics forever: abortion.

For years, there had been very little outrage among my parents and their friends at the Good News Center, or anywhere else in the world of American evangelicals, about *Roe v. Wade*'s legalization of abortion.

In 1968, *Christianity Today* conducted a symposium among two dozen theologians on the morality of abortion, which wound up undecided. A few years later, the Southern Baptist Convention passed a resolution approving of abortion, not only in cases of rape and incest but also in "the likelihood of damage to the emotional, mental, and physical health of the mother."

The former SBC president and fundamentalist icon, Pastor W. A. Criswell, actually praised the *Roe* decision: "I have always felt that it was only after a child was born and had a life separate from its mother that it became an individual person," he said, "and it has always, therefore, seemed to me that what is best for the mother and for the future should be allowed."

In a cover story, *Newsweek* called 1976 "The Year of the Evangelical," reporting on all the key issues important to this newly coveted voting bloc, but nowhere in this lengthy article does the word "abortion" appear. It simply wasn't on the political radar for anyone other than Catholics, whom most conservative evangelicals held in suspicion, if not complete contempt.

Legal access to abortion had been the law of the land for five years—without a peep from evangelicals—when Paul Weyrich came to Iowa in 1978 to observe the race for the U.S. Senate. The incumbent Democrat, Dick Clark, had been polling far ahead of his Republican challenger, Roger Jepsen, right up until election day, his victory a foregone conclusion by every local pundit. Jepsen's promise for a constitutional ban on abortion, however, had won him the support of Iowa's working-class Catholics, who engaged in a massive leafleting campaign for him on election day—with images of mangled, bloody fetuses, and text comparing abortion clinics like Planned Parenthood to the gas chambers of the Holocaust—that turned the tide of the election toward the Republican challenger.

Inspired, Weyrich implored many of the most prominent evangelical leaders of 1979—Pat Robertson, James Robison, and Jerry Falwell, among others—to denounce abortion vehemently as a sin, an act of murder, and to declare shame on America for allowing it to happen.

A pool table in your community!

Even though he had insisted that "preachers are not called to be politicians," Jerry Falwell would claim that it was the abortion issue that made him, and other evangelical leaders, change their tune (despite their lengthy silence on the issue). Falwell, Weyrich, and others (including the future co-author of *Left Behind*, Tim LaHaye) founded The Moral Majority, an evangelical political organization that would shape the outcome of the 1980 presidential race.

Like many of her peers, my mother identified herself as a Christian feminist, which was not considered an oxymoron in the 1970s. Egalitarianism had been a central tenet of the "social gospel" evangelicals of the early twentieth century, and much of the women's liberation movement of the 1970s found a home in the Jesus Movement, leading to the Evangelical Women's Caucus in 1974. But the anti-abortion propaganda coming in the wake of Weyrich's Moral Majority drove my mother, and many others, to aggressively oppose legal access to abortion. They were horrified by videos like *The Silent Scream*, though many doctors would speak out against that film's premise that a twelve-week-old fetus would feel pain, let alone thrash about in terror during an abortion, and also pointed out that the ultrasound footage was heavily manipulated and misinterpreted.

A lot of misinformation about abortion spread across the nation in this pre-internet age. Newly formed anti-abortion campaigns claimed the procedure caused breast cancer and mental-health disorders, or interfered with future fertility. As conservative men spread their dark wings across America, birth control was similarly demonized and subject to obfuscation.

A few months into her marriage, my mother was pressured by friends to go off birth control. At eighteen, she had planned to wait at least a year to get pregnant, but everyone she spoke with (none of them doctors) assured her it would be at least a year before the birth control left her system and allowed her to get pregnant. Instead, she found herself pregnant weeks later, and would go on to have three unplanned kids before her twenty-first birthday. (My dad would get a vasectomy shortly after I was born.)

Deep down, both of them were overwhelmed and terrified, but they would never have admitted that aloud. My mom wasn't about to prove my grandmother right that she was in over her head as a teenage bride, and Dad shrouded himself in an unbridled optimism about the future and the riches it would bring him.

The election of 1980 brought a new Republican presidential candidate, who reinforced Dad's belief in an abundance of riches coming just around the corner. While Jimmy Carter was telling America to stop being so greedy and materialistic, to grapple with the energy crisis by setting their thermostats to fifty-five degrees and embracing solar panels, he was being challenged by a Hollywood cowboy my parents knew from their childhoods, a hypermasculine father figure promising to "make America great again" (thirty years before this campaign slogan would be adopted by another alpha-male candidate).

Despite his Hollywood background, Ronald Reagan was an icon of the "new right" movement of conservatives like Paul Weyrich. After his acting career fizzled out in the early sixties, Reagan turned his attention to politics; his handsome face and comforting demeanor wowed audiences at the 1964 GOP convention, where he attacked programs like Social Security and Medicare as trading "our freedom for the soup kitchen of the welfare state."

Though he would be elected governor of California, Reagan's hard-right stance turned off many moderate Republican voters when he ran for the GOP presidential nomination in 1976. But by 1980, the "new right" conservatives were able to rebrand libertarianism as sensible, patriotic, and what was best for you and your family, while slowly convincing working-class Americans that the progressive FDR policies they'd once championed were actually bad for them.

Following an oil shortage, the Iran hostage crisis, and Carter's "malaise" speech, Reagan was able to capture the American spirit with the hope of a better tomorrow just around the corner, if the liberal government would simply get out of the way. Despite not belonging to any church or being known to quote the Bible, Reagan—with some help from Falwell and Weyrich's Moral Majority—galvanized evangelicals in a way never seen before.

Weyrich, Falwell, and others helped Reagan package his brand of free-market individualism and criticism of "the welfare state" for the same evangelical audience who had embraced Carter's humanitarianism four years earlier. Falwell was fond of quoting passages like 2 Thessalonians, "If anyone is not willing to work, let him not eat," or Proverbs, "The soul of the sluggard craves and gets nothing, while the soul of the diligent is richly supplied." Meanwhile, he deliberately ignored Jesus's direct admonishment for the rich, "It is easier for a camel to go through the eye of a needle than for a rich person to enter the kingdom of God."

Ultimately, America chose Reagan's brand of American exceptionalism over Carter's more prudent sensibilities, ushering in the age of right-wing, laissez-faire capitalism that industrialists had been working toward since they first began courting evangelicals decades earlier.

Reagan's promises of an economic revival convinced my parents to plow forward with an entrepreneurial spirit of their own, launching a tanning salon and a waterbed retail store. (Reaganism wasn't the only California trend coming to North Iowa in 1980.) Before this, Dad had been making decent money working at the Winnebago factory, offering a modest but stable lifestyle to his new family. But this wasn't nearly enough to assuage his adolescent fantasies, or to give us the resources we'd need to live through the time of Tribulation.

Looking back years later, my mother says it was high inflation (which was at 13.5 percent by 1980) more than anything else that drove her conversion from Carter to Reagan.

This belief is echoed by historian Fareed Zakaria in a 2022 CNN editorial, where he notes that high inflation often corresponds with political unrest, as it did in Germany in the twenties and Iran in the seventies. Zakaria places the Reagan Revolution in that company, seeing it as the death of the New Deal era of American economics. (Inflation would play a similar role in the rise of Donald Trump's presidency a generation later.)

With inflation so high in 1980, the only business loan my parents could get came at 21-percent interest, and they needed my mom's older brother to cosign on the loan. My dad also got his brother and uncle to invest in Sleepy Hollow Waterbeds. After all, waterbeds made up 20 percent of the mattress market at the time. And what could possibly stand in the way of the rising popularity of tanning salons?

My mother would later admit that, deep down, she was hoping their business loans would be denied. She felt the risk was too high, and the stress of bringing her big brother into the mess was keeping her up at night.

Though she didn't have the language to express it at the time, with each pregnancy my mother was burdened with a weighty postpartum depression, which never got the chance to abate before another zygote arrived. She could feel her former confidence and clarity beginning to slip away.

But there was no room for doubt or depression. After all, unwavering faith was the road to financial success; the sin of disbelief would lead to bankruptcy.

The Gordon Gekko line "Greed is good" is often proclaimed to be the ultimate summary of the 1980s; in evangelical churches of the time, "Greed is God" would've been a more appropriate adage. Thousands of Reagan-loving preachers across the nation were subtly blending into their sermons the social Darwinism of Ayn Rand, the myth of American upward mobility in Horatio Alger novels, and the "New Thought" movement, which taught that maintaining a positive mindset would lead to riches.

This thinking had its roots in the "Protestant work ethic" champi-

oned by Graham and Falwell, which—in its sixteenth-century Calvinist origins—suggests that those who not only work hard, but *enjoy*
working hard, are predestined to be God's chosen people, earning
them riches in Heaven as well as on Earth. To be lazy, or to grumble
about working conditions or wages, was a sign you were predestined
for Hell.

Evangelicals in the Reagan era were encouraged to be exhibitionists in their labor, gleefully working themselves to the bone without
complaint, while engaged in an unspoken competition with their
peers to accrue the most hours, to push through the highest levels of
exhaustion. To be unsatisfied with work was a sign of dwindling faith.
This was also the message of Agapé Christian Temple, the Clear Lake
church my parents helped found in 1980.

Agapé began with the same humble origin story as the Jesus Movement, first hosting informal Bible studies in living rooms, then renting
the local movie theater on Sunday mornings for church services (a
common practice for suburban evangelical churches without a sanctuary to call their own, leading to many parents bribing their children
with popcorn to stay quiet through the service). They would eventually purchase a large pyramid-shaped building on the north end
of town. Agapé leadership had nothing to do with the design of the
building, but this was a serendipitous coincidence: the message of our
church would come to resemble the "fake it till you make it" ethos of
multilevel marketing enterprises, also known as "pyramid schemes."

Rarely did anyone transcend the "fake it" stage.

At Agapé, we were taught that the image of success was a currency
that not only projected to the world you were in God's favor, but
inspired an envy among your peers, making them curious about the
apparent bliss of being born again and thus opening the door to getting them saved (and attending our church). If you're unhappy with
your work, your family, or your faith, no one is going to want what you
have, and you'll thereby miss out on the chance to rescue them from
the fires of Hell.

So my mom tried to keep a winning smile plastered across her face
at all times, ignoring the impulse to speak up when she had doubts
about the risks they were taking in their business ventures. The big-

ger the risk, the bigger the evidence of your faith, and the bigger your reward.

At first, it seemed to be working.

Sleepy Hollow Waterbeds would gross $325,000 in its first year. But my dad was in a manic state of optimism, and kept reinvesting everything into the business. Soon they opened a second waterbed store in Algona, a sixty-mile drive from Mason City.

Dad quickly set to work filling the house with new furniture, an entertainment system, and appliances (all bought on credit)—all those prizes he'd dreamed about while watching game shows on TV as a boy. More babies, more businesses, more, more, more.

After all, time was running out.

Despite evangelicals' embrace of materialism—with many church leaders proudly displaying their mansions, jets, and luxury watches as evidence of God's blessing—the conviction that God would soon destroy it all in a coming Apocalypse remained strong, bolstered by the incessant anxieties of the Cold War.

"Never, in the time between the ancient prophecies up until now, has there been a time in which so many of the [Bible's] prophecies are coming together," Reagan said in the documentary *Ronald Reagan and the Prophecy of Armageddon,* at the time of his campaign. "There have been times in the past when people thought the end of the world was coming, and so forth, but never anything like this."

Trouble with a capital T!

Hal Lindsey was still selling books, quietly updating his doomsday clock as his prophecies failed to materialize, while others were selling survival kits for the dark days to come, before our economy was devoured by the Antichrist and his socialist Mark of the Beast.

Like those he descended from, my dad was a working-class laborer with little education or financial literacy, operating on gut instinct. He believed it wasn't necessary to write a business plan—as so many "educated" bankers and advisers asked of him—because he had God on his side. He was making financial decisions based on the guidance of his emotions, which was how God communicated with those who lived by faith, not by sight.

The secret truth was, my dad was just as terrified as Mom.

He was shuffling around money from business to business, paying his personal bills with business revenue, solving every problem with more debt, all of it compounding into sleepless nights, explosive rage, and mounting anxiety.

Mom and Dad hadn't taken the time to establish the trust in each other necessary for healthy communication. So, instead of growing closer by confessing their mutual concerns and collaborating on pro-active solutions—because acknowledging those fears would be a sign of doubt, not faith—they grew apart, with Dad shielding himself in defensive rage, and Mom growing ever more silent and resentful.

Whenever my dad got even the slightest bit of pushback from Mom or a financial lender about his business decisions, he would turn a dark shade of red, tremble with rage, and shout, "Why don't you just *believe in me*!? You think I'm just an ignorant dumbass farm boy, don't you?"

His fear of humiliation in the eyes of intellectuals was an epigenetic inheritance that could be traced all the way back to the Scopes Trial; he couldn't bear to be caught without an answer to any question, or to be confronted by any holes in his logic, without erupting in defensive indignation.

The gregarious, optimistic boy my mom had met at Revelation Bible Study had disappeared, and so had her ability to connect with the community she had worked so hard to build. "Your dad became so insecure that I couldn't leave him alone at parties or else he'd get angry, complaining of not knowing anyone and feeling rejected," she recalls.

My mom didn't consider all the advantages she had that her husband didn't—growing up in a financially secure, two-parent household full of books and without violence or sexual abuse—and my dad never thought to consider all the life advantages he had acquired in simply being born a man.

When it came to the household chores, Dad went from defense to offense, berating Mom for letting the house fill up with trash, for taking us out of the house with stains on our clothes and food on our faces. "What kind of a mother are you!?" he screamed. As someone who grew up taking care of many siblings in a one-parent household, he had little patience for Mom neglecting her domestic duties. He didn't take the time to consider that she grew up never learning these skills—primed by her mother for the life of an academic and not a housewife—and certainly didn't recognize that she was spiraling into an abyss of severe depression and anxiety.

"Most of my memories of being pregnant with you are of your dad screaming at me," my mom later recalls. "And then I went back to work only two weeks after having you, which was far too soon."

"She just shut down," my dad recalls. "Stopped talking, stopped getting out of bed, stopped taking care of the kids, just disappeared in front of the TV."

One thing both my parents agree on: the marriage was more or less over by the time I was born.

CHAPTER SIX

Blood on the Scarecrow

"In sorrow thou shalt bring forth children."

—GENESIS 3:16

1986

I'd been running through the cornfields for some time, desperate to hear my mother's voice. I was four years old, and the infinite rows of cornstalks towered over me like everything else in this world, creating a dark canopy that blocked out the setting sun.

"Phin? Faith?" I called out for my older brother and sister, anxiety building as the wet leaves of the cornstalks slapped me in the face. "Mom? Dad?"

We'd come out to this field on the Agapé bus with the rest of the congregation to raise funds for our church by detasseling corn. Farmers paid us each $3.35 an hour to work these fields, money we then donated to the church.

Most of the services at Agapé in those days opened with an announcement of the state of our church fund-raising goals; we'd chant slogans like "Debt Free by '93!"

Panicking, I jumped through the rows of corn, thinking perhaps my mom had gone into a different lane. I felt I couldn't breathe until I heard her voice. I'd been chasing after Phin and Faith, but they were too fast in their efforts to ditch me. After running for a few minutes, I caught the sound of two ladies talking in the row next to me.

"He killed his *wife*?" one older lady in overalls and a John Deere hat asked the other. I crouched down in the dirt, then lay flat, curious to hear more but not wanting to be seen.

"Worse," replied the other woman, wearing an Iowa Hawkeyes

stocking cap and a Carhartt jacket. "Before that, he shot the president of the bank he owed nearly a half-million dollars to. Then he shot his neighbor, who just won a land judgment against him. Tried to kill the neighbor's wife and kids, but they escaped. Then he drove off in his pickup and shot himself."

"Uff da," the older lady replied, shaking her head. "Those poor children."

"You betcha," she agreed. "He left a note for his son that just said, 'I'm sorry, I can't take the problems anymore.'"

Stories like Dale Burr's triple homicide/suicide in Lone Tree, Iowa, were not uncommon during the 1980s farm crisis. Across the Midwest, men who'd never cursed or so much as raised their voices to their families had suddenly become drunken, violent wrecks.

"Did you hear about Eva's husband over in Keokuk? Kids came home from church and found him swinging by a noose in the barn. The suicides are bad in every county."

The word "suicide" had been ringing in my ears ever since our church's Passion play last Easter. Typically, the plays were about the life and crucifixion of Jesus, but recently we had been incorporating modern scenes in which different people died and went to either Heaven or Hell. In one story, a crying woman put a gun to her head and pulled the trigger, then awoke to find herself in Hell, being tormented by Satan.

"Ready to go, bud?" I heard my mom say.

She was filthy and looked exhausted as she walked down my row of corn.

I felt every muscle in my body relax at the sound of her voice.

The night before, she and I had been working late at North Iowa Christian School, cleaning the bathrooms in exchange for reduced tuition for Phin and Faith. (I was still a couple years away from enrollment, but not too young to be put to work.)

My brother and sister were both at Mom's side now, smiling, out of breath, with mud smeared across their apple-cheeked faces and their arms. Dad was finishing up his last row of corn; he looked heavy and exhausted, and wasn't saying a word. We all got into our grandpa's pickup truck, which smelled of hay and had heavy, rusted doors that took all my strength to close.

As we drove down the road, I saw "For Sale" signs peppering the landscape, slapped on tractors, combines, pickups, and staked into the wet soil of farmlands. We passed one farm where an auction was being conducted. Wealthy men were shouting over one another, bidding for the tools, machinery, and livestock at cents on the dollar, while the family who had worked the land for generations watched on.

Historians like to point out that the biggest difference between the Great Depression and the farm crisis of the 1980s was isolation. During the Depression, the pain was shared among the whole nation (some fell into extreme poverty and others simply stopped being rich, but almost everyone was affected). But the farm crisis—initially, at least—had an impact only on farmers, and those farmers were isolated even from one another in their cold, dark fields. This created a pervasive sense of shame in farmers across the Midwest, most of them believing it was their failure to live up to the Protestant work ethic of their granddads that lost them their family farm.

Throughout the 1960s and early '70s, low interest rates and high land values had caused bankers to encourage farmers to take on large amounts of debt, expanding their operations and buying ever more expensive farming equipment, leading to unprecedented levels of food production.

When the Soviet Union invaded Afghanistan in 1979, the United States placed a grain embargo on exports to the Russians; this created a massive surplus of food in the States, causing prices to plummet far below the costs of production. Given this situation, plus skyrocketing inflation and an oil crisis, farmers across the Midwest found themselves in a head-scratching conundrum that no amount of Protestant work ethic could solve.

Across the next four years, land values would drop 60 percent, and by 1990, three hundred thousand farmers had defaulted on their loans, leading to thirty-eight bank failures in Iowa alone. Unlike during the Great Depression, the state of Iowa never implemented a moratorium on bank foreclosures during the farm crisis. The number of farms in my home state went from 6.8 million in 1934 to 2.1 million by 1990, as the wealthiest and most secure agribusinesses bought up the land and equipment in foreclosure auctions.

Besides this concentration of land ownership, there was also a vertical integration of all aspects of farming: single companies controlled the seeds, fertilizer, machinery, and marketing of the end product, thus controlling virtually all aspects of the industry.

As corporations began to sink their roots into agriculture, conservatives like Reagan—who'd been critical of bailing out individual farmers—softened on the idea of government subsidies for the industry. With the size and scope of farms swelling, diversity of crops and livestock shrank, until the two productions became completely separate: most livestock were now raised in giant (terrifying) industrial warehouse operations, and giant fields grew enormous amounts of either corn or soybeans, most of which would never reach a human belly, to be used instead for ethanol or animal feed. As a result, rates of food-borne illnesses rose, as did cancer rates in Iowa (which are currently the second highest in the nation), due to massive amounts of pollution in the water. The once-fertile soil slowly became bankrupt due to the lack of crop rotation and overproduction.

Farmers continued to sell crops below the price of production. The majority of subsidies from the U.S. government went to large corporations, rarely to the type of small farmers you see on Folgers commercials during the Super Bowl.

For many Iowan farmers—whose way of life stretched back to the farmlands of Norway—the loss they suffered during the 1980s farm crisis was more than their business, but their way of life, their identity, and their trust in the Protestant work ethic, which had been central to their sense of pride and existential identity.

Suicide rates in Iowa spiked 400 percent during the farm crisis, as the foreclosures continued and many blamed themselves for the loss of family inheritances, even though they had been as smart and hardworking as their forefathers.

Some farmers organized to protest the U.S. government's failure to respond to the crisis, with tractor rallies and white crosses posted on courthouse lawns (one for every farm foreclosed upon). And celebrities were drawn into the cause as well. John Cougar Mellencamp wrote "Rain on the Scarecrow," a gut-wrenching, darkly sentimental song about losing the family farm to the bank. Willie Nelson and Neil

Young launched Farm Aid, and Sissy Spacek and Jessica Lange (both of whom had recently starred in movies about the farm crisis) spoke about it before Congress.

But, for whatever reason, fewer than 2 percent of farmers joined these efforts.

Phin, Faith, and I rode in the bed of the pickup on the drive home, watching fireflies dance above the cornfields to a symphony of crickets and night birds. Grateful to be out of the spooky cornfields, I smiled into the humid wind, looking for God's face in the setting sun, while Mom feverishly worked the accounting books of the waterbed business, the lines in her face growing deeper before our eyes.

CHAPTER SEVEN

On Fire for God

1987

"Janet, you are *not* making us late for church again!" my dad yelled up the stairs, his voice shaking the windows like thunder.

I was wading through the mess of dirty clothes in my bedroom, desperate to find my church shoes before Dad screamed again. Phin and Faith were ready, but my thoughts were moving slowly, and moved even slower every time that voice boomed through the house; I was certain I'd done something wrong.

"Being late tells people that your time is more important than their time," he often said in moments like this. This principle would serve me well years later, when I became a freelance journalist, but at that time it filled me with shame and helplessness.

Mom sprinted down the stairs, putting on lipstick with one hand and carrying my church shoes in the other. She tossed them to me without looking, and we all rushed out to the car; Dad hit the gas before I'd even closed the door.

We were indeed late for church that morning.

"Glory, glory, glory!" the worship leader proclaimed as we walked into Agapé Christian Family Church. (The name was changed from "Temple" to "Family Church" around this time, because we were often accused of being a cult associated with Jim Jones's Peoples Temple, more than nine hundred members of which committed mass suicide in 1978.)

The sanctuary was filled to capacity, with about three hundred people. Typically, we'd shake hands and say hello to everyone before the worship music started, but we were late, and the first song had just finished. It was amazing to me how quickly both Mom and Dad were transformed once they began singing along with the worship band: their eyes closed, grins peeling the corners of their mouths upward. Mom picked me up in her arms and rested me on one hip as her other hand gently waved in the air.

I raised my hands, too, closed my eyes, and sang along, just like her.

"Surrender yourself to the Holy Spirit this morning," the worship leader said. I looked around and saw all the other happy families, smiling and worshipping God in their best suits and dresses, shoes shined and faces clean. I felt ashamed, knowing that our family had fought in the car on the drive out here.

The band had three guitar players, four singers, a keyboardist, and a muscle-bound drummer with a ponytail who played on an electric drum set. Everyone onstage had bright smiles, swaying to the music, seemingly experiencing the happiest moments of their lives.

The music slowed down, the keyboard offering a soft melody as the drummer ran his stick along a row of chimes. "How many of you believe God will make a way, amen?" our pastor asked, as everyone swayed to the music, eyes closed, some crying. "God blesses those who prove their faith to Him. God doesn't want your money, He wants an exercise of your faith, amen?"*

"Amen!"

"Has He given you a spirit of poverty?!"

I ain't never been on welfare.

"NO!"

"That's right!" he said, skipping and dancing across the stage in a way that made me giggle. "If you can, turn in your Bibles to the Gospel of Mark, chapter 12, verse 41. Here Jesus visits the Temple and sees all the people giving their weekly tithe of ten percent. The wealthiest proudly filled the collection plate with riches, but then, the Bible says,

---

* These quotes are from my memory, and so they are not verbatim. Several former members of Agapé have read this chapter and said it reflected their memories of the sermons, too.

'a poor widow came and put in two very small copper coins, worth only a few cents. Calling his disciples to him, Jesus said, "Truly I tell you, this poor widow has put more into the treasury than all the others. They all gave out of their wealth; but she, out of her poverty, put in everything—all she had to live on."' "

I looked around at the sanctuary and saw all the farmers, laborers, and small-business owners pulling out their checkbooks, or counting the cash in their wallets. Dad was doing the same, writing math equations on the palm of his hand.

"No, we need to tithe on the *net,* not the gross," Mom said to him quietly.

"I know, I *know,*" he said through gritted teeth. His face was turning that angry shade of purple, his knuckles glowing white as he filled out the check.

At the time, I was unaware that my family's businesses were going bankrupt.

The new waterbed store in Algona had suffered from thefts, management turnover, and bad bookkeeping, eating up all the profits from the Mason City location, along with twenty thousand dollars in losses. In desperation, they had made a promotional offer of a free bedroom set to anyone who could catch a piglet on a greased waterbed mattress, but this failed to bring in customers.

Mom was growing colder and more distant each day, as her undiagnosed postpartum depression pulled her mind into a subterranean misery.

Years later, my grandmother would recall a time when she saw Mom putting me in pajamas that were clearly too small, and said "Janet, he's outgrown those!"

"Yes, but he's my baby, and I want to keep him small forever," she'd said, very slowly, looking straight ahead with a thousand-yard stare.

"You were like a weed left to grow at the back end of the yard, totally unnoticed," Grandma would recall.

As Mom grew colder, Dad became red-hot. He was a ticking time bomb; a toy dinosaur under his foot, or a bad smell coming from the refrigerator, turned him suddenly into the Incredible Hulk, shaking the house with his booming voice.

Around once a month or so, Dad would give me a tremendous series of spankings for something I did wrong, and a few times even slapped me across the face. This violence was obviously distressing, but even more so was my awareness of his anger, his fear, his discontentment with life, all being transferred into my little body. After this release, he would often break down in a fit of sobbing and desperate apologies.

"If you find yourself missing out on the blessings God has for your life, it may be time to look at the attitude with which you give to God," Pastor Jim said, pacing across the stage in his boxy three-piece gray suit. "Are you giving with a spirit of joy? Are you giving with complete faith that God will bless your obedience?"

Shiny brass offering plates were passed throughout the sanctuary, and I could hear my dad sigh as he dropped his check into it.

I watched as the plates were carried out of the sanctuary.

Everyone always talked about "giving to God" with their weekly tithes, but they never mentioned *how we get the money to Him*. I had seen *Raiders of the Lost Ark* and understood that we couldn't be in the same room as God (because God can't be in the presence of our sin, which was why Jesus had to be sacrificed on the cross as payment for our sins, so we can be clean enough for God to stand looking at us), so I assumed that giving Him our money was done quite carefully.

Perhaps they put the money out in the lobby while we were in the sanctuary, and it disappeared to Heaven when no one was looking?

Two hours into the sermon, I told Mom I needed to use the bathroom.

I didn't really, but wanted to see if our money was waiting for God in the lobby.

It was not.

I wandered around for a bit anyway, enjoying the quiet solitude of the hallways. There had been a lot of yelling at home recently, and it was nice not to be on guard for a moment. I often said I needed to go to the bathroom when I didn't, just wanting to be alone in a quiet space.

I stared at the carpet, the ceiling tiles, and heard the muffled garble of the Sunday-school activity through the closed doors. (I had gone with the other kids to Sunday school a few times, but was dreadfully shy and begged my mom to let me stay with the grown-ups in the adult church service.)

Then I came upon a series of framed paintings depicting the Tribulation.

The first was of the Four Horsemen of the Apocalypse, with each ghastly rider bringing different horrors to the Earth: famine, pestilence, war, and death. The next painting depicted a timeline of Christ's second coming, explaining the wars on Earth, the Mark of the Beast, and the Antichrist ascending from the Bottomless Pit.

Sometimes, when we were running too late for Agapé, Dad would throw his arms up and say, "Screw it! We're gonna have home church!" Then he'd tell us we were likely living in the "last days," and we'd soon have to live off the grid, retreating from society, sleeping in the wilderness, growing and hunting our own food, hiding from the armies of the Antichrist and his Mark of the Beast.

Looking at these paintings, I felt stupid and terrified: There was so much I didn't understand about all of it. If I didn't understand this stuff, would I know whether I was making the right choices to avoid eternal torture in the Lake of Fire?

When I walked back to the sanctuary and cracked open the door, I saw that things had ramped up again.

"You will *laugh* at your bills," Pastor Jim shouted at the congregation, who were all out of their seats and standing below him at the altar. "You will *expect* miracles, glory to *God*! Plant your *seed of faith* and you will reap a *tenfold* harvest."

I never saw adults behave elsewhere like they did at Agapé.

I knew we were different from those who belonged to other churches in Clear Lake. Adults who were usually as normal as pumpkin pie became totally different people at Agapé, almost a different *species*, during these Sunday church services. People who were usually so quiet, never showing much excitement or drawing any attention to themselves, seemed to be up for anything once they passed through those doors and heard the music: sprinting up and down the aisles, crying, laughing, screaming, moaning, spinning in circles, jumping from side to side, beating their chests, pulling their hair, rolling on the floor. But what would echo in my ears for decades to come was the cacophonous waves of humans speaking over one another in some kind of *non*-language.

"Shon-dah-lah-skah-bah-rah-tah-tah-tah-roh-koh-la-see-see-see!" shouted a woman who was rolling in the aisle as I returned to my parents' seats. I recognized her as one of Phin's teachers from the Christian school he attended. I knew a lot of these people: our mailman, a grocery store cashier, one of my babysitters, all of them sweating and heaving, spitting out syllables like bullets from a machine gun.

"Boh-roh-ta-see-yonda-yonda-untie-ya-boh-honda!" my pediatrician yelled.

"Hah-ha-bah-kah-la-dah-dan-dah!" exclaimed the woman who delivered our pizza.

My parents were slightly more reserved, staying in their seats but still singing with their eyes closed, Mom quietly speaking in tongues while Dad smiled brightly with tears streaming down his cheeks. It was strange to see these figures of authority behaving in such a vulnerable, childlike way.

The room smelled of sweat and brand-new carpet.

Up front, some of the people were lying on the ground, twitching like they were being electrocuted. The rest were standing side by side before the altar, eyes closed, waving their arms as they sang:

There is a fountain filled with blood,
Drawn from Immanuel's veins,
And sinners, plunged beneath that flood,
Lose all their guilty stains:
Lose all their guilty stains,
Lose all their guilty stains . . .

Pastor Jim approached these people one at a time. Most of them fell to the ground the instant he touched them, often shaking and speaking the non-language. Others stayed standing as he held the sides of their heads, pressing his forehead to theirs, praying loudly, usually shouting, "In the name of *Jesus*!," before touching them on the chest or stomach.

Rarely did anyone remain standing after that.

The ritual of "speaking in tongues" comes from the book of Acts, where, on the day of Pentecost (after which our Pentecostal denomination is named) the disciples all gathered together after Jesus's ascent to Heaven. And as they prayed, "Tongues that looked like fire appeared to them, distributing themselves, and a tongue rested on each one of them. And they were all filled with the Holy Spirit and began to speak with different tongues, as the Spirit was giving them the ability to speak out."

In the Bible, they were speaking *actual languages,* the miracle being that those languages were unknown to the speakers before they were entered by the Holy Spirit with a message, which would then be interpretable by those who *did* know the language. Modern Pentecostals are just speaking a kind of gibberish. Many linguists have studied recordings of Pentecostals speaking in tongues and found no discernible pattern in their speech, none of the ranges of tone or inflection found in all languages. It's mostly just a staccato burst of syllables.

The University of Pennsylvania once conducted brain scans of Christians in the act of speaking in tongues and found that the language regions of the brain—as well as the frontal lobe, the part of the brain that controls thinking and volition—were quiet, while the deeper, more instinctual and emotional regions were alight, suggesting that this is a state of pure feeling, a primal expression with little or no conscious thought. This intense emotional state quiets a person's intellectual defenses, opening them up to absorb any messages that follow.

The other traits of a Pentecostal church service—trembling, weeping, collapsing, dancing, crying out, then smiling euphorically—have Biblical and historical precedents, but speaking in tongues has only become common practice in the last century.

Though many faiths define themselves by various doctrinal or theological belief structures, Pentecostalism is the most emotionally driven form of Christianity. Your relationship with God is primarily defined by how He makes you *feel,* how He is moving through your heart and body. This, we believed, was how God made His presence known, through euphoria, catharsis, ecstasy, the hairs that stand up on your arm when you care about something *so deeply* that time seems to slow down and speed up all at once.

Your conversion was a "born again" experience, transforming your heart into something previously unrecognizable. For years, this was the only version of Christianity I was familiar with; I had little concept of Catholics, or the galaxy of other Protestant faiths (other than attending Grandma Marilyn's Methodist church a handful of times). And I was certainly unaware that so many of the tropes of an Agapé church service—the chairs instead of pews, the video projector instead of hymnals, the modern instruments, the stylish suits worn by the church leaders, and the relaxed, stand-up-comedy–like sermons—had been brought to our land by the likes of Burroughs Waltrip half a century earlier.

Feeling an anxious rumble of nausea in my belly, I left my parents' side and walked up the aisle of the church, stepping over the men, women, and children of all ages laid out on the floor, and approached Pastor Jim at the altar.

"You must be *on fire* for God!" he said, "lest he spew you from his mouth."

I was close enough to see the pores in his nose, made shiny with sweat, and to hear his voice boom *"in the name of Jesus"* before the words even hit the microphone, as he touched (pushed?) a pigtailed girl on the forehead, causing her to plummet to the floor.

I thought of the Tribulation.

I thought of my mother's sadness, my father's anger.

"Have you been washed in the blood of the lamb, Josiah?"

"Yes," I whimpered, not really understanding the question.

"Then be cleansed *in the name of Jesus!*" he shouted. My knees buckled, and I tumbled to the ground the instant he touched my forehead. Waves of joy, pulses of euphoria, all moved through me as I lay there for twenty minutes, smiling brightly.

I was clean.

I was safe.

Or at least I hoped I was.

CHAPTER EIGHT

Prophets of Profit

My dad returned to Agapé later that Sunday night, sighing as he flipped on the lights to the sanctuary. (I was not there, but I would hear this story from him years later.)

He'd just put in thirteen hours at the waterbed store, then driven straight to church, where he'd volunteered to man the phones of the suicide hotline overnight.

The hotline had been in high demand during those dark years of the farm crisis, and lately Dad had been volunteering more and more often for the graveyard shift.

But he was not there for altruistic reasons.

"Tithe on the *net,* not the *gross,*" Dad said to himself in a high-pitched voice, mimicking his wife, as he sat down at the hotline's rotary phone with his multiple bags of McDonald's cheeseburgers.

Mom had been right to remind him of this, because Dad wasn't great at bookkeeping. Neither of them was. They both realized this when they ran some numbers and learned they'd given Agapé over ten thousand dollars in a single year, while paying themselves the same amount (and even in 1980s Iowa, ten grand was insufficient income for a family of five). So, instead of giving the church the standard 10 percent of their income, they'd matched 100 percent.

Dad opened one of his McDonald's bags, then looked up and saw the scripture Luke 6:38 written across the sanctuary wall.

Give, and it shall be given unto you; good measure, pressed down, and shaken together, and running over, shall men give into your bosom.

So—is the check just lost in the mail, or what? Dad thought. *I've certainly been holding up my end of the deal, and I'm about to file for bankruptcy.*

But then Dad recalled the words of Oral Roberts (whose Oral Roberts University was attended by some of the Agapé leadership) in his book *The Miracle of Seed-Faith.*

"The spirit with which you give is the most important part of giving," Roberts says. "You need to *expect* a miracle. Do not sow seeds of doubt. When you believe God exists and wants to meet your needs, that God is the Source of your supply, and therefore should be first in your life, He will multiply back to you. With faith you do something *first* and thereby make it an act of faith . . . Doubt (or unbelief) is the *reversed form* of faith. It's when you believe God doesn't exist . . . It is bad, very bad for you. As SEED-FAITH is multiplied back, so is SEED-DOUBT."

Roberts was one of the most famous and influential preachers of "prosperity theology," the teaching that any additional "gifts" to God (beyond the weekly 10 percent of your income) will be returned tenfold in literal cash, through some fortuitous change in your circumstances.

Harold Hill offered a very similar strategy for success in *The Music Man.* After the boys are all dressed up in their band uniforms, instruments in hand, they naturally ask Hill how these things are played. Having no clue himself, he tells them they only need to *hear* the music in their heads, *feel* it in their hearts, and when the time comes, they'll know what to do. Professor Harold Hill calls this "The Think System."

We were given similar instruction from Pastor Jim when told, "Go home and laugh at your bills!" and "Give to God with a spirit of joy!" The same approach would be sold to us in multilevel marketing schemes like Amway, in which we were encouraged to "fake it till you make it."

You just needed to *believe* hard enough that God would bless you, and he would.

Just as you could learn to play a musical instrument by simply imagining yourself doing it.

Prosperity gospel is a very seductive promise made by American evangelists touring developing nations, where starvation, genocide, natural disasters, and colonial exploitation have left people vulnerable to the promise of supernatural solutions to their complex, systemic poverty.

It was equally seductive in Iowa during the great farm crisis of the 1980s.

The concept was born out of the faith-healing revivals of the sawdust trail, where preachers like Kathryn Kuhlman would insist that those whose faith was strong enough could be healed of literally any physical ailment.

During the televangelism boom of the 1980s (when Christian broadcasters like the Praise the Lord network had their own private satellites circling the globe), round-the-clock evangelical entertainment was blended with fund-raising telethons, raking in millions of dollars in small donations from working-class Christians who were struggling throughout the recession, told that their donations were actually a supernatural investment strategy that would make them rich in no time.

We were taught to view the rich with an aspirational envy, never questioning why prosperity gospel seemed to pan out only for the church leadership.

I don't know how many sermons I heard from Pastor Jim at Agapé (while he was dressed in a designer suit) about how God had blessed him so vigorously that he could afford to buy a brand-new car, with cash, any time he wanted. His family lived in one of the most expensive neighborhoods in Clear Lake, on waterfront property across the street from a golf course.

Meanwhile, I knew of many families attending Agapé (including our own) who lived on food stamps, hand-me-down clothing, thirty-year-old cars with torn mufflers, and homes with leaky roofs, all while donating *at least* 10 percent of their meager paychecks to the church (often more). Whenever gossip about an affair or drug use by one of these working people surfaced, a common response was to nod, think of their poverty (or, say, their failing waterbed store), and say, "That proves it: God doesn't bless sinners."

Have I been reaping seed-doubt? Dad asked himself.

Of course you have, because you're a weak, lazy sinner, a hateful voice replied within his head.

Roberts also writes that the soil of your seed is your personal relationship with God, and if something is getting in the way of that relationship, like sin, you will have a disappointing harvest. (These metaphors of planting seeds and reaping a harvest found a receptive audience in Iowa.)

Dad never had to stretch his imagination very far to identify a handful of sins that could be disconnecting him from the love (and soil) of Jesus Christ. Many of them had occurred right there in the sanctuary.

And as the sound of a ringing phone pierced the silence of the church—right on schedule—Dad knew he would be chalking up a few more tallies on that scoreboard of sin tonight.

Meanwhile, I watched Mom put Amy Grant's *Age to Age* LP on the stereo, tie up her hair in a bandanna, and smile at me. This meant she was ready to clean the house.

Mom really hated cleaning, but this ritual (and Grant's music) often psyched her up enough to get through it.

When she was a teenager, her bedroom and car had always been in chaos, and she'd gone from being berated by her anxious mother for it to being relentlessly bullied by her new husband. "I come home from work and it looks like a bomb went off in here!" had become Henry's typical greeting, as he trembled with anger and stomped through the house. "What's the matter with you?! How hard can it be to clean up every now and again? What kind of *mother* are you?"

It wasn't uncommon in Iowa for wives to help out with the family business, like my mother did (an extension of the agrarian model of the family farm), but always in a subservient capacity, never as the leader that Mom naturally was. And whatever work the wives contributed to the business, it was *never* an excuse to fall behind on housework and child rearing, the silent labor of a dutiful, Christian wife.

As much as she hated to admit it, Henry was right about one thing: the house was a disaster. Everywhere she looked, some neglected chore had caused a catastrophe, often thanks to her long stretches of dissociation and depression while taking care of three kids under the age of eight.

I watched from the hallway as she knelt to scrub the kitchen floor, only to abandon the task moments later and begin tackling a stack of mail that'd been piling up on top of the fridge for the last year. Wedding and graduation invitations, junk mail, stacks of bills marked "overdue" and "final notice," scores of yellowing *Globe Gazette* newspapers, tax returns, *Focus on the Family* magazines, Republican campaign fliers . . . She knew she needed to throw some of this away, but she couldn't discern what, or how to organize what she had to keep. (I didn't know this was going on inside of her mind at the time; I'd learn it much later.)

Each decision seemed to weigh more than the last.

It was the same with food in the fridge: a lot of it (usually at least half) was spoiled, some of it nearly spoiled, with edible food mixed in somewhere, among shelves and drawers caked with old syrup or spilled vinegar. The solution to each of these tasks was somewhere in her head, but a rush of contradicting thoughts bottlenecked together whenever she'd try to find it.

Her mind dissected every issue with an infinite amount of complexity: Is this food healthy for my child? Can we afford it? Does this meat come from Iowa? What are the rates for beef exports these days? Is chicken the better choice? Is this chain grocery store really stimulating our economy?

All day, every day.

A superpower transformed into a disability.

My mom was very tired.

She'd never regret having kids, but the high standards for motherhood within fundamentalist Christian culture (and the judgmental side-eyes that come with it) weighed heavily on her self-worth.

They were broke and working around the clock to keep the kids fed and the mortgage paid. Dad was working weekends as a furniture-store salesman. In addition to raising three kids, Mom was also volunteering at the Agapé nursery several days a week, and cleaning at North Iowa Christian School at night.

My mom set the mail back on top of the fridge (all of it) and returned to washing the kitchen floor. Amy Grant's "I Have Decided" roared on the stereo, that anthemic country guitar rousing her spirit, while the lyrics reminded her to forget "your self-righteous pain."

She was thinking of 1982, the year this record came out, the year she was pregnant with me, and the year she accepted that her marriage was a mistake.

Often, when she looked at me, she couldn't help remembering the months when her husband wouldn't stop screaming at her, and the stress she'd surely been passing along to me, twitching in her belly like a fetal Pentecostal.[*]

Amy Grant's record was her lifeline that year, reminding her of Carole King's *Tapestry*, her favorite album when she was a teenager, but with an evangelical twist, including aching love songs to Christ instead of to some long-lost boyfriend. Post-rapture ballads like Amy Grant's "In a Little While" were rousing beams of hope for people like my mom, promising, "In a little while, / We'll be with the Father; / Can't you see him smile?"

It was only a few weeks earlier that Mom had sung this song to herself while lying alone in her bed in the Fountain Lake Treatment Center. When she was admitted, she hadn't slept in days and was running a fever with high blood pressure. It was her husband who'd initially been checked in to the drug treatment center—paid for by his boss at Henry's second job, at the furniture store—but he disappeared after

---

[*] Research published in *Frontiers in Psychology* shows that "maternal stress during pregnancy exerts strong influence on the development of the unborn . . . [including] metabolic functioning, cognitive and emotional development . . . Consequences might be increased cortisol levels, increased cortisol reactivity and, in the long run, an increased risk for developmental problems in the offspring."

three days of treatment, picked up by a woman who had been plaguing Janet's mind night and day.

But we'll get to that in a minute.

After Dad disappeared from the clinic, Mom suffered a mental breakdown and was admitted under the center's "codependent program." There she slept for seven days straight. When she returned home, Dad informed her he wouldn't quit using drugs or stop sleeping around.

"I had the worst panic attack ever through that argument, and locked myself in the bathroom," she recalls to me, years later. "I thought for sure my legs were going to come off, so I held on to them tightly. I don't remember long parts of that day."

After that, Mom began experiencing agoraphobia.

"I had been having panic attacks in crowds or large groups," she tells me when I ask why we stopped going to Agapé for periods of time. "You may remember you and I leaving during a service. My heart was pounding so loud I couldn't hear what anyone was saying, and I knew the severe shaking would begin soon. So I grabbed you and left. I likely sat in my room when we got home, to ride through it."

(I recall leaving the church suddenly, but never knew why. Mom—like many Iowans—had become very good at hiding all emotions other than anger.)

For a year after that, Dad's behavior was all over the place, playing the loving husband and father one week and a ferocious hurricane the next. He'd move out for a few weeks, with all of us crying and begging him to stay; then we'd celebrate his return, and everything would go back to normal. Sometimes Mom would find herself staring off into the distance, not knowing how much time had passed, only that a dark merry-go-round of guilt and shame had been circling in her mind.

Stop with your self-righteous pain, Janet, a voice reminded her. *You are made to suffer, and to want otherwise is disobedience.*

2 Corinthians 4:17: "For our light and momentary troubles are achieving for us an eternal glory that far outweighs them all."

Romans 5:3: "We also glory in our sufferings, because we know that suffering produces perseverance."

Ephesians 5:22–23: "Wives, submit to your husbands as to the Lord. For the husband is the head of the wife as Christ is the head of the church."

Her back was killing her, and she had a headache the size of the USSR.

Speaking of, Mom had just turned off the record player and switched on the radio, which was reporting on the international arms-control negotiations between the United States and the Soviet Union, in Moscow. She could've been involved in that, working as a diplomat for the State Department, rather than feeling helpless before a refrigerator as toxic as Chernobyl. Instead of getting her degree, traveling the world, and lending her brilliant intellect to international affairs, she had three kids with a near stranger who was addicted to sex and drugs, and was spending half her life at a waterbed store where she was universally referred to as "my boss's wife," despite being a co-owner of the business.

You've made so many bad decisions, she thought, *dropped out of college, married the wrong man, buried yourself in debt. It's no wonder you crumble under the weight of even the smallest decision.*

She'd been so desperate for her family's approval, to be viewed the way she believed her siblings were—as successful, wealthy, ambitious, full of love and God's favor—it killed her to see that her mother may have been right: she should've stayed in school and declined Henry's offer of teenage marriage.

Every day, she told herself to just keep pushing forward. Keep cleaning, cooking, changing diapers, answering the phone, going to church, volunteering for everything—anything to avoid thinking about the thousand-pound weight of depression chained to her ankle.

Keep believing in the power of seed-faith.

Remain on fire for God.

No room for doubt, or "self-righteous pain."

A 2011 Gallup poll revealed that adults living in poverty are nearly twice as likely to be diagnosed with depression as those who have financial security. And according to a 2013 study published in the journal *Science,* living below the poverty line reduces cognitive function on average by thirteen IQ points. This doesn't even account for the ancillary effects of depression: lethargy, lack of motivation, decreased exercise, poor nutrition, impaired social skills, oversleeping or insomnia.

Not to mention suicide. A study from Emory University found that increasing the minimum wage by just one dollar would decrease the suicide rates of those with only a high-school diploma or less by up to 6 percent.

Poverty is a massive weight on your every thought and movement; the only thing it doesn't depress is the incessant, bullying voice of self-loathing reminding you of how far you're falling behind.

Mom flinched as a loud thud came from the second floor.

She was just about to rush up there when the phone rang.

"Hi," she said, out of breath. "Hello?"

"Is Henry there?" a voice asked.

"Who is this?"

"Why, who is this?" the woman replied.

"Henry's wife."

"His *wife*!?" the woman shouted. "He said he was single! We just spent the night together at the Hanford Hotel."*

My mom felt the floor drop out from beneath her; everything sounded far away.

Two weeks after this phone call, she would have coffee with her mother-in-law, who would say, "Well, at least the woman wasn't telling you she was pregnant with your husband's baby and was going to marry him, like mine did." It was not until then that Mom learned of Henry's father's proclivity for drunken philandering.

A second thud rang from upstairs, followed by screaming and a trickle of water falling from the ceiling. Mom hung up the phone and leapt up the stairs before she even knew what she was doing.

On the top landing, she looked to her bedroom on the left, then to the kids' bedroom on the right. She gasped each time her eyes moved,

---

* My dad denies having an affair with this particular woman, but my mom remembers the call very well.

there was so much horror to take in. Phin and Faith had been alone for less than fifteen minutes, but that was enough to transform their bedroom and hers into an unrecognizable crime scene.

In her bedroom, pillow feathers gracefully fell to the floor, where various lipsticks and nail polish had turned the yellow shag carpet into a Jackson Pollock art piece. A kitchen knife (where did he even get that?) was in Phin's hand, and with it he was carving elaborate designs and poorly spelled words into the wooden bedroom set my parents had bought (on credit) only months earlier. A bottle of baby powder had been chucked at the ceiling fan just before she walked in, creating a snow-globe effect in the room.

Across the hall, in the kids' room, Faith was screaming. The floor was covered with inches of water, presumably from the waterbed, which was now missing its essential ingredient.

She would later learn that Faith had wanted to see what would happen if she violently stabbed her waterbed a few dozen times and got her little brother (me) to jump on it with her. Water had sprayed and splashed across the room, and then I slipped on the polyvinyl material and slid into the water on my back (causing the splash that eventually reached our mom downstairs), accidentally kicking Faith off the corner of the bed and onto the ground, where the tiny metal edge of a heat register made the one-in-a-million puncture of a tiny artery on her scalp.

My mom could feel reality pulling away from her; she was desperate to check out mentally, for just an hour or two. But her maternal instincts ripped her back into gear.

With Faith in her arms, a rooster tail of blood spraying from her skull, she reached down and pulled me out of the water. I coughed, then saw so much blood it made me think of the crucifixion scenes in Agapé's annual Passion plays. Mom placed a towel firmly on my sister's head, then yelled for Phin to put his clothes on. We were going to the hospital.

As the weed and methamphetamine partied through his veins, my dad found himself standing naked in the church sanctuary, about to enter a woman who was not his wife, with pornography playing on both projector screens above the altar. And he asked himself: *Well, how did I get here?*

After finding that marriage was unlikely to satisfy the incessant demands of his body (no matter how much he prayed, read the Bible, or chastised himself), Henry had begun eating several extra meals a day—quickly shoveling fast food down his gullet, as if he were in a race—and had gained a hundred pounds since his wedding day. Masturbation had been a regular practice since he was twelve, but now he'd been doing it three or four times a day (in the car, public bathrooms, wherever the all-consuming impulse struck). When traveling to waterbed trade shows or making deliveries, he'd buy pornography magazines, look at them once, do his business, then throw them away and promise himself this was the last time.

Then he'd do it again, and again.

Sometimes he'd buy pornographic videos and check into motels in Mason City, just for the twenty minutes it took him to watch them.

"You're a disgusting, weak, pathetic sinner," he'd tell himself in the motel bathroom mirror every time. "This is the *last time* you *ever* do this. Think of the *shame* you're bringing on your family. What kind of a *father,* what kind of a *husband* behaves this way? Why can't you just be *satisfied*?"

At this time, my dad was unaware of the integral relationship between shame and addiction, even though he was painfully acquainted with the gossip about him spreading through Agapé. Friends he'd known for years no longer acknowledged him in the halls; others would offer no sympathy, only point to his failing businesses and say, "God doesn't bless sinners."

"As I think back on those years, I remember feeling like I really needed help," Dad recalls during an interview with me years later. "All I got was judgmental attitudes: critical, simplistic answers, like 'You need to dig into God's word more' or 'Just stop what you're doing.' Years later, I found more acceptance in bars than in any church."

Like the ring-toss game I'd run at the carnival as a boy, my dad was constantly told that chastity, sobriety, a happy marriage, and becoming rich were "easy" games to win.

His wife was suffering a mental collapse, he was constantly screaming at his kids, and it seemed like everywhere he turned someone
was disappointed in him. Dad became wildly defensive in the face of
this—despite a whirlpool of self-loathing circling within him—and
would snap at accountants, employees, anyone who disagreed with
him about anything.

As a child charged with being the man of the house, he'd learned
early on to keep his inner world a secret, to maintain stability at all
times. He was successful at this in church and at work, but once he
got home, the pressure cooker of his emotions would explode across
all of us. Then he would be smothered in regret and shame, hungry
for soothing.

By the time he'd checked himself into rehab earlier that summer,
Dad's heart and mind were so calcified he wouldn't listen to a word
his wife or any therapist had to say. He was myopically focused on
defending himself, never daring to admit, even within his own mind,
how scared and lonely he was. Dad believed that the thoughts and
impulses raging through his body were freakish anomalies that no man
in history had ever grappled with. He had no idea just how much extramarital fucking was going on all around him.

Decades later, when I returned to interview many of these people,
I'd learn our family was no different from the others at Agapé Church:
substance abuse, violence, affairs (sometimes between church leadership and congregants), learning disabilities, depression, social anxiety, poverty masked by thrift-store deals on brand-name clothes, and
massive credit-card debt propping up a lifestyle that was used to market evangelical success were dirty little secrets kept behind the closed
door of each family.

Of course, it would be unfair to single out my church for this behavior: such secrets can be found in every church in America, particularly
those that espouse "family values."

Religious empires are often built on silent sex scandals, and by the
late eighties, many of the most prominent evangelists were literally
getting caught with their pants down.

The evangelical cutie-pie couple Jim and Tammy Faye Bakker were
two of the most powerful names in televangelism at the time; their

Praise The Lord network had its own satellite orbiting the Earth (in 1983, mind you), which allowed them to raise tens of millions of dollars in nonstop telethons to fund their Heritage USA amusement park (the third-most-popular tourist attraction in the United States in the 1980s, according to *The Washington Post*). Jessica Hahn (later known for starring in Sam Kinison's raunchy "Wild Thing" video) accused Jim Bakker of raping her, and other close associates accused him of pursuing sexual encounters with men. Bakker would claim that the encounter with Hahn was consensual and deny pursuing sex with men, but the damage was done. Meanwhile, sweet Tammy Faye was sleeping with her record producer and losing her mind on so much Ativan she attempted to rip open the emergency exit of a private plane mid-flight.

In 1986, the Assemblies of God megastar (and cousin to Jerry Lee Lewis) Jimmy Swaggart exposed his fellow AG minister, Marvin Gorman, for having an affair (leading to his defrocking)—only to have Gorman turn around and hire a private investigator, who obtained photos of Swaggart visiting prostitutes in a roadside New Orleans motel.

Even the "father of Christian rock," Larry Norman, had multiple affairs—one with the wife of his best friend and collaborator, Randy Stonehill—and fathered a child out of wedlock, from whom he remained estranged for most of his life.

Evangelicalism is littered with such stories, though it's usually the women who suffer the shame of being "harlots," "jezebels," and "temptresses," while the men often retain their power, status, and money.

Susanne had called the suicide hotline the first night my dad volunteered.

She was a German immigrant who'd moved to Iowa to escape years of sexual and physical abuse by two family members in Berlin. As a result of this trauma, she had been diagnosed with dissociative identity disorder (what was once called "multiple personality disorder"). Her life had been a dizzying carousel of abusive men, mental illness, and drug abuse, and she was desperate to get her feet on the ground.

"I need help!" she'd sobbed on the phone that first night. "You sound like such a nice, religious man. Can you help me?"

With barely a high-school education, my dad had zero knowledge of psychology, therapy, or the conduct of emergency mental-health services. Our church had given each of the suicide hotline operators some instruction on how to counsel people in a crisis, though much of it was centered on spiritual, rather than medical or psychological, interventions. Dad was confident that becoming born again and experiencing the transformative love of Christ was enough to heal any wounds (with himself as the hopeless exception). He told Susanne about the love, healing, and forgiveness that could be found in surrendering your life to Christ. He read her some scripture, prayed with her, asked her to recite Billy Graham's "Sinner's Prayer" (which was taped to the wall above the phones), then told her that she was now born again, and Heaven awaited her in the afterlife.

She was ecstatic, and began calling my dad at the hotline regularly, desperate for healing, for peace in her troubled heart. Slowly, their conversations drifted away from sin and redemption, and into playful banter.

You're flirting with someone in a crisis, who you're supposed to be helping, Dad told himself. *Why are you such a piece of shit?*

That was when he started watching pornography in the church sanctuary.

Agapé had invested in a massive satellite dish to bring in Christian programming to our church, like Jim and Tammy Faye Bakker's Praise the Lord network and Pat Robertson's Christian Broadcasting Network. But, as my dad discovered, it could just as easily offer access to pornography channels, the images displayed on two projector screens above the altar.

Dad couldn't figure out how or why, but somehow he'd become addicted to conjuring and executing the worst behavior imaginable. The pressure to feel, think, and behave in a very rigid way had boomeranged into his seeking out what every authority figure in his life would abhor. Years later, I would show him research revealing that repressive religious societies often bred the most extreme sexual taboos, like dominant alpha-male conservatives who disproportionately enjoyed being "cuckolded"—i.e., watching their wives have sex with other, often more attractive or endowed, men.

The prince of his father's evangelical empire, Jerry Falwell, Jr., was one of the most powerful names in the Christian right, until a twenty-year-old pool boy revealed he'd had sex with Falwell's wife for years, while her husband watched from a darkened corner. (Falwell, Jr., admits to his wife's affair, but denies his participation.)

According to a study in *The Journal of Sex Research*, "religious adolescents are higher in [compulsive sexual behavior] than secular ones," and the repression of sexual thoughts among those raised in religious households has a "rebound effect," creating an even greater preoccupation with—and compulsion toward—sexual behavior.

Quite often, this cycle of repression and compulsion will spiral into ever more extreme behavior, the pursuit of a gambler's thrill of risk and reward.

It's what made some of the leadership of the hipster megachurch Hillsong engage in drugs and sex on the same stage from which they'd preach chastity the next morning. It's what made the co-founder of Moms for Liberty (who fought to ban LGBTQ books from libraries) engage in a threesome with another woman.

It's what made Kathryn Kuhlman so irresistible to Burroughs Waltrip.

It's what made the Music Man crave Marian the librarian, the one woman who could bring his whole con to an end.

After a handful of calls, Dad eventually suggested that he and Susanne meet up. He told her, and himself, that this was just to take their counseling sessions to another level. "I had convinced myself I was helping someone not die," he reflected years later.

During the meet-up, a simple hug was all it took, and they were unable to stop themselves. "Both of us felt extremely guilty," he reflected, years later. "Susanne never wanted to be the 'other woman.' I believed it was okay to behave terribly so long as I beat myself up about it."

In addition to the extreme ethical violation of sleeping with someone you've agreed to counsel out of suicide, I often think of how tragic it was that Susanne proactively called the hotline, seeking necessary help to her urgent problems but, for this effort, was not only treated to the guilt of playing mistress to a married man—unhelpful to a woman with profoundly low self-esteem—but would also forever carry with her that she played the role of the druggy temptress who lured our dad away from a happy marriage.

Dad also admits, years later, that Susanne became his connection to marijuana, which he then began smoking again constantly—with a little meth here and there. He kept the drugs in his car and in his desk drawer at Sleepy Hollow.

Though he hated himself more and more after each meet-up with Susanne, Dad felt unable to stop himself. Soon no amount of weed or meth could push away the guilt he suffered. He'd lie awake at night, heart pounding, that awful voice circling in his brain:

You're such a disappointment, such a lousy father.

Why did you think you could ever run a business?

What right do you have to raise children?

You're no man of the house; no wonder your dad left you.

You should just skip town and stop bothering people who don't want you.

One night, he drove himself to the hospital emergency room, certain he was having a heart attack. "The pain in my chest is unbearable!" he told the attending physician. "I can't breathe! My vision is blurry, and I feel like I'm dying!" After several tests, the physician failed to find anything physically wrong, and told him he was likely experiencing panic attacks and should reduce the amount of stress in his life.

He'd strongly considered suicide on a number of occasions.

He had longed for it, in fact, with a hunger to match his culinary and sexual appetites. But in his training for the suicide hotline, Dad had learned that children whose parents had committed suicide were three times more likely to commit suicide themselves. He couldn't do that to his children, so he would keep on living, if you could call it that.

Am I even enjoying this anymore? my dad wondered, while having sex, stoned, with Susanne inside the Agapé baptismal tub.

He was not.

CHAPTER NINE

Reaping the Whirlwind

1988

By 1988, Dad had moved out and was filing for divorce.

The night my parents called us all together for a talk in the living room, I knew what was up. Before letting them speak a word, I said, "I'd like to clean the whole house tomorrow!"—as though this intervention would put a stop to the coming news. It wasn't so much that I was upset about their divorce (a concept I hardly understood); I just didn't want them to be sad. Everyone was crying hysterically, and I searched my mind for a way to make it stop.

As my dad had when his dad left him, I was sure that this split was my fault. I had tried to keep the house in shape in the face of my mother's inability to do so. I'd take on large projects, like cleaning out some area of the house that had been neglected for years (the porch, the basement, the cabinet under the kitchen sink), but then become overwhelmed and unsure how to proceed, having somehow made things worse.

Of course, as bad as the house was while Dad lived with us, it sank into a biohazard after he left.

Dishes smeared with rotten food covered every surface and lived beneath all the furniture. Months (years, in some cases) of dirty laundry piled up in every corner. The washing machine was often full of clothes that had been washed, then forgotten and left to mildew. And, speaking of mildew, black spores covered the basement walls, which flooded every other summer. Down there, mushrooms grew out of the carpet, and centipedes slithered across long-abandoned toys.

The refrigerator looked like a penicillin lab and smelled like a dumpster in July.

Mom suffered another breakdown after Dad left, often staying with friends or not leaving her bedroom for long stretches of time, while we were cared for by friends or relatives. She eventually pulled herself together and enrolled in the "displaced housewives" program (yes, it was really called this) at the local community college, which helped get her on the path toward a degree. She was working days, cleaning rooms and running the front desk of a roadside motel, and also cleaning office buildings on the side. When she started attending night classes, I saw less and less of her.

Mom felt so humiliated when applying for food assistance, she insisted that she only needed it for a couple weeks. The woman at the Department of Human Services gave her an incredulous look and handed her six months' worth of food stamps. We would be fed by this program for several years, plus receive assistance with our heating during those merciless North Iowa winters.

Even though the Bible contains more than two thousand verses about caring for the poor, the Christian right of the 1980s really had it in for those living below the poverty line.

President Reagan and his Moral Majority Music Men found a way to convince working-class voters that welfare programs actually *harmed* the poor, that locking up drug users would keep everyone safe, that mental-health services were a form of socialism, and that gutting unions was the best way to fight communism and grow the economy for everyone.

In 1980, Jerry Falwell expertly blended the rhetoric of the conservative movement with fundamentalism, railing against a secularized government that had reared young people in "socialism and welfarism." "They have been taught to believe that the world owes them a living whether they work or not. I believe that America was built on integrity, on faith in God, and on hard work . . . We now have second- and third-generation welfare recipients . . . We have reared a generation that understands neither the dignity nor the importance of work."

In his 1981 inaugural speech, Reagan said that the recession of the late seventies was "proportionate to the intervention and intrusion in our lives that result from unnecessary and excessive growth of government."

By the time he left office, Reagan would cut twenty-two billion dollars from welfare spending, while still tripling the federal debt with massive increases in military spending.

In addition to cuts to the very welfare that was keeping my family alive, by the end of the Reagan administration there were more than a half-million fewer manufacturing jobs than when he started (whereas the previous eight years had seen a net gain of 360,000 manufacturing jobs). His relaxing of antimonopoly laws resulted in concentrations of power among the corporations employing Iowa laborers, resulting not only in massive layoffs, but shrinking wages.

Essentially, Reagan transformed America from a labor economy to an investment economy, and the labor jobs that remained were butchered.

When the Professional Air Traffic Controllers Organization went on strike for better pay and working conditions in 1981, Reagan sent an unprecedented message to unions across America by firing every one of them.

In his book *Methland: The Death and Life of an American Small Town,* journalist Nick Reding traces the loss of manufacturing jobs (along with the death of the family farm) and the rise of illicit amphetamine use in Oelwein, Iowa (a short drive from Mason City). Within heartbreaking portraits of Midwest addiction, Reding examines the larger economic winds shaping the destiny of a working-class community. For instance, the corporate agribusiness giant Cargill enjoyed tremendous growth in the 1980s and '90s, yet one plant in Oelwein saw workers' wages drop by as much as 300 percent. Facing longer hours for less work, workers found a drug like meth, which would make it possible for them to work double shifts while keeping their spirits high, very attractive.

. . .

A few months after the divorce, I woke up to hear Mom screaming.

"We have to clean the house!" she shouted while running down the stairs, randomly placing mops, brooms, and rags in our hands. "Like *now*!"

I didn't know what was going on, but I actually enjoyed cleaning (still do) and was excited to see my grandparents and uncle arriving to help out. "He's gonna try and take my kids!" I heard Mom shout to her parents from the basement, while I scrubbed the bathroom floor.

Years later, I would learn that my dad had called the Department of Human Services, saying his children were living in dangerous and unsanitary conditions at their mother's house. Dad had tried to get full custody of us in the divorce, but he was broke and living in a seedy motel on the north side of Mason City, where there was far too much drug use and prostitution for any judge to place us in his care. "The courts always side with the mother," he often grumbled. "The government plays *way* too large of a role in American families. Everything works better when the government stays out of our lives." He resented having to pay child support, and was always telling us how our mom was spending the money on herself and not us.

We pulled so much trash out of that house that day that it required two pickup trucks to get it all to the dump. Because I knew how much this humiliated my mom, I worked extra hard, and gave her a lot of affection and praise whenever I could. In the end, we cleaned the house enough that when the social worker arrived, there was no longer sufficient evidence to grant my dad sole custody.

Then I learned that later that night we would be hosting a fundraising meeting for North Iowa Christian School (NICS) at our house. I felt rattled, nauseated, and exhausted. But I was getting used to surprises by that point.

NICS was a small private school with only a handful of kids in each grade, so there were only around a dozen parents walking into our living room, shaking snow off their heavy coats. Still, they all brought their kids with them, so there were more people in the house than I'd ever seen.

Phin and Faith had been going to NICS for a few years (I wouldn't start kindergarten there until the next fall), so they knew most of these kids: they'd shared recesses, craft projects, and nap times with them. I'd been too shy to make any friends at preschool and was intimidated by these older kids and their cool haircuts.

"What? You don't even have a *Nintendo*?" one of the boys said, kicking off his shoes and dropping his coat on the floor. "*Tell me* you at least have *cable*!"

We did not.

"We have an Atari!" I said, excited to be a good host to our guests.

A few of the older kids turned to me, were quiet for a second, then burst out laughing all at once. I didn't understand what they found funny, but then I took a second to look at their clothes—and their cars in the driveway—and realized that they lived in the kinds of houses that have Nintendos, get pizzas and pop delivered, and buy brand-name clothes at the mall during back-to-school shopping.

My cheeks turned red, and I felt humiliated. But it could be worse. We could be hosting this party on any other night, when the house didn't look so immaculate. That night it resembled pictures I'd seen from when Mom and Dad first moved in, when it was just Phin and Faith, back when the businesses were thriving, the walls were freshly painted, and all the furniture, carpeting, stereo, and TV were brand-new, before the drugs and the infidelity. Before my parents accidentally found themselves with a third helping of pregnancy they hadn't really wanted.

"Strike Force!" one of the kids yelled, before leaping into the air and dropping his elbow on another boy. I smiled at this, remembering the *Strike Force* show that had come to our church last summer. They were bodybuilders who smashed flaming bricks and blocks of ice with their heads and hands, then told us about the love of Jesus and the dangers of homosexuality. The boy was wearing a *Strike Force* T-shirt that read "HELL IS FOR WIMPS!" across the back.

Easily spooked by loud noises and intimidated by pretty much any game involving physical activity, I kept a good distance from these kids. I knew that I would be flattened to the ground every time I tried to wrestle anyone (boy or girl, older or younger).

For the rest of my years in Iowa, at any social gathering—holidays, birthday parties, funerals, Bible studies—I'd find myself quietly drifting toward the women in the kitchen, sincerely enjoying the cooking, cleaning, and gossip of female company over the football, racist jokes, and "no one wants to work anymore" conversation from the men slouched in their La-Z-Boy recliners.

It was just pie and coffee at that night's meeting, and there were only so many mugs I could fill, so many second helpings I could serve, until there was nothing left for me to do. (No one ever asked me to do this, I just really enjoyed domestic work.) So I stood on the landing between the adults seated in the kitchen and all the boys wrestling in the living room, unsure where I belonged.

No one can see you, a voice spoke within me. *You're invisible, a ghost.*

I saw a group of girls my age on the couch and shyly asked if I could play with them. They were braiding one another's hair and agreed to let me hang with them if they could braid mine, which I pretended I didn't want but reluctantly agreed to.

I sat on the floor as a girl in a *Rainbow Brite* sweatshirt brushed my long locks into sections held between her fingers, causing goose bumps to ripple across my scalp.

A bearded man in a John Deere hat had left the other adults in the kitchen to come watch our TV. He sat down on the couch next to us and switched it from an episode of *MacGyver* over to NBC, where a handsome man named Geraldo Rivera was just beginning a special news report called "Devil Worship: Exposing Satan's Underground."

"Our reporters have been investigating Satanism in America for months, and have a good idea of what's happening in our country," the mustached host said. "Satanism is cause for concern, and its roots can be anywhere, even in the heartland of our country."

While the girl continued to braid my hair, my goose bumps went from pleasure to terror as I watched the program, eyes wide and unblinking.

"Estimates are that there are over one million Satanists in the United States, in a highly organized, secretive network."

I felt dizzy watching this and worried that I might throw up.

I often felt like I was about to throw up, and would run to the bathroom, but most of the time nothing would happen. I'd just sit on the toilet, rocking back and forth, waiting to feel normal again. The best I could describe it at the time was a sudden plummeting sensation in my stomach, like the drop of a roller coaster. It would come on every evening, when the sun began to set, and get worse and worse until I fell asleep. (I hated sleep.)

After the girl finished braiding my hair, she and the rest of them ran up to Faith's room to play with her Barbies. I was following them and had gotten halfway up the stairs when I heard one giggle and say, "Quick, shut the door before he can get in!"

No one wants you here, the voice inside me said.

I didn't want to keep watching TV, so I wandered out onto the porch.

Scores of shoes lined the floor, illustrating the wealth and poverty of each family: farmers' boots caked in mud, ladies' high-heeled dress shoes, brand-new Air Jordans, and Chuck Taylors from the seventies. We'd never made a practice of it, but I'd asked everyone to take off their shoes when they first came in, because I thought this was what rich people did in their houses. (Again, no one asked me to do this, or was even paying attention to me; I was just really excited to be playing host.)

I grabbed a pair of high-heeled stilettos and liked the way the top of my foot slid into the front of them (with an inch or two gap at the heel). The challenge of walking in high heels was a thrilling game, like walking on stilts. I strutted across the porch, swishing my hips and flicking my recently braided hair. A window separated the porch from the living room; when I caught my reflection in it, I was delighted by my appearance, feeling a primal strength in looking exactly the way I wanted to look.

It was the same way I felt when dancing in my grandma's bedroom to MTV music videos (Grandma Marilyn *did* have cable). I'd always lock the door, and keep the volume low and my steps light, but mimicking Paula Abdul and Madonna made me feel so free and playful. ("Authentic" would be the best word to describe it, but I didn't understand such a concept at that time.)

It just felt right, like cold water on a hot day.

After I spent a few moments posing before the window reflection, my gaze went past my reflection and into the living room; one of the boys was looking at me. At first, I was excited by the attention, thinking he might want to join in the fun.

"Fag!" he shouted, pointing and laughing at me.

It was the first of thousands of times I'd hear that word while growing up in Iowa. On this night, I had no idea what it meant, but I could tell from the other boys' laughter that it wasn't good. That sick feeling in my stomach grew stronger, and then, suddenly, I felt very far away, as if this house, these people, even I myself, were all total strangers to me, like I'd just dropped into this life and had no idea what I was supposed to be doing.

Several years later, I learned the term "panic attack." It was another several years before I learned that Dad had had the same nightmares, insomnia, and loneliness as a kid that I did. I'd learn that Mom had felt invisible to her older siblings as a kid, just like I did, and would do anything—including marrying a stranger—to grab their attention, even for just a moment.

Fag, the voice within me teased. *Ghost boy.*

"Hey!" I heard myself shouting. "Hey! Everyone! Check this out!"

Though I had no idea what I was about to do, I watched myself do it just the same.

I didn't want to be invisible, didn't want to be a ghost boy, didn't want to be a "fag."

I made a fist, closed my eyes, and slammed my right arm through the window separating the porch and the living room. A piercing, shattering sound radiated throughout the house, silencing everyone's conversation.

There wasn't any pain at first, just a wild spark of pleasure, as if all the bad feelings had been zipped right out of me. This was a sensation I would chase for years to come, the feeling of having all fear and sadness float away on a damp cloud of blood.

Have you been washed in the blood of the lamb?

I turned around and was excited to see all the boys paying attention to me; even the adults had run onto the porch from the kitchen. But when Mom joined them, I saw the look of astonished horror on her pale face and realized I'd done something bad.

I'd caused her more humiliation in the eyes of church people.

I'd made a mess and was feeling too woozy to clean it up.

Our life was supposed to make people jealous, so they'd become born again.

A boy in high heels and braids spilling his blood on the carpet was nothing to envy.

I looked down at the shattered glass on the floor, then up to the hole in our porch with my arm thrust through it.

When I pulled my arm out of the broken window, I saw a thick purple line about six inches long running down the inside of my wrist. Then the line seemed to grow wider, as pulses of thick blood spread the skin so far apart I could see tendons twitching up and down in pace with my fingers. Dark-red liquid gushed down my arm, pooling in my hand, and started to splash onto the floor like an upturned pitcher of Kool-Aid.

There is a fountain filled with blood, I thought, remembering the song from church, *and sinners, plunged beneath that flood, lose all their guilty stains.*

Then I began to scream.

Interlude: God-Fearing Child

2023

As I stare into the wide, unblinking eyes of a goat marionette, I wonder if I'm addicted to fear. It's a rainy summer afternoon, and I'm standing in the MacNider Art Museum, housed in a spooky old mansion in downtown Mason City.

It's tucked away in a quiet, charming corner of the city, surrounded by willow trees, antique streetlamps, cobblestone walls, and a plethora of Frank Lloyd Wright architecture.

It's one of the last remnants of charm and style in old Mason City.

I've taken a break from my research at the library and walked over to this eerie vestige of my childhood. The puppet room of the Mac-Nider Museum terrified me as a child (often reminding me of the hall-of-heads scene in *Return to Oz*), and yet I was equally drawn to it. Here you can see the marionettes from *The Sound of Music*'s "The Lonely Goatherd" scene—creations of the late Bil Baird, famous Mason City puppeteer—who live behind glass walls in a dark room on the second floor.

Looking at them as an adult, I can't help but think of the modern horror-film series *Annabelle*, wherein a demonic spirit possesses an antique doll not unlike the ones I'm looking at now. The film series is one of many based on the lives and work of Ed and Lorraine Warren, a pair of Christian "demonologists" who rose to fame in the 1970s for their association with the *Amityville Horror* story, as well as the wildly successful *Conjuring* Universe horror-film series (which to date has grossed $1.2 billion in box-office sales).

The real Annabelle doll that inspired the films resides behind glass in the Warrens' Occult Museum in Connecticut, a fate not unlike these *Sound of Music* puppets.

Along with William Friedkin's *The Exorcist* and Roman Polanski's *Rosemary's Baby*, the Warrens played a massive role in shaping Christian mythology in twentieth-century America, possibly more than any actual Christian institution.

You may assume that, growing up in an evangelical household, I was not allowed to watch horror movies as a kid. And though my mom did try to maintain this policy, she was eventually so buried by two jobs and night school that I was more or less raised by late-night television.

Perhaps not unrelatedly, at around the same time that I slammed my fist through the porch window, I began hearing voices. Well, *a* voice. Not quite an auditory hallucination, but a voice that was clear, loud, and bullying enough to take up all the room inside my head, shutting down all thoughts or actions.

Then the voice began appearing in my dreams as an old woman.

Her name was Caldonia, and she embodied the classic "old hag" or "witch" archetype—weathered face under a black hood, using dark magic to lure children into their lair. This trope of Christian propaganda dates back centuries, used in part to frighten children, but also literally to demonize women of a certain age who'd acquired knowledge about sex, nature, and medicine, and were viewed as a threat to a patriarchal society.

The mythology is also associated with sleep paralysis, wherein the old hag sits on your chest and prevents you from moving when you wake from a dream. The condition itself is real, and I had an episode of sleep paralysis around once a week as a kid.

Caldonia wouldn't be sitting on my chest, though: she'd be standing over me.

I couldn't move, couldn't look away.

She'd be giggling to herself, the pupils in her wide eyes made of tiny flames that looked a thousand miles away. I would groan with disgust when she caressed my skin while reciting my sins, as if she were counting her own money.

Sloth! Lust! Lies!

The more I heard her voice, the more I was convinced that she was a demon that had taken possession of my little body.

The films I was watching, like *The Amityville Horror* and *The Exorcist,* didn't invent the concepts of demonic possession or supernatural warfare—angels and demons surrounding us in an invisible realm, warring for possession of our souls—but they did dramatize and contextualize it for modern audiences. Though they were pieces of entertainment, they were also cemented in a religious context and conviction felt deeply by their creators.

In nearly every supernatural horror film, there is, inevitably, a "liberal skeptic" character who insists on grounding his worldview in logic and science, unable to accept what is happening around him. This character is likely to be either killed by whatever ghost or demon the movie is centered on, or forced to accept that science and logic can no longer save him, so he must develop some kind of faith beyond the laws of physics.

Most of these films exist within a tradition of Christian propaganda extending back to the original Passion plays of the Middle Ages, exhibiting Christ's bloody demise and using the very instrument of torture (the cross) as the ultimate symbol of Christianity.

Epic paintings like *Dull Gret* and *The Garden of Earthly Delights,* which depict in vivid detail the gruesome and creative forms of eternal torture awaiting all sinners, played a major role in the conceptions of sin and damnation in the minds of sixteenth-century Europeans.

Mainstream horror movies aren't strictly Christian propaganda, but they are often heavily rooted in Christian themes, tropes, and characters. And they would eventually inspire a full circle of pop propaganda when evangelicals began making their own books, films, and songs of supernatural terror, often borrowing from the horror movies initially inspired by Christianity.

Before *The Exorcist, Rosemary's Baby,* and the Warrens, the concept of witches, ghost hunting, and exorcisms had nearly vanished from most Christian institutions. The Age of Enlightenment of the seventeenth and eighteenth centuries had made the barbarism of the Spanish Inquisition and the witch hunts of early modern Europe look like embarrassing chapters of a primitive era. But in the 1970s and '80s, the idea that witches and Satanists toiled in dark corners of American society—and evil spirits regularly possessed human bodies, driving them to commit murder against their will—was revived in the American consciousness. Suddenly the Catholic Church was inundated with requests for exorcisms (which they'd not performed for centuries), and Christians in law enforcement and the media slowly conjured the conspiracy theory known today as "the Satanic Panic."

Much like during the Inquisition or the witch trials, throughout the 1980s it was widely believed that a cabal of as many as a million devil worshippers had infiltrated schools, day-care centers, Hollywood, police departments, and all levels of government, and were ritualistically raping, murdering, and eating scores of American children. There would be over twelve thousand claims of Satanic ritual abuse against children, with absolutely zero evidence outside of coerced and leading confessions from children.

Scores of lives were lost to social persecution, suicide, and years of incarceration, not to mention millions of dollars in wasted law-enforcement resources.

Both *The Satanic Bible* and the Church of Satan were the creations of Anton LaVey, in 1969 and 1966 respectively. He was a showman and satirical trickster who didn't even believe in a literal Satan, let alone worship him. Before this there had never been a legitimate religious sect worshipping Satan, as it would ultimately just have been another Christian denomination, since the Devil doesn't exist outside this paradigm.

Throughout the 1970s and '80s, there were certainly a number of paint-huffing metalheads and coked-out pagans engaging in wild shit involving robes, masks, and Aleister Crowley's writings on sex magic, but none of it was ever linked to a larger network of believers with a consistent and coherent theology.

Throughout my childhood, I was glued to the TV during news reports (and the infamous Geraldo special previously mentioned) alleging that these evil and powerful baby-eaters surrounded us, and that rock music and drugs were used to lure young people into their dens of iniquity.

These reports would be loaded with B-roll footage of Anton LaVey's ceremonies, paintings depicting Dante's *Inferno,* faces of serial killers like Charles Manson, or random imagery associated with Wiccans or the Masonic Temple. Most common was the "pentacle," a star encased in a circle (often misnomered as a "pentagram") popularized in the eighties by metal bands like Slayer. This image, at the time referred to as "the symbol of Satan" by TV sensationalists like Geraldo, is actually historically associated with King Solomon, or various pagan faiths. News reports would show photos of a pentacle spray-painted on the undersides of bridges across America, which suggested a unified network of murdering devil worshippers from coast to coast (as opposed to the popularity of Mötley Crüe's "Looks That Kill" music video).

When hard evidence of these conspiracies failed to materialize— and alleged perpetrators of Satanic murder like the West Memphis Three and caretakers at the McMartin Preschool were exonerated of their crimes—the Satanic Panic hysteria cooled and became an embarrassing chapter of American criminal-justice history.

Both in the 1980s and today, evangelical conservatives have tapped into the pop-culture paranoia that supernatural evil is all around us, requiring political and spiritual interventions from church leaders.

The creators of the 1972 rapture film *A Thief in the Night* were heavily influenced by the cinematic techniques of horror films. The Hell House craze of the 1980s and '90s (Christian haunted houses using fear to proselytize) was clearly inspired by both slasher and horror films, dependent on jump scares and an overabundance of gore. My best friend, Thad, and I often borrowed imagery from films like *Tales from the Darkside* and *Hellraiser* when constructing our makeup, costumes, and performances as demons in church plays and Hell Houses. And the Christian author Frank Peretti was influenced by Stephen King for his wildly popular evangelical horror novel series, *This Present Darkness.* In addition to my gluttony for secular horror films, I was immersed in all the macabre media the Christian conservative world had to offer on a nightly basis, shaking like a shitting dog at the idea that I was possessed by a malignant spirit from Hell.

Most children today might wake from a nightmare and be comforted by their parents with the classic reassurance "That was only a dream, it's not real," but I was taught that such fears were completely justified:

That wasn't just your imagination; there really *is* a monster under your bed.

My only defense, I was told, was to pray, fast, and read my Bible. If I were to curse, masturbate, listen to certain music, watch certain movies, or allow unclean thoughts to enter my mind, these goblins would sink their claws deeper into my soul.

Today I know that Caldonia was a manifestation of all the fear and shame I'd absorbed at the hands of the Christian right. I now know that witches never really existed (at least not the type of witch I was taught to be on the lookout for). I know that Satanism was also a fictional concept, used to inspire fear of a malevolent "other," justifying the prosecution, torture, and execution of anyone engaged in a belief system outside Christianity.

I know all of this, and yet, looking into the face of this goat puppet behind the glass of the MacNider Museum, thinking about Annabelle in the Warrens' Occult Museum, thinking about the incessant visions of Caldonia that made my childhood one long marathon of self-harm and panic attacks . . . I must admit that the fear is still in me and will likely never leave. After my two decades of being pickled in Christian terror, no amount of logic can prevent the hairs on my arms from standing on end, goose bumps from rippling up my spine, my muscles from trembling like scurrying bugs under my skin, whenever I'm confronted with the tropes of supernatural warfare.

There's a dopamine release with this surge of fear, and even if it is compulsive and involuntary, it's still a kind of addiction that I wouldn't know how to live without.

As an adult, I've written multiple horror novels, hosted creative-writing retreats in notoriously haunted hotels, gorged myself on Stephen King books, and watched a scary movie almost every night before bed.

I no longer believe, but I still feel the fear, horrible and wonderful as it is.

As a freelance journalist, I am fueled by fear—of poverty, of missed deadlines, of the dying out of my career or talent—and find it difficult to be productive without having a panic attack driving my ass into gear. I suffer from an overactive nervous system, ramped up when my trauma is triggered, which I then monetize into the form of wild sentences. My relationships, both personal and professional, are often mired in conflict. My therapist has wondered if I suffer from "chaos addiction," whereby children reared on adrenaline will unconsciously pursue drama as adults, because it's the only relational dynamic they're equipped to navigate.

Fear is quite possibly the most powerful tool for social control in human history. It can be used to justify war, to get people to vote for or against a political candidate, or to invest in a boys' marching band before a pool table corrupts their souls. This is why media outlets that frighten are more popular than those that inform, and why churches that preach hate and division are so much more popular than those that preach love and tolerance.

I may no longer believe in any of it, but I still experience the fear of a believer.

And am quite likely addicted to it.

But there's one thing I've never quite been able to understand. On the rare occasion in my dreams when I'd find the strength to face Caldonia and bravely shout, "What do you want? Why are you tormenting me?," her consistent reply was always:

"I'm here to keep you safe."

CHAPTER TEN

The Wages of Sin

1993

After watching Jesus get punched in the face for the hundredth time—blood spraying from his mouth onto the stage—I really wasn't buying it anymore.

I'd watched this play so many times over the years, I knew every line of dialogue, every note in every song, and could perform the entire thing as a one-man show (and often did, in front of the mirror when home alone). Our church had been putting on these musical Passion plays—telling the story of Jesus's birth, life, gruesome death, and resurrection—since the eighties.

The aim was always to personalize the death of Jesus, directly associating your own sin with his torture. Crucifixion remains one of the most brutally creative ways to slowly kill a human, and to observe its re-enactment through the lens of sin—*your* sin—is to hate yourself beyond comprehension (or to be angry with the Jews for orchestrating this, which, historically, was another motive of Passion plays).

You see, Jesus had to die for our sins; otherwise, we'd all go to Hell.

It's a bit of a convoluted theology, but the idea, as I understood it at the time, was that God once had a relationship with humans—namely, Adam and Eve—but when they sinned, they became so impure that God could not stand to be in their presence. Before Jesus, the Jewish tradition had been to slaughter a lamb as a penance for our sins, but—as the Christian story goes—Jesus was "the lamb of God," slaughtered to take away the sin of the world. The fact that Christ's gruesome death happened two thousand years ago is irrelevant, because his sacrifice is paying out supernatural dividends throughout eternity.

Mom was always in the choir of our Passion plays, so I hung out in the theater late into the night during every rehearsal, until I was old enough to perform in the play myself. The way Jesus was whipped, beaten, and bullied by the Roman soldiers used to scare me—along with the booming thunder and lightning that followed his "It is finished!"—but once I started helping out with the makeup team on the bruises and bloody, torn flesh crisscrossing Jesus's body, a lot of the magic of the crucifixion disappeared.

Though for me, being allowed to play with makeup was more than enough magic.

We would start on Jesus's wounds several hours before showtime. First we'd create bruises from a combination of yellow, brown, and blue makeup. Then we'd start on the lacerations, using latex and tissue paper, blow-drying them into scabby, shiny welts of ripped skin. Once they were dry, we'd smother the wounds with different types of blood—some syrupy and coagulated, some wet and thin—spraying across his back, arms, and legs.

This year, we'd started doing a new play called *Heaven's Gates, Hell's Flames*. It was still the story of Jesus (with the essential crucifixion scene), but peppered throughout with one-act plays featuring modern families, switching back and forth between 1993 and 30 A.D.

The modern stories followed two types of people: born-again Christians and sinners who have rejected Christ. One family is driving to church, smiling and wholesome, like the Flanders family from *The Simpsons*; in another car, a father and son are skipping church, mocking believers, rejecting God.

The two cars crash, and everyone dies.

Both families find themselves before the pearly gates and the Lamb's Book of Life. If your name is written in that book (which is what happens when you pray to be "born again"), the gates open, a choir sings, and angels, dead relatives, and Jesus himself usher you into Heaven. If you've rejected the opportunity to accept Christ into your heart, as the boy and his father did, the room turns black, then red with strobe lights, and a laughing Satan bursts onto the stage, followed by painted demons who sprint toward the damned souls, ignoring the father's desperate pleas to spare his boy, and pull both of them, screaming, offstage.

Jesus's death didn't scare me anymore, but that sure did.

When I was old enough to play a demon, I was so good I scared myself.

The play ended with another modern story, this one a news report about millions of people suddenly vanishing off the face of the Earth, which leads to chaos when airline pilots, truck drivers, and world leaders disappear, and panic when doctors report that babies have suddenly vanished as they're being delivered.

All the Christians of the world have been raptured, and those remaining will face unspeakable horrors in an age known as: the Tribulation.

Ya got trouble, my friend!

The stage went black; then a spotlight descended on three women, who sang an a cappella song that I recognized from my parents' record collection, a song depicting war, starvation, dead children, and those who are out of time, and will be "left behind."

A chill shuddered through me as one of the three women sang the bridge (in a high, vibrato scream not unlike Yoko Ono's): "The Father spoke, the demons dined, how could you have been so blind?"*

Trouble with a capital T!

I was watching all of this from backstage, through a peephole in the curtain.

"God has given us the free will to choose to follow Him, or follow sin to Hell," Pastor Jim said once the song was finished. "Now I'm going to ask for every head bowed and every eye closed in this auditorium tonight. And I want you to ask yourself, if you died tonight, do you know where you would go? If you're not one hundred percent certain you'd go to Heaven, I'm here to tell you there's a way you can know for sure."

He then shared the story of a mother who'd attended our Passion

---

* This lyric was slightly changed when the band DC Talk covered the Larry Norman song, which was the version my generation was most familiar with.

play the year before, and during the altar call—the time when all are invited to come to the stage for prayer—her ten-year-old son had given his life to Christ. Two months later, during a tornado, the roof of their trailer was ripped open, and her son was plucked from her arms, to die in a nearby field. But, thanks to our play, she had the reassurance that her son was waiting for her in Heaven.

People poured out of their seats so quickly that the ramp to the stage was bottlenecked with sinners, hungry for salvation. Once there, they were paired with a counselor who led them in the "Sinner's Prayer." Then the newly born-again Christians filled out cards with their contact information. In a week, they would receive a call (or several) inviting them to Agapé Christian Family Church on Sunday, or any of our other services and events throughout the week.

Watching through the peephole in the curtain, I wondered how many of these converts would continue to live a Christian life once they left the auditorium.

Belief was so much easier to maintain on their side of the curtain.

In the dark of the audience, it's all so urgent, dramatic, and simple. It was a fork in the road, with Heaven pointing to the left and Hell to the right, and you just needed to say, "Oh, I'll take eternal bliss over eternal torture, thank you very much."

But it was never so clear on my side of the curtain.

After the age of twelve or so, I began attending several different churches on my own (all of them Protestant evangelical, of course; we thought of Catholics as closer to voodoo than Christianity) and was getting conflicting information about a great many things, particularly salvation from Hell. They all agreed that reciting the "Sinner's Prayer," inviting God into your heart and life, and becoming "born again" would get your name in the Lamb's Book of Life. But would it stay there no matter what?

I'd read in the book of Hebrews, "It is impossible for those who have once been enlightened . . . and who have fallen away, to be brought back to repentance."

At church camp, I often heard the term "backsliding" to describe a born-again Christian who'd fallen into sin, and it was often insinuated that that person was no longer exempt from eternal torture.

Unlike Catholics, we never had a system for ranking sins or specific methods of atoning for them; they were all equal in God's eyes, I was told. And God's eyes cannot look upon sin without our first calling upon the forgiveness that was bought with Christ's death. So, if I have an impure thought about my teacher just as a speeding car crushes my head, and I die before asking God to forgive me, would I go to Hell?

It seemed so.

Pastor Jim reinforced this idea when he said, "Now, some of you still in your seats may be thinking, *I dedicated my life to Christ when I was a child,* but you may be feeling this tug in your heart tonight to get right with God, that there's something that's keeping you from the redeeming blood of Jesus. I invite you to come onto this stage and pray with our counselors, rededicating your life to Christ. Don't let this opportunity pass you by, because your eternity is at stake, and there may never be another night like tonight."*

To be honest, I didn't really understand what "sin" even was.

Jesus talked a lot about *forgiving* our sins, and said that we should forgive one another for wrongs done to us, but he didn't get into specific sins very often. When he did, it was stuff about not "lusting in your heart," or the vague yet ominous "Whoever blasphemes against the Holy Spirit can never be forgiven, but is guilty of eternal sin."

What the heck did that even mean?

Had I done this without knowing I did it?

I knew some Christians who cursed and drank beer, claiming these weren't sins, and I knew others who believed playing cards was akin to murder. Standing behind that curtain, I thought about the Latchkey Boys.

On the south end of Clear Lake, a collection of trailer parks hosted a small handful of boys I'd befriended who had a lot of time on their hands.

My brother, Phin, referred to them as "the Latchkey Boys," telling me they were nothing but trouble (yet he still showed little concern about the amount of time I was spending with them). Despite stereo-

---

* Again, these quotes are from my memory and are not verbatim.

types about trailer parks, all of their parents were still together but worked around the clock.

A few of them were bright and playful, the exception being an over-developed twelve-year-old everyone called Hooch. Muscled, with straight black hair and eyes to match, Hooch was always playing mind games with everyone, pressuring them to skateboard down a steep ramp, shoplift booze, or break into the trailer with all the porn.

The trailer had seemingly been abandoned months ago, and inside was a virtual library of pornographic videos and sex toys I couldn't begin to imagine how to use. I knew nothing of sex, but was drawn to the dark, warm feeling in my lower gut, which spread throughout every cell once the first video was thrust into the VCR (the trailer's electricity still worked). I was terrified of the feeling, but the craving to pursue it was so enormous it eclipsed the warnings to stay away. I watched the other boys touching themselves and felt compelled to do the same—not from social pressure, but from the pressure that seemed to be building in my groin.

Two of the boys were talking to the screen, encouraging the naked people as if they could hear us. "Yeah, do it, baby!" one said. "Ride him like a bull!"

Afterward, while biking home, I cried and panicked, begging God to forgive me.

You don't deserve forgiveness, the voice of Caldonia spoke within my head. *You had your chance to run away, but now there's no time to change your mind; you've done what you've done, and you'll be left behind.*

"If there is something separating you from God's love, please come to the stage tonight and pray with us," Pastor Jim again urged.

Despite the profound self-loathing it induced, I found myself coming back to that trailer, again and again, feverishly watching strangers do things to one another that confused yet enticed me. Worst of all, I found myself just as drawn to the men's bodies as I was to the women's, and would often picture myself in women's clothes while being touched by the men.

"There may not be another night like tonight."

I walked around the curtain, right up to Pastor Jim, with tears in my eyes. "I am a sinner that needs forgiveness. I don't want to go to Hell."

I would feel good after he prayed with me, but—just as I wondered about the rest of these people on the stage—the feeling wouldn't last. And neither would the commitment to avoid sin. At least once a week over the next eight years, I would find myself walking to the altar of churches, camps, conventions, concerts, and plays whenever someone asked the question "Do you know where you'll go if you die tonight?" And every time, the assurance that I'd be going to Heaven would escape my grasp.

Every moment of every day throughout my childhood, I lived with the conviction that I would burn in Hell for my sexual sins; I'd be lonely, terrified, and tortured by demons for all eternity.

CHAPTER ELEVEN

Suffer, Little Children

"Sleep, those little slices of death—how I loathe them."

—ATTRIBUTED TO EDGAR ALLAN POE

1993

Mom and I walked into the dark house, both of us exhausted and silent.

The temperature had remained below zero for more than a week, with only a few hours of gray sunshine each day. Our furnace was running around the clock, but couldn't keep up with the brutal cold of a North Iowa winter.

Phin and Faith had gone to live with my dad by this time, while I chose to stay with Mom, not wanting her to feel left behind, though I did visit Dad on weekends. My siblings would later admit they felt guilty for abandoning Mom, but Dad's house had good food and cable and was, above all, clean.

"Do you have any homework?" Mom asked as she set down her purse and turned on the lights.

Mom always asked this question, and tried her best to read my report cards and meet with my teachers. We were both left-handed, and she'd coach me to "write *beneath* the copy," keeping my pencil under the words I was writing so I wouldn't smear the page with my hand while it moved left to right (something right-handed people don't have to worry about).* I was resentful of her efforts, though years later I'd come to see the benefits of the Midwestern manners, eloquent

---

* Only a couple generations earlier, our southpaw inclinations could have been viewed as a sign of demonic possession, and at the very least would have been strongly discouraged, if not punished.

speech, and attention to detail Mom worked to instill in me. But lately she had so little time to help me with my homework, and couldn't even find my report cards buried in the mess of junk mail piling up on the porch.

"Nope," I lied. I actually had a lot of homework to do, but it was stuffed deep in my backpack, under random cassettes, a *Tiger Beat* magazine, and a sweater that had been used to clean up a jug of milk I'd spilled at school.

I didn't want to open my backpack. I didn't want to think about school, or homework, or how weird my classmates thought I was.

"Great," Mom said. "Hey, bud, I'm pooped, and I'm gonna go to bed. You do the same, okay?"

I told her I would, knowing it was another lie.

As soon as I heard her bedroom door close, I turned on the news, eager for more updates on the Branch Davidian standoff in Waco, Texas. Their leader, David Koresh, had been saying for years that he was the second coming of Jesus Christ, and prophesied that he and his followers would be killed by the U.S. government, which would bring about the Tribulation. It was fifty-one days since the ATF had stormed their compound, just like Koresh said they would, and I was glued to the news each night.

Most people I knew thought Koresh was insane, or possibly the Antichrist, but isn't that exactly what the Bible predicted people would say about Christ when he returned? Isn't that what happened the first time he came? That night, I watched footage from earlier in the day, where tanks sprayed tear gas inside the compound, which then caught fire and burned seventy-six people alive, including dozens of children.[*]

It's almost time, Caldonia reminded me, *for you to be left behind.*

I hoped I'd never have to shoot a gun, because I was terrified of loud noises.

As I watched the flames of burning humans rise into the air, I bit

---

[*] The antigovernment militia movement swelled in the aftermath of Waco, and came to a head on April 19, 1995, when Timothy McVeigh bombed a government building in Oklahoma City, killing 168 people in an act of retaliation for Waco and the Ruby Ridge standoff.

down hard on my tongue. I always did this whenever I wasn't sure if I was awake or dreaming. Sometimes there'd be no pain, only dull pressure, and I'd know that I was dreaming and terrible things were about to happen. But when I'd feel pain spark out from my tongue—just like the sensation I felt when punching that window, the jagged glass slicing through my tender skin—a warm blanket of reassurance would fall over me, for I knew that the demons would remain in the invisible realm, at least a while longer.

I turned off the news and put in a videotape of *Friday the 13th: The Final Chapter,* which I'd recorded off HBO at Dad's house. About twenty minutes into the movie, I started to feel sleepy, so I fixed myself a cup of coffee.

This is something I'd learned from characters on *A Nightmare on Elm Street,* who used caffeine to push away sleep (as it was only in dream-land that they were haunted, tortured, and often killed by Freddy Krueger, whose carnage would manifest in the real world). I knew that sleep would eventually overtake me, as it usually did, around three or four in the morning, but I tried to stave it off for as long as possible. Sleep was not my friend, and it never got me without a fight. My entire life, I'd suffered not just from nightmares and sleep paralysis, but also from sleepwalking. It wasn't uncommon for me to be found walking in the backyard or around town wearing nothing but my Carman T-shirt. Sometimes I'd wake up trembling, unsure where I was, swatting at my skin and clawing my face, shouting, "Don't touch me, Caldonia! In the name of Jesus, stop touching me!"

Throughout my childhood, I'd been told that when I was being pursued by evil from the supernatural realm, all I had to do was shout the incantation "In the name of Jesus, I cast you out!" But this never worked in my dreams, because I was always verbally paralyzed. I once asked one of my church-camp counselors about this and he said, "If God isn't coming when you call, I would question your relationship with Him. Is there something keeping you from God's love, Josiah?"

I hadn't entered my bedroom in years; I spent each night on the couch.

My clothes rarely saw a washing machine and never made it to a dresser drawer.

Once it got dark, TV became a kind of talisman that I clung to for reassurance. Anywhere in the house outside of the comforting glow of that screen might have held demons, so I'd delay going to the bathroom or the kitchen as long as possible. I'd slap my face to stay awake, reminding myself of what awaited me behind my eyelids.

When I eventually succumbed to the pull of sleep that night, I found myself in the backyard.

I bit my tongue, felt nothing, and knew the coffee had failed me once again.

I was walking down the back stairs and saw that our yard had turned into a baseball diamond. The sky was black and starry, with the full, bloodred moon shining down on the freshly mown grass. In a flash of smoke and fire, Caldonia rose out of the pitcher's mound. Gooseflesh crawled across my skin, and my gut stirred with dread. She was smiling with those wide, jittery eyes, tiny flames dancing in the deep recesses of her pupils.

I tried to speak, to rebuke her in the name of Jesus, but as was so often the case, my mouth was paralyzed, as was my body.

Dread mixed with arousal stirred in my belly. It was sexual, but horrible at the same time. I attempted to repeat my incantation, but could only stammer nonsense.

"God *knows* who you are," Caldonia said with a snicker, her eyes growing even wider. Suddenly I felt an overwhelming erection growing in my pajamas. "God cannot stand in the presence of sin, and you are *too weak* to resist sin."

She threw her head back in a loud cackle, then pointed to my crotch.

A cartoonishly large bulge pushed against the fabric of my pajamas, throbbing and driving me mad with horrible pleasure. It kept growing, tearing through my pants, and rising into the air. It burned, ached, and stung, but felt so good at the same time that I thought I might go mad.

Then my penis detached from me and floated away, bursting into sparkly confetti in the night sky. I lowered my eyes back down in time to see Caldonia hungrily leaping toward me, with her bulging eyes and spiked teeth. Her flaming pupils roared into a wildfire that consumed her sockets as her hands dug into my sides.

CHAPTER TWELVE

Walking Under Water

1994

Throughout the Satanic Panic era, we had several guest speakers at my church who claimed to be former Satanists and were now born-again Christians.

There seemed to be a lot of them.

They wrote books, gave speeches, appeared on Pat Robertson's *The 700 Club;* all had wild tales of drugs, sacrificial murder, orgies soaked in blood, and demonic possession, and even claimed to have witnessed the physical manifestation of Satan himself. I still didn't understand that passage in the Gospel of Mark about "blaspheming the Holy Spirit" being an "unforgivable sin," but apparently making sacrifices to the Devil wasn't a deal-breaker for salvation.

In the summer of 1994, I walked to City Beach after our Sunday-morning service at Agapé let out. I'd just sat through a sermon from a former Satanist who said he'd been infected with "the demon of homo-sexuality" as a child, which made my blood go cold. I was still shivering on the beach, despite the sweltering heat.

I'd heard a lot about the "demon of homosexuality" at church camp and youth rallies, often when some effete boy was in the middle of a kinetic prayer circle—everyone huddled tightly around him, sweat-ing, twitching, praying loudly, a jungle of hands touching his upper body—and a middle-aged male counselor would be shouting, "We bind the demon of homosexuality attacking this boy, in *Jesus's name!*"

I knew I was attracted to boys as much as to girls, and assumed this was the spirit realm at work within me, with demons seducing me toward the former, and angels pushing for the latter.

Church had been over for hours, and I'd spent the afternoon on the beach, getting too much sun while reading one Chick Tract after another.

These little three-by-five-inch comic booklets were one of the most ubiquitous and influential sources of evangelical propaganda of the twentieth century. Nine hundred million copies of their 250 titles have been printed, and they have been translated into 120 languages. Named for their creator, Jack Chick, the easy-to-read and well-illustrated comic book stories infused conspiracy-theory propaganda with relatable American characters, warning about the insidious agendas of hippies, communists, evolutionists, gays, Catholics, Jews, witches, abortionists, the government, and "false religions" (which was all of them except fundamentalist Christianity).

Aimed to grab your attention before you got the chance to flush the truck-stop toilet, the Chick Tract stories were notoriously brutal and sensationalistic. I'd amassed a huge collection of them from the various evangelical churches I'd been attending.

Doom Town describes an insidious plot by LGBTQ activists to infect the nation's donated blood supply with AIDS, as a form of political violence. In *The Poor Little Witch,* a high-school teacher turns her student on to witchcraft; she eventually participates in a child sacrifice to Satan, in which she's forced to drink the blood of the deceased or be murdered herself.

Reading Chick Tracts left me with a hypervigilance about guarding my thoughts from the evils that surrounded me, particularly those in my own mind. I couldn't trust my thoughts, instincts, or impulses, because they were likely demonic influences.

After hours on the beach, I was feeling dizzy and tired, the hundred-degree sun beating down on my head like a hammer to an anvil.

I turned to the tract *Wounded Children,* the story of a boy named David who is encouraged by Satan to read his father's pornography magazines. "Think of all those pictures in your daddy's book," Satan whispers into little David's ear as the boy lays anxiously awake in bed.

Ten-year-old David begins masturbating, then escalates to fooling around with a girl, until she rejects him. Estranged from his hypermasculine father and confused about his sexuality, David becomes lonely and depressed. While he's in this vulnerable state, Satan pays David another visit, subliminally telling him he's confused about his gender.

The next day, Satan tells David's father (again, subliminally) to bully him for being a sissy who plays with dolls. At the top of the page, a narrator explains, "The demonic force working on David is molding him into a feminine role . . . In this case, it is using David's father to help plant those thoughts in David's mind."

Sitting on the beach, I wondered if any of the Satanists who, I was told, had infiltrated my school, police force, and government were engaged in supernatural warfare to turn me gay. Whenever I lusted after Kurt Cobain or Michael Hutchence in a music video, or secretly adorned myself in the girls' clothes I kept hidden under the basement stairs (dresses, pearls, heels, makeup), I'd wonder: was all this due to a cabal of devil worshippers casting spells at me, infecting me with "the demon of homosexuality"?

Was that how Caldonia got into my head?

Was she a witch demon sent to torture me?

Deuteronomy 22:5: "A woman shall not wear a man's garment, nor shall a man put on a woman's cloak, for whoever does these things is an abomination to the Lord your God."

Even though I was attracted to girls as well as boys, the word "faggot" seemed to chase me everywhere I went. It accompanied punches to the back of my head in school, my pants ripped down in the hallways, my weak body thrown into a locker or recycling bin.

And I heard it that day on the beach as I read the Chick Tract.

I was about to stand up and walk home for some Hamburger Helper and Hi-C Ecto Cooler when I heard a familiar voice say "Whaddup, faggot?"

"Hey, Hooch," I said, standing up straight, feeling woozy from too much sun.

"What are you doing, praying Jesus will give you a big dick?" he asked, and the two other Latchkey boys with him laughed. They'd all grown a head taller than me, and developed low voices and broad shoulders, while I had remained short and weak, somehow both pudgy and skinny. "What do you got there?" Hooch asked, snatching the Chick Tract out of my hand. I expected him to explode with laughter and show the other boys the pictures of frightened little David, playing with dolls.

But instead he just grinned to himself, shoved the tract in his pocket, and said, "Looks like the lifeguard forgot to lock up that canoe," pointing at the boat resting by the lifeguard chair. Seconds later, the two other boys were dragging it to the water, hopping in, and pulling out the paddles. "Let's go, Josiah."

At first, I smiled brightly at the Latchkey Boys.

I'd been told again and again to make my face an advertisement for the joy of Christianity, reinforced in Christian-rock songs like the Newsboys' "I'm Not Ashamed" or "Shine," which instructed me to "shine, make 'em wonder what you've got."

But then I began to wonder: Were the Latchkey Boys part of Satan's army?

"Naw, I gotta get home," I said to Hooch. "My mom has chores for me to do."

"That's bullshit," Hooch said, planting one hand on the back of my neck and squeezing, hard. "We both know you and your mom live in filth, and neither of you do chores. Now, let's go fishing, you little bitch."[*]

I could not swim, and Hooch knew it.

I was terrified of water, and Hooch also knew this.

I got in the boat, just as Hooch knew I would.

Even though Mom had enrolled me in swimming classes at the beach, I could never manage to keep water from gushing into my nose and choking me every time I submerged myself. While the other kids effortlessly floated across the surface, I couldn't keep myself from sinking like a cannonball.

Part of this was due to my body type—small, yet dense, with little

---

[*] For storytelling purposes, I've combined two different incidents with the Latchkey Boys into this one scene.

muscle—but it was largely because I was never comfortable in water, and would reflexively tense every muscle whenever the water reached above my waist, pushing air out of my diaphragm. To float, you must have a level of trust with the water, and I never got beyond viewing it as a threat that would render me helpless, breathless, and, eventually, dead.

The handful of times we stayed in hotels on vacation, I was content to splash around in the shallow end of the pool, but Phin always insisted that I could learn to swim if forced to. If I dared to stand at the edge of the deep end, he'd often sneak up behind me and push me in. I'd then prove my inability to float by patiently sinking to the bottom of the eight- or nine-foot-deep pool, and then walk my way up the incline toward the shallow end.

Jesus could walk on water, but I could walk underneath it.

As our boat traveled farther from the shore, Hooch watched me, seemingly searching my face for panic. It was almost as if he was hungry for my fear, feeding off it like Caldonia in my dreams. Thinking of the Chick Tract, I was convinced that Satan was using him to get to me.

"Where have you been lately?" he asked. "Haven't seen you all summer."

"I was at camp," I said, pretending to look at fish in the water.

"Jesus camp," Hooch sneered.

He was right. Around this time, I started attending a weeklong camp with the Assemblies of God church every summer, followed by a second week at the Open Bible campground (one year, I attended the junior-high *and* high-school camps at both churches, resulting in four straight weeks of church camp). Both AG and Open Bible also had weekend retreats during the fall and spring of each school year, in which we stayed in hotels in big cities like Des Moines or Cedar Rapids. And then there was the Acquire the Fire convention each year in Minneapolis, plus the Sonshine Festival in the summer, and at least a dozen Christian-rock concerts throughout the year.

My weekly church schedule had become even more congested. Even though I wasn't a student there, I often went to events at Forest City Christian School; I was desperate to enroll there, to escape the anti-Christian propaganda of public school, which I'd been attending since my parents split up and North Iowa Christian School became unaffordable. While I was in Forest City, I'd often attend the Baptist youth group there on Mondays. On Tuesdays, it was the Evangelical Free Church youth group in Britt, followed by the E-Free youth group in Clear Lake on Wednesdays, then Open Bible youth group on Thursday nights, then Agapé's youth group on Friday. I was usually pretty tired by that evening, especially since I had a Promise Keepers breakfast at six a.m. before school every Friday.

After Sunday morning's service at Agapé, there was usually a rehearsal for something—the Easter Passion play, or a Christmas service, or a Fourth of July Parade performance—followed by the Sunday-evening church service.

On average, this came out to around nine church events each week.

There was literally nothing in my life—no friends, activities, or ambitions—that wasn't linked to an evangelical church. I was desperate to find some understanding of it all, desperate for the click of salvation in my head, the one that would tell me, "Relax, sleep well, Josiah, you're a good boy who won't be tortured for all eternity."

But, alas, that never arrived.

Out in the middle of the lake, the August sun shone even brighter and hotter. My vision was becoming blurry, and my head ached. I longed to be home with a giant glass of Kool-Aid.

"You haven't even seen how hairy Bobby's dick has gotten," Hooch said, and everyone laughed at this. Hooch rocked the boat from side to side while staring at me, and I knew he could see my fear. "You gotta show him."

Bobby complied, and I was treated not only to what looked like an ant colony of black hairs reaching out in every direction from his crotch, but also to the sight of Bobby's frighteningly large penis. "Pretty crazy, eh?" Hooch said, smiling. "Kiss it."

The sun shone brightly off the water, projecting a celestial chaos onto Hooch's face. As I looked at him, I checked out temporarily, then pulled my gaze up to Bobby, who for a split second seemed just as alarmed by this command as I was. Then he returned to that dumb, vacant laugh.

"Kiss it," Hooch repeated.

I might have been aroused whenever Jared Leto appeared on *My So-Called Life*, but at this moment there wasn't a single solitary shred of temptation in me. Bobby was a chubby, pimpled boy who smelled as though he showered less than once a year. I wanted to kiss his penis about as much as I wanted to kiss a dead animal.

Besides, I knew there were demons all around us, and this was a test.

I wouldn't fall for it like little David in the Chick Tract.

"No," I said, the defiance causing adrenaline to surge through my body.

I thought of Matthew 5:12: "Rejoice and be glad, for your reward is great in heaven, for so they persecuted the prophets who were before you."

"What did you say?" Hooch asked. "You kiss it, or else I'm gonna push you into the lake."

"In the name of Jesus, you will not!" I said, stomping my foot on the canoe floor. I could hear my voice slurring a little, as my consciousness drifted in and out, and I interpreted the early signs of sunstroke as the presence of evil in this canoe.

Hooch's face morphed from confusion to disbelief to outright hilarity.

"What was that, some kind of a spell?" he asked, laughing while looking at the others.

You must have faith to be healed.

He was on his feet and moving toward me in a flash.

Something is keeping you from God's love.

The world turned green before I could fully comprehend what was going on. All sound became muffled—waves hitting our canoe, jet skiers roaring by, Hooch barking orders at his minions—replaced only with an intimate warbling. I was submerged in the pale-green water, falling away from the sunbeams near the surface; everything was growing cold and dark. My arms and legs thrust spastically in all directions, free of strategy, uselessly clawing at the dark, murky water.

This was my Tribulation, my test to see if I was worthy of Heaven.

As the rippling sun above me faded, I turned and looked down.

Instinctively, I waited for my feet to land on the bottom of the lake, which would reassure me that the Earth was still there and I could once again walk across it. But this was much deeper than a nine-foot hotel pool.

I have no idea how far I sank. Possibly only a few feet beneath the rowboat, but it felt like a mile. My lungs grew hot and twitchy, and my vision filled with spots as my muscles tensed.

I looked down, hoping to see a muddy earth covered with seaweed lazily drifting around. But I saw nothing but green. Then a pair of tiny red lights.

They were profoundly small, these lights, yet somehow bright enough for my eyes to see them. Time both slowed down and sped up, as the one pair of red lights became two pairs, then grew larger, seeming to approach me. Two sets of eyes with tiny flickers of fire for pupils. Eyes became faces, faces became bodies, and then two witches, both Caldonia, were swimming toward me from the bottom of the lake.

They were cutting upward like Olympic swimmers, with a desperate hunger in their eyes. They'd come up from Hell and planned to drag me back down there with them.

I stopped allowing myself to sink and grabbed spastically at the water, desperate to remember any detail from my swimming lessons. Should I cup my hands or make them flat? Kick while pumping my arms, or only do one or the other? I couldn't recall, and wound up doing all of the swimming strokes at the same time, like a panicking cat dropped into a pool.

Like Hooch, the double witches seemed tickled by my fear.

I was about to succumb to the dizziness, to the comforting darkness wrapping itself around me, when I felt hands gripping my armpits and pulling me upward, toward the surface. After a couple of desperate, coughing breaths I looked over and saw it was Bobby who had jumped in and pulled me out of the water. He was holding on to me while grabbing the canoe with his other arm.

"You want us to bring you to shore?" Hooch asked, hyperventilating with laughter while wiping a tear from his eye.

I could barely muster a "yeah."

On the walk back home, I felt very far away from myself, almost outside of my body. My wet clothes slapped against my skin, and my shoes squished and squeaked along the sidewalk, but somehow it all felt far away.

The house was empty when I got home.

I lay down on the floor, not bothering to change into something dry, and turned on the TV.

CHAPTER THIRTEEN

Child Left Behind

1995

Every generation inevitably faces the moment when the fashion of their youth is revived by those twenty years younger.

And, to the adults, it always looks awful.

I've dealt with this in 2023, with the revival of enormous JNCO-esque pants and the return of floppy boy-band hair parted in the middle. Gen Xers faced it a decade ago with the revival of the mullet and hair metal, followed by plaid shirts and baby-doll dresses. And in the mid-nineties, my parents faced this when I began sporting bell-bottom leisure suits with puka-shell necklaces.

But we nineties evangelical kids were actually a copy of a copy.

Ever since Larry Norman and the Jesus Movement created the genre of Contemporary Christian Music (CCM), the industry has always reflected the popular (secular) tastes of the time—from Stryper, representing glam metal; to Jars of Clay, with coffeehouse rock; to Carman, emulating the worst elements of every genre. And this continued when secular bands like The Dandy Warhols, Deee-Lite, and Oasis were mimicking the pop sounds of their parents' generation. Christian rock was happy to appropriate their appropriations—like a series of postmodern Russian dolls.

Hip yet family-friendly Christian bands like Audio Adrenaline were dressing like the Allman Brothers and covering seventies classics like Edgar Winter's "Free Ride." The Newsboys appeared to have raided

ABBA's wardrobe, wearing eyeliner and recording an album titled *Love Liberty Disco*.

When I saw the faux-TLC Christian girl group Out of Eden covering the Bill Withers song "Lovely Day," I thought they were pop geniuses, because I'd certainly never heard the original. Similarly, the Doobie Brothers' "Takin' It to the Streets" was a common hype song at church camp, where a crowd of nineties teens would sing along to lyrics we believed were about going downtown and warning strangers about the coming rapture (unaware that it was actually a song about income inequality written under the influence of cocaine).

But the crown of Classic Rock Christianity has to go to DC Talk. Often referred to as "the Beatles of Christian Rock," this rap/rock vocal trio had been covering boomer songs like The Doobie Brothers' "Jesus Is Just Alright" and the actual Beatles' "Help!" for years. With their boy-band handsomeness and high-energy live performances, DC Talk were icons for a generation craving a little cool with their Christ. Just before they changed the CCM genre with their double-platinum album, *Jesus Freak,* in 1995, the band dropped a promotional single of the title song, and gave it out for free to youth pastors across the nation.

The CD was designed to resemble a 45-rpm single, with a groovy bubble font reminiscent of *The Living Bible* of the seventies. Though the term "Jesus Freak" had been a slur against the Jesus People of the 1970s, by the nineties it had been reclaimed as a badge of honor, conveying a heady sense of martyrdom.

On the B-side of this CD single was a cover of Larry Norman's rapture anthem, "I Wish We'd All Been Ready."

I was one of many glassy-eyed Christian teenyboppers in the audience of DC Talk's performance of this song in Cedar Rapids, Iowa, in 1995, one month before the album dropped. Our youth group had shuttled us down there, and I cried with fear as the dreamy vocalist Kevin Max sang, like Johnny Cash with vibrato, about the terrors we would all suffer if we were "left behind" in the rapture.

This song had a similar effect on my parents decades earlier, when it was played over and over in the 1972 rapture film *A Thief in the Night,* filmed in the nearby Iowa capital of Des Moines.

The same year when DC Talk was selling millions of *Jesus Freak* albums, the Christian-right icon (and founding member of the Moral Majority) Tim LaHaye teamed up with the author Jerry B. Jenkins to publish the rapture novel *Left Behind: A Novel of the Earth's Last Days.*

Just like *A Thief in the Night, Left Behind* placed end-times prophecy in contemporary life (also owing a debt to Norman's song, particularly for its title), and successfully scared the shit out of young sinners throughout the Clinton era. I can easily think of a dozen young people I knew who had been actively rebelling against Christianity but then stepped squarely back into line after sweating through that book. Twelve sequels and three prequels would follow the first novel (selling a combined total of eighty million copies), along with five films and several video games.

Saturated as I was in this content, a day never went by without my weighing the strength of my faith versus starvation and torture.

I was certain I'd never make it, and Caldonia often reminded me of this.

You can't even fast for a whole day, you weakling, she'd say. *How could you possibly handle sleeping in the woods, or refusing to renounce Christ even when your teeth are ripped out, your feet are boiled, and bamboo is shoved under your fingernails?*

You can't even handle a roller coaster, you little wimp.

The year before the release of *Jesus Freak,* on the afternoon of May 10, 1994, I was certain my time had come.

It was recess at school, and I'd been reading *Where the Red Fern Grows* under a willow tree when the afternoon sky suddenly turned from sunny to nearly pitch-black. When I looked up, I saw that the sun had turned dark and had a red, bloodlike haze vibrating around it. Instantly I flashed on the prophecy of Revelation 6:12: "When He had opened the sixth seal, and, lo, there was a great earthquake, and the sun became black as sackcloth of hair, and the moon became as blood."

I stood up in a panic, then fell to my knees in the dirt, scratched at my face, and pulled my hair, urgently begging God to forgive me for every sin I could think of. (Fortunately, none of my fellow students witnessed this—I often sought out privacy during recess.)

I knew what would come next.

Any second an ear-splitting trumpet would roar from the now-blackened sky, the stars would fall to the earth, the ground would split, emitting a black smoke that would shroud the earth, followed by a swarm of locusts with the faces of men, wearing long hair under golden crowns, with the teeth of lions and scorpion tails, given authority to torture all of us for five months, as prophesied in Revelation.

Though it just turned out to be a solar eclipse.

I dusted myself off and returned to class.

(It's possible our teachers had warned us about the eclipse and I just wasn't paying attention, as I often slipped into bouts of dissociation during school.)

For years, I interpreted the world around me through an apocalyptic lens: Mom was home late (the rapture must have occurred); a tornado siren was being tested (that must be the horn of Gabriel). I was eight when Mom took us to the Holocaust Museum in Chicago (Dad hated museums, but Mom insisted), and afterward I kept getting the history of European Jews in the 1940s confused with Christian films like *A Thief in the Night,* which portrayed Christians in similar circumstances (swapping Hitler for the Antichrist).

I can vividly recall my watching an episode of the ABC miniseries *War and Remembrance* with my parents, which graphically followed Jews being led to and locked in a gas chamber. Women, children, and the elderly were screaming, pushing one another over, desperate to escape the poison gas in a scene that lasted nearly twenty minutes. My eyes remained wide as I lay in bed that night, knowing I wouldn't be strong enough not to renounce Christ in the face of such terror.

By 1996, many evangelists were hyping the Y2K theory—positing that every computer on Earth would fail on January 1, 2000, leading to global chaos—as the event that would usher in the Tribulation. This included the godfather of rapture fever, Hal Lindsey, who published *Facing Millennial Midnight: The Y2K Crisis Confronting America and the World* with co-author Cliff Ford.

Even though his 1988 prophecy had lapsed without fanfare, Hal Lindsey had never really gone away. After *The Late Great Planet Earth,* he continued to write books warning about the coming apocalypse, with titles like *The 1980's: Countdown to Armageddon, Planet Earth 2000 A.D.: Will Mankind Survive?,* and *Planet Earth: The Final Chapter.*

Lindsey's quantifiable predictions, and anticlimactic letdowns, were seen by some evangelical leaders as an embarrassment, making them hesitant to say that Y2K was the real deal. But you could bet nearly everyone in their church was talking about it, and devouring books with titles like *Y2k Equals 666* and *Judgment Day 2000.*

Some prominent televangelists weren't afraid to go all-in on Y2K.

"The Trinity has come down and looked us over," Jerry Falwell said in a sermon at the time, comparing Y2K to the Tower of Babel, the story in Genesis in which God thwarts the Babylonians' attempt to build a structure so high it would reach Heaven by causing them all to speak a different language (which was, we were told, how the world wound up with so many forms of speech). "And it seems that God doesn't like what He sees. We are fast moving toward a cashless economy, a one-world government, a one-world court, and a one-world church. We are building a universal city with a one-world church whose tower reaches into heaven. He may be preparing to confound our language, to jam our communications, scatter our efforts, and judge us for our sin and rebellion against His lordship. We are hearing from many sources that January 1, 2000, will be a fateful day in the history of the world."

I could feel the clock ticking.

I only had so much time to wrestle my impulses into submission, to pray them all away, before there was no time left to change my mind and I'd be left behind. I needed to double my efforts—more fasting, praying, Bible reading, witnessing, speaking in tongues, attending classes, sermons, concerts; spending time only with other believers; not watching or listening to any more horror movies, secular music, or pornography.

Deep down, however, I was convinced it was already too late for me.

CHAPTER FOURTEEN

Guilty Stains

"In your struggle against sin you have not yet resisted to
the point of shedding your blood."

—HEBREWS 12:4

1997

One stormy summer night, I walked down to the basement carrying a
boom box, a Bible, and every large knife in the house.

My feet landed in an inch of floodwater.

Epic thunderstorms often flooded our basement in the summer,
creating black mold that lined the walls of the basement. The air was
thick and musty, like the inside of a decaying whale. The green tint of
the sky earlier in the day had suggested that this storm could become
a tornado at some point. I put a CD in the boom box and hit "play";
the harmonies of DC Talk's cover of "I Wish We'd All Been Ready"
filled the basement.

Mom was usually home late, but never this late.

I'd called my grandma, Dad, my youth pastor; no one was answering.

This is it, Caldonia said to me. *The rapture has happened, and you
weren't taken.*

*Your weakness brought you here, and you have no one to blame but
yourself.*

The Antichrist's army will soon be looking for you.

Some part of me was honestly ready for it all to be over. I was so
tired.

One summer at church camp, a guest speaker had told us about the
millions of babies who'd been murdered by abortion since *Roe v. Wade,*
and someone raised their hand to ask what happened to the babies
after they died. "Why, they go to Heaven, of course," he explained.

Suddenly I felt envious of aborted babies. They were never forced to endure this life. They'd never have to navigate the trials of a nervous system, of puberty, adolescence, bullying, education, or earning money. They'd never have to decode the mysteries of the Bible or the metric of sin, or decipher what thoughts and sensations were their own and which were the devil's trying to seduce them into their own demise.

Smile, your mother chose life!

After the popularity of the movie *Wayne's World* brought Queen's "Bohemian Rhapsody" back onto the radio, I thought often of the lines "I don't wanna die, / I sometimes wish I'd never been born at all." I knew from our church plays that people who committed suicide didn't go to Heaven, and that made me feel stuck, enduring a contest I was ill-equipped to handle.

A flash of lightning briefly lit up the basement, and in that split second, I saw the demons from my dreams, all of them with the face of Caldonia, those hypnotic flames dancing deep in their eyes. The sound of rain pouring outside was so loud, it was like a thousand wineglasses shattering every second.

I turned up the volume on my boom box.

My family, friends, everyone I'd ever known had left this Earth.

They were in the euphoric bosom of Jesus, and I'd been left behind.

I unzipped and lowered my pants, then reached for a large knife.

I heard the demons stalking me in the darkness, their talons scraping the stone floor, their hot breath on the back of my neck. Water trickled in through the basement windows, splashing onto the floor.

I ran the knife along the soft flesh of my upper thigh, a wet, red line following in its wake.

There is a fountain filled with blood . . .

"Do not be deceived!" I shouted, reciting my Bible from memory. "Neither the sexually immoral, nor idolaters, nor adulterers, nor men who practice homosexuality, nor thieves, nor the greedy, nor drunkards . . . will inherit the kingdom of God!"

And sinners, plunged beneath that flood
Lose all their guilty stains . . .

I shivered at the relief of one cut, then another, and another.

This released all the pressure boiling through my veins like hot soda water. It made me think of the Passion plays, where Jesus suffered for my sins.

The cutting had begun a year earlier. The feeling of a blade penetrating skin, the exclamation points of wonder sparking behind my eyes—it was the same relief I got from biting my tongue to determine if I was dreaming or not. The same comfort I felt when I slammed my fist through the porch window. I'd cut only so deep, and only in places no one would see, always smearing the cuts with Neosporin afterward, trying to keep any scars from forming.

One time, I put a drill between my two front teeth. It was a flathead bit, and fit snugly between the Madonna-like gap between my incisors.

Pulling that trigger, and feeling the white-hot flash of pain, was a transcendent pleasure (and excruciating pain) I will remember for the rest of my life. It's a miracle my teeth didn't snap; perhaps they would have if it hadn't been a cheap drill powered by AA batteries.

A handful of times, I tried to see how far I could cram my finger or a pencil up my nose, wondering if I could lobotomize myself. This was after watching *One Flew over the Cuckoo's Nest*; I envied Jack Nicholson's blank face following his brain surgery and remember thinking, *He'll probably never be tempted by sin again.*

These injuries usually followed some sexual dalliance that I had craved desperately in the moment, then regretted to the point of madness immediately after. The teeth-drilling incident followed an afternoon with a teenage boy in his trailer home. His parents hadn't been around for months, but they'd left stacks of pornography videos around, which their son kept watching on the TV all day and night, while living on Black Velvet whiskey and ramen noodles.

I'd witnessed to him and led him to the Lord.

Then he led me to his bedroom.

Back in my mother's basement, lightning struck the lake a few blocks away, flashing in the basement windows like searchlights, filling up my world with explosive sound.

I punched myself in the groin. Over and over.

The pain was comforting, snuffing out any potential pleasure.

"The cowardly!" I shout, quoting the book of Revelation. "The faithless, the detestable, as for murderers, the sexually immoral, sorcerers, idolaters, and all liars, their portion will be in the lake that burns with fire and sulfur, which is the second death!"

I was ready for the seven years of Tribulation.

I would live in the wilderness, hiding from the socialist Antichrist and his Mark of the Beast economy. I would survive, proving my worthiness to Yahweh, earning a place beside my family in Heaven and—

"Josiah, are you down there?"

It was the voice of my mother, soothing, like a hot bath.

"Yep!" I shouted to her. "Be right up!"

The rapture hadn't happened . . . yet.

I was safe for another day.

I didn't have the heart to tell Mom how often I did this.

CHAPTER FIFTEEN

Protecting Belief

I was late to school more often than not—having overslept following a night of coffee and horror movies.

From the ages of twelve to eighteen, I always slept on the couch.

After forcing a quick shower, I'd walk to school sleepy and disoriented, my wet hair turning to icy dreadlocks in the below-zero winter air.

After the divorce, Mom and Dad couldn't afford to send me to North Iowa Christian School, so I was thrust into the godless world of public education in second grade, going from a class of ten to two hundred, into a world I'd been warned was a den of sin, liberal politics, and, perhaps worst of all, the theory of evolution.

Clutching a *90210* Trapper Keeper to my chest, I studied the public-school kids, mimicking their speech and body language, trying to make myself as invisible as possible. This was a challenge, given the sudden bursts of fear I'd experience for no apparent reason. Every day since I'd entered public school, the same thing would happen: I'd be sitting in class, listening to my teacher's lesson, and before I knew what was happening, I'd find myself standing up and shouting, "I need to go!"

Though I never knew what was wrong, I always wound up in the hallway, walking to the nurse's office almost involuntarily. When the nurse asked me why I was there, I couldn't articulate anything beyond a vague sense of feeling profoundly unwell. It wouldn't have made any sense to be honest and tell her, "I know nothing is wrong, but I feel like I was just pushed off the roof of a tall building."

In fifth grade, I was sent to the "special class" for children with learning disabilities. According to aptitude tests, I didn't have a learning disability and was actually quite bright, but I was flunking several classes and barely passing the rest.

That same year, a doctor prescribed me ten milligrams of Ritalin twice a day, which only amplified my paranoid feelings. The only increase in focus it provided was on Caldonia's voice, which incessantly reminded me that I was lazy, and weak, and a poor example of Christianity to the lost souls around me.

All day, I would picture the faces of my fellow students writhing in agony as they burned alive in Hell, tormented by monsters with bloody claws and fangs, knowing it was my fault, because I wasn't witnessing to them enough, I wasn't presenting a life of cheer and success, something for them to envy enough to join me in church.

Years earlier, as a kid at church camp, I asked my counselor how we get to Heaven (actually wanting to know how to avoid Hell). "Well, Josiah, the Bible is quite clear on that," he said. "In John 3:16, we're told that God 'gave his only Son, that whoever *believes* in him should not perish but have eternal life,' and if we flip over to Romans, it says, 'If you confess with your mouth that Jesus is Lord and *believe* in your heart that God raised him from the dead, you will be saved.' So you see, Josiah, it's very simple: all you have to do is *believe* in God to get to Heaven."

Around that time, I read my mom's copy of the Christian novel *This Present Darkness*, about a small town caught in the middle of an interdimensional battle between Heaven and Hell. One of the headquarters of the demons is the local university, where professors teach evil things like environmentalism, yoga, and psychology. The demons used education to chip away at students' faith in God, mostly through manipulative questions that made them think God didn't exist and churches were bad.

Learning about evolution, slavery, unions (communism?), the Big Bang, Native American genocide, racism, outer space (is Heaven not above the sky?) in public school would often lead to a spiral of questions I couldn't square with my evangelical beliefs—which was how I knew they were traps of Satan.

Still, I was terrified of threats to my belief each day in public school. I was certain that the wrong thought could irrevocably damn me to Hell.

In Mark 3:29, Jesus says, "Whoever blasphemes against the Holy Spirit will never be forgiven; they are guilty of an eternal sin."

In eighth grade, I had a history teacher who was very excited to teach us about Greek mythology. I was a big fan of the show *Hercules: The Legendary Journeys,** and movies like *Clash of the Titans,* so I was excited to learn more about this world of ancient fantasy. I thought of these stories as tall tales, like Paul Bunyan or Pecos Bill, and enjoyed the way hearing about Zeus transforming himself into various animals, or Atlas holding the world on his shoulders, stirred my imagination.

But then my teacher probed us by saying, "Isn't it interesting how these Greek mythologies are so similar to the stories in the Bible?"

My blood ran cold.

Caldonia shouted five things at once in my head as my publicschool teacher went on to elaborate.

"Pandora's husband is given a box and told not to open it," he continued, "but she does it anyway and lets sickness and death into the world. Similarly, in the Bible, Adam is told not to eat of the fruit of knowledge, but his wife does and lets sickness and death into the world. When Zeus tries to kill all of humanity with a flood, Deucalion builds a wooden chest to float in with his family and eventually lands on a mountain, just like Noah did. When Prometheus brings fire to humans, he's chained to a rock with his arms spread wide; when Jesus brings wisdom and forgiveness to humans, he's nailed to a cross in the same position."

My breath was like rapid gunfire; cold sweat soaked through my T-shirt.

---

* Starring Kevin Sorbo, who would go on to become a conservative icon and one of the biggest stars of the Christian film industry, particularly for his portrayal of an atheist college professor who bullies his Christian students in the smash hit *God's Not Dead.*

How could I dismiss all of the Greek myths as silly when the Bible had the exact same stories? Before I could stop myself, I raised my hand and asked whether the Greeks copied their stories from the Bible.

How dare you betray your Lord by talking to this man! Caldonia shouted. *You'll be flayed alive in Hell for this!*

"Excellent question, Josiah!" my teacher said, excited that I was participating for once. "It's unknown exactly who wrote the stories of the Old Testament, but we do know they came along five hundred to a thousand years after the era of Greek mythology, and the New Testament a couple thousand years after that."

Did that mean that the men who wrote the Bible copied the Greeks? part of me wondered. Who wrote the Bible, anyway?

That's it! Caldonia announced. *You've blasphemed the Holy Spirit! You will never be forgiven for this!*

I bit down hard on my tongue and was relieved to find I wasn't dreaming, even as blood trickled into my mouth.

"Actually, Christian stories borrow from all kinds of mythologies, not just Greek," my teacher continued. "The story of Jesus alone borrows from so many gods that came before him, it's like he's a Greatest Hits of Mediterranean Mythology! Three thousand years before Jesus was born, the Egyptians worshipped Horus, who was born on December 25. In 900 B.C., in India, Krishna was said to be born of a virgin; he performed miracles and was resurrected after his death. The Greek Attis and Mithra in Persia were also both born on December 25. Attis was killed on a tree, buried in a tomb, resurrected after three days, as was Mithra, who also had twelve disciples. The same could be said for Dionysus, who . . . Josiah, are you okay?"

With my palms pressed firmly against my ears, I rocked back and forth, humming to myself. A lot of the kids were laughing at me, but I didn't care. Too much was at stake to let this information—and the questions that came with it—into my head.

CHAPTER SIXTEEN

Unworthy of Healing

"Tuesday night at the Bible study
We lift our hands and pray over your body
But nothing ever happens"

—SUFJAN STEVENS, "CASIMIR PULASKI DAY"

1998

"Ewww, here comes Joesmellah!" my classmates would say to me every morning, holding their noses and running away.

This began after I accidentally wore a pair of jeans smeared with cat shit to school in the seventh grade, and cleared out every classroom with the violently offensive odor. My reputation for poor hygiene had not improved by my sophomore year, when I refused to shower with the other boys after gym class.

These weren't stalled showers with walls and curtains, just a large, tiled room that made me think of the Holocaust movies I'd watched as a young kid. Beyond shyness and fear of having erections, I hid in a toilet stall while the boys showered each day after gym for an even more alarming reason: my left testicle had swelled to a gargantuan size.

It was as large as a lightbulb, or a man's clenched fist.

I had been experiencing a mild discomfort in my testicle for a while, but the pain had steadily grown until it consumed my thoughts for large portions of the day, rivaled only by Caldonia's incessant monologue. The testicle had become as solid as concrete, the weight of it pulling aggressively and unnaturally at my cremaster muscle (a term I didn't know at the time, but a piece of my anatomy I was viscerally aware of due to the pain). I would keep this softball in my pants a secret for three years, fearing that it was God's punishment for fooling around with boys.

Smile, your mother chose life!

I never thought of it as a medical issue that I needed to bring to my parents' attention. Seeking help from a doctor would have been evidence of my lack of faith. It was a shameful secret, and I was terrified that anyone would find out about it. If I was going to tell anyone, it would've been a youth pastor or counselor, asking them to pray over me for healing. But it didn't seem appropriate to ask God for healing if He was the one afflicting me.

Miraculous healings were a big topic at youth groups and camp. "I've seen limbs grow out from stubs; I've seen crutches and glasses left at the altar," our youth pastor at Agapé told us multiple times. One of my Assemblies of God camp counselors told me he'd once witnessed a man being raised from the dead at his own funeral. "He'd been embalmed and had his organs removed, but when he was prayed over, he got up and walked. He was actually upset that he'd been taken away from the bliss of Heaven!"

I'd heard these stories for years, but had yet to witness a miracle myself.

I was told this was possibly due to my lack of faith.

During an Open Bible convention, a boy who was born without his left eye was singled out by our youth pastor, who grabbed him on each side of his face, shouting, "In the name of *JESUS*, I *command* an eye to grow in this socket!"

But nothing happened.

Afterward, the boy's brother told me this same routine occurred every time he came to one of these meetings, and how upsetting it was for him.

Walking back to my hotel room that night, I silently asked God why he hadn't healed the boy this time, or any of the others. "Was it because he lacks faith? Or because I do?" I pleaded, with no answer given. At this point, I'd heard of the evangelical faith healer Kathryn Kuhlman, who was said to have cured over two million people of diseases, disabilities, and chronic pain (though I knew nothing of Kuhlman's sordid history in Mason City). This stuff seemed to be happening all around me, but never when I was looking.

That's because you're a disgusting sinner, filled with shameful lust and the seduction of glamour, Caldonia said to me. *God can't even look at you, you're such a nasty, sinful boy.*

It would be another three years before I learned my swollen testicle was due to physical trauma, and would require surgery. It would be another fifteen years before I would learn about panic attacks, religious trauma syndrome, or attachment disorders.

At the time, I was convinced that all this suffering originated either from God or from Satan. And it seemed that Satan had already claimed me.

CHAPTER SEVENTEEN

An Education

Dad wound up marrying Susanne, the woman he was supposed to be counseling out of suicide but had an affair with instead. This eighteen-month marriage had its moments of love and domestic bliss, but they were mostly overshadowed by violence, drug abuse, and madness, because Susanne was never able to find the treatment she needed for her mental illness (which I'd attributed at the time to demons, knowing nothing of dissociative identity disorder). I had a stepbrother for a while, though we lost touch after the divorce; he was twelve at that point, and began smoking and cooking meth, and burned down half the house in the process.

Mom's marriage to Barry, a local radio DJ eight years her junior, was even shorter. Barry turned me on to a lot of old noir movies and even let me read the news on the air (my first journalism gig), but he suffered wild swings of mood and behavior (looking back, I suspect he was bipolar), and just disappeared one afternoon, leaving my mom with a brief note explaining that he wouldn't be coming back.

By 1995, Dad had landed a job with KAAL, the local ABC station in southern Minnesota, selling airtime to local advertisers in North Iowa. He was earning fifty thousand dollars a year, which might as well have been fifty million in our eyes. He bought a house on North Shore Drive, in the same neighborhood as our pastor, where Phin and Faith lived with him, and I would visit on certain nights.

Dad was so proud that he'd made it to a middle-class income without ever having gone to college, and would remind our mother of this every chance he got. When visiting his side of the family for holidays, I'd sometimes hear them talk about higher education as at best "a waste of money," and at worst "a liberal brainwashing factory."

I could sense a strong unease whenever the word "college" entered the room, an insecurity about their status in life and their intelligence, masked with contempt.

Dad's side of the family were primarily generations of manufacturers extending back to the industrial revolution, made up of hard-drinking fathers that could, more or less, still provide for their families with very little education if they put in the hours at the factory. They were the same people humiliated by the Scopes Monkey Trial in 1925, forever distrustful of those "educated" people from the media (or government) who caused them—secretly, deep down—such shame.

His mother, my grandmother Doris, never finished high school; she'd had to drop out and go to work in a hospital her senior year. Though she eventually got her GED, years later she would tell me that, throughout her life, "I didn't think I was as good as the rest of them." My mom, on the other hand, was raised by Methodist Democrats who championed higher education as an essential tool of the American Dream. Her mother, my grandmother Marilyn, had stressed the urgency of education to me before I entered preschool and asked about my "studies" every time I saw her.

I didn't know what to think when Mom graduated from the local community college at the age of thirty-seven. Looking back, I see it as a profound accomplishment that took a lot of hard work and sacrifice, and would eventually lead her to a middle-class income many years later (by which time I'd be long gone). But back then, watching her walk across that platform in her cap and gown, accepting her degree in business administration, I alternated between indifference and contempt.

College was a nest of demonic vipers.

College had taken my mother away from me.

Dad was in the bleachers with us during the ceremony and later complained about how sitting there for so long hurt his back. "Well, to sit in the chairs, you have to earn a degree," Mom said, and I watched

Dad turn red with anger. Even at thirteen, I knew they were arguing about more than just lumbar support.

It made me think of an argument I'd overheard years earlier, when they were still married. Mom wanted to move a small portion of their savings (back when we had savings) to a college fund for us. "Those kids are *never* going to college!" Dad proclaimed. "And if they do, *I'm* certainly not paying for it."

This would turn out to be true: Phin and Faith both financed their higher education with student loans, and I wouldn't set foot in a college classroom until I reached the age of thirty—when I would be paid to speak at them.

CHAPTER EIGHTEEN

Campy Boy

As I ran across a grassy field with a trash bin over the upper half of my body, I couldn't help but wonder: *How will this make me a better Christian?*

It was my fourth year attending Open Bible summer camp, which was just on the other side of the lake from my house. It was a bit more rustic than the Assemblies of God camp, which I'd attended each summer since I was ten (they were always held at different points in the summer, allowing me to attend both each year). The AG camp had an air-hockey table and air-conditioned rooms, but Open Bible had trampolines and mini-golf, so they both had their merits.

Large gatherings in the woods had been a staple of Protestant Christianity ever since the Great Awakening in eighteenth-century England and America. During the industrial revolution in America, concerns about boys growing up in cities—where they were exposed to a diversity of cultures, faiths, morals, and vices such as billiards—led to sending them away each summer to "toughen up" in nature. When the Christian right exploded in the 1980s, evangelical summer camps became a rite of passage for young believers in need of spiritual cleansing.

In 2006, the fly-on-the-wall documentary *Jesus Camp* shocked secular audiences with scenes of young children weeping, screaming, speaking in tongues, and praying to a cardboard cutout of George W. Bush. But many evangelicals, including some those featured in the film, saw it as an accurate representation of their culture.

The camps combined games with church services and classes, usually a 70/30 ratio, with church in the lead. Each service typically opened with a series of "y'all ready for this"–type Jock Jams, combined with footage of sports highlight reels to get everyone psyched up before the worship songs, sermon, and inevitable altar call.

The game we were playing with the trash cans at Open Bible Camp was something new that the older counselors—who seemed intent on making our camp experience more akin to a fraternity hazing ritual—had just dreamed up.

A metal trash can was placed upside down over my head, extending down to my waist, and I was instructed to run straight (or what I assume to be straight) across a large field to the other side. At the other end of the field, someone else wearing a four-foot trash can over their body would be running toward me, attempting to get to where I had started from. And, just to make things extra fun, two more blind sprinters would be doing the same thing from the right and left sides of the field at the same time.

The object was to try to get to the other side without smashing into another runner. It soon became apparent that this game was created solely for the counselors' amusement.

Dripping sweat soaked my WWJD ("What Would Jesus Do?") bracelet as I looked down at my feet, shuffling across the sunny grass. The sound of my breath echoed within the aluminum trash can, accompanied by the thud-thud-thud of my pounding heart. I'd been running for a while, and thought I was about to make it to the other side when—*wham!*—an explosion ripped through my senses like shrapnel, so loud my ears would ring for the rest of the night. My vision went from the grass to the sky, and suddenly I was lying on my side next to two other kids, all of us moaning in pain. (The fourth kid actually made it to the other side.)

I looked up and saw the counselors, pointing and doubling over with laughter.

They were college freshmen, and seemed to be competing over who could administer the first nervous breakdown in a camper. I received about two dozen wedgies over the course of that week, often while chatting up girls I'd been crushing on. On the second night of camp, five kids had been caught outside their cabins after lights out. At three a.m., wearing nothing but their underwear, they were made to hold up a heavy picnic table together, while the counselors all shone flashlights on them, drawing an army of mosquitoes to their tender young skin. The next morning, every one of them looked like he had a severe case of chicken pox.

Unlike a lot of the kids, who had church forced on them by their parents, I genuinely enjoyed the services, classes, and Bible quizzes of each camp. Many of the outsiders were weirded out by the Pentecostal rituals of sprinting, dancing, spinning around, and falling to the floor with tremors while speaking in tongues. But I loved it, and almost convinced myself it was why I was there . . . except that the voice of Caldonia kept reminding me: *You're not a real Christian, and you only come here to see the big-city kids in their big-city clothes because you're a pathetic, glamour-obsessed heathen.*

Admittedly, fashion was always on my mind at church camp.

After moving along from pop bands like DC Talk and the News-boys, I became obsessed with the sights and sounds of the West Coast Christian punk scene. Labels like Tooth & Nail Records brought punk, ska, and hardcore bands with a Christian message into Midwestern ears like mine, thanks to our local Christian bookstore, and tours passing through Des Moines or Minneapolis.

I dyed my hair a different color every week (most often blue, green, or pink), wore absurdly tight band T-shirts with enormously wide-legged jeans, and dripped chains from my neck, arms, and wallet. At the time, I was unaware that punk rock was not an exclusively evangelical institution, and that all of these bands had their secular equivalents on the radio. I saw punk-rock music and fashion as part of my Christian identity, as much as my Bible or WWJD bracelet.

My fashion choices at Clear Lake High School (where the rich kids looked like they fell out of an Abercrombie & Fitch catalogue and the poor kids fought over donations from Goodwill) alienated me even more than my proselytizing.

"I feel bad for you getting bullied," my dad said to me one morning as I was leaving the house for school, "but sometimes I look at the clothes you wear . . ." He sighed, then confessed, ". . . and I just think you're asking for it."

But although I may have been a pariah at school, I was a big man on the Jesus campus.

I had a handful of friends at each camp, and even one or two girl-friends. But they all lived across the state, and we only saw each other during the summer and conventions during the school year. Campers from big cities like Des Moines and Omaha looked like they had just stepped out of a music video, with their frosted hair, tech vests, and Spice Girl platform shoes. Some of them I'd never even spoken to, but I'd been watching their hairstyles and jewelry choices shift over the years, taking exhaustive mental notes to file away for my own use.

I couldn't afford the gas to drive to the big cities, let alone buy clothes there. Thankfully, around my sophomore year I met a pair of hipster girls at the youth group who told me they got their best outfits by raiding abandoned farmhouses.

I began tagging along with them, and, sure enough, the Iowa coun-tryside was littered with condemned homes (roofs collapsed, raccoons living in cabinets, etc.) that were still filled with clothes, furniture, dishes, accounting ledgers, picture albums, and other remnants of lives abruptly halted. Most of these properties were bought up by wealthy neighbors during the farm crisis. All they wanted was to expand their farms into neighboring fields; they were uninterested in the decrepit homes. The original owners of all these items were either dead or in nursing homes by now (and their children, typically, had moved out of state), so we figured there was no harm in appropriating their sixties and seventies wardrobes before the coyotes got to them.

Like those at my home church, the camp elders were enthusias-tically split on my boisterous fashion choices, either celebrating or condemning them with equal zeal. There was a song we'd been sing-ing every year since I was a kid at the Assemblies of God camp that embodied conservative attitudes toward popular culture:

Who needs the Rolling Stones, when the stone's been rolled away
And who needs a pervert like Prince, when the King is here to stay

I don't need no Cinderella, or any other kind of sin
I don't need no Ozzy Osbourne, because I's been born again

The references were profoundly dated for the late nineties, but the message was clear: rock stars were false idols, and we had to turn away from them if we were to worship Jesus.

But ever since Larry Norman and the Jesus Freaks brought the music of Laurel Canyon to a generation of young Christians, followed by pious hair metal bands like Stryper and Petra in the eighties, there'd been at least a counterargument to the fundamentalist idea that we should be "*in* the world but not *of* the world."

Around this time, megachurches—with their fog machines, turntable DJs, light shows, rockin' worship music, hip fashion, and stadium-sized crowds—were just beginning to spread across America, and the fight against worldly aesthetics in evangelical culture was beginning to fade away. The split between the older and younger generations on this issue left me with a bit of mixed messaging when it came to how God wanted me to dress, and what music would or wouldn't open me up to demonic possession.

For years, I'd alternate between imposing a complete ban on secular music and movies, and then returning to the embrace of MTV, HBO, and *Spin* magazine weeks after camp let out.

When my dad became a Christian, he burned all of his Alice Cooper, Led Zeppelin, and Deep Purple LPs, replacing them with Petra, Keith Green, and Carman. Burning secular albums had become an evangelical rite of passage by the nineties, and I burned my Salt-N-Pepa, TLC, and Janet Jackson CDs before heading to the Christian bookstore to find their evangelical doppelgängers.

But, quite often, I'd end up just purchasing another copy of the secular CDs I had once destroyed.

In time, I justified listening to secular music on the radio in the interest of guiding lost souls toward Christian rock—*You are such a liar,* Caldonia shouted, *you're just seduced by sin!*—and couldn't help but notice that CCM wasn't its own musical genre, like country or rap or classical, with its own sound, style, and perspective. All of it appeared simply to mimic the secular songs we claimed to hate on the radio, but with all the swear words taken out and "Jesus" swapped for "baby."

At some point in the mid-nineties, Christian bookstores started hanging posters above their CD racks with a list of all the secular Top 40 artists placed alongside their CCM equivalents: "Do you like Fiona Apple? Try Jennifer Knapp!" "Is your son a fan of Everclear and Weezer? Buy him Audio Adrenaline, Switchfoot, and Bleach!" Even musicians often labeled "Satanic," like Marilyn Manson and Rob Zombie, had their Christian carbon copies in Zao and Klank.

A lot of these bands didn't just sound similar to secular bands, they were identical to them. DC Talk's smash hit "Jesus Freak" was such a mirror of Nirvana's "Smells like Teen Spirit" that you could play them at the same time and they'd sync perfectly. (DC Talk even hired the director for Nine Inch Nails' "Hurt" to direct the video for "Jesus Freak.") The Newsboys' "Shine" was built around the same riff as Hot Chocolate's "You Sexy Thing." And pretty much every megachurch worship song was just a generic version of U2's "Where the Streets Have No Name" or the second half of Springsteen's "Jungleland" (or, in the years ahead, songs by Coldplay and Arcade Fire).

I would often enter worship mode while listening to Christian-rock bands—hands raised, eyes closed, whispering desperate pleas for forgiveness—just as I did with the easy-listening worship music in church. At camps and conventions, it was not unusual for Christian punks to form a mosh pit near the stage while rocking out to "Jesus Freak" or some MxPx song. This kinetic, primal form of dancing always gave me a surge of euphoric goose bumps. Mosh pits weren't all that different from Pentecostal rituals—sweaty, primal, a little scary—and gave me the same feeling I got when dancing to worship music, so I assumed it was the Holy Spirit moving through me during these moments of adrenaline-charged jubilation.

On the third morning at Open Bible Camp, I'd been rocking out to a song with some other boys in our cabin, jumping around in our underwear and slamming our bodies together, when I noticed the lyrics "When masturbation's lost its fun, you're fuckin' lonely!" and froze.

I'd been feeling that same blitz of joy while pogoing and moshing with the other boys, recognizing the drum fills and chord changes from the thousands of other Christian punk-rock songs I'd been listening to.

"Who is this?" I asked one of the boys who was still moshing.

"Green Day!" he said, nearly out of breath.

"Is that a Christian band?"

"Oh, no way, they hate Christians!" he said, gleefully. "They're all about drugs and sex and making fun of church."

How could that be? I wondered. How could I feel the presence of the Holy Spirit while slam dancing to a secular band? Was this one of Satan's tricks? Or did I just enjoy this specific style of music?

You're beginning to doubt again, aren't you, Josiah? Caldonia said. *Your sins have infected your mind and body, and now you don't even know what's righteous and what's sinful anymore.*

Luckily, there was a camp class on sexual purity right around the corner to set me straight.

CHAPTER NINETEEN

Pure

In 1990s evangelicalism, teenage virginity was the ultimate commodity.

It was a gift from God that must be protected, we were told, because once it was gone you were significantly devalued in the marketplace of Christian courtship.

It's somewhat awkward for me to write about evangelical "purity culture" (as it came to be known), because it was the girls who bore the brunt of these teachings. They were charged with the responsibility of managing the hypersexuality of teenage males, mindful never to cause their "brothers in Christ" to "stumble."

In the late nineties, books like *I Kissed Dating Goodbye* instructed us on parent-controlled courtship rituals, while songs like Michael W. Smith's "Old Enough to Know" or DC Talk's "That Kinda Girl" and "I Don't Want It" (a rebuttal to George Michael's "I Want Your Sex") made waiting for marriage the cool thing to do.

In 1994, the teen-purity advocacy group True Love Waits hosted a DC Talk concert in Washington, D.C., followed by various speakers denouncing the Clinton administration's "safe sex" education programs in public schools, which were making condoms available to teenagers.

Some of us kids wore promise rings to pledge ourselves to our future spouses—to whom we were encouraged to write letters praising our imagined wives or husbands for remaining chaste. These letters were intended to be presented to our partners on our wedding nights, and

I knew some people who actually followed through with it. But most of the letters wound up in the trash: far more of us failed to remain virgins until our wedding nights, and absolutely hated ourselves for it.

A 2001 survey of Southern Baptists—the denomination that launched the teen-purity movement—showed that 70 percent of regular churchgoers admitted to having sex before marriage, and 80 percent of these regretted it.

I thought the promise rings looked tacky and never wore one, but I did recite the True Love Waits abstinence pledge at summer camp (forever ruining an otherwise wonderful Radiohead song with the same name):

> "Believing that true love waits, I make a commitment to God, myself, my family, those I date, and my future mate to be sexually pure until the day I enter marriage."

The pledge intentionally went beyond your relationship to God, and placed your community within the promise to remain pure, creating a pressure cooker of shame and fear surrounding your sexuality.

The movement also popularized "Daddy Daughter" dances, in which a man's female offspring is ritualized as his property to be defended at all costs. It was a revival of the fever that gripped the Klan in the 1920s, the belief that (white) female virtue was under siege in a changing society, and it was up to the well-armed men to protect it.

Abstinence-only sex education programs began receiving federal funding during the Reagan administration in 1981. But it wasn't until Newt Gingrich and the Christian Coalition pushed the Clinton administration to the center-right with the 1996 welfare reform legislation (drastically cutting benefits to America's most vulnerable citizens) that purity culture was given a fiscal steroid by the U.S. government. Inserted into the welfare reform legislation was the Title V "Abstinence-Only-Until-Marriage Program," which stated that sex-education programs should teach that "a mutually faithful monogamous relationship in the context of marriage is the expected standard of sexual activity" and "that sexual activity outside of the context of marriage is likely to have harmful psychological and physical effects."

Additionally, these sex-ed programs were not allowed to discuss condoms or other contraceptives except to note their unreliability, pushing against liberal efforts in the nineties to increase condom access to teenagers.

From 1981 to 2017, the U.S. government spent over two billion dollars on abstinence-only sex education—and that's just domestically. An additional $1.6 billion was spent to export these teachings to developing nations around the world.

In 2017, the Society for Adolescent Health and Medicine reviewed the history of these programs, particularly their efficacy and impact on developing sexuality, concluding, " 'Abstinence-only-until-marriage' as a basis for adolescent health policy and programs should be abandoned."

In addition to free condoms for kids, a backlash to the feminist movement of the seventies and eighties drove purity culture. One of the galvanizing forces in the early days of the Christian right was conservative opposition to the Equal Rights Amendment, which sought to remove gender as a factor in legal matters surrounding employment, divorce, property, and more. The amendment failed, partially because of campaigning by evangelical leaders like Tim LaHaye and Phyllis Schlafly, and "feminism" has remained a dirty and dangerous word in evangelical circles ever since.

This was probably articulated best by the failed evangelical presidential candidate and *700 Club* host Pat Robertson, in a 1992 Christian Coalition fund-raising letter: "The feminist agenda is not about equal rights for women. It is about a socialist, anti-family political movement that encourages women to leave their husbands, kill their children, practice witchcraft, destroy capitalism and become lesbians."

In response to the political correctness of the nineties, many evangelical preachers began making "jokes" about the traditional gender roles championed by purity culture (and criticized by outsiders). "What do you do when the dishwasher stops working?" one Assemblies of God camp speaker told us from the stage. "Slap her."

The children around me laughed at this, but when I repeated the joke to my mom, she looked horrified.

At Open Bible Camp, the boys were taken out into the woods for our session on sexual purity and male leadership in the household.

"Sex is God's gift to us," our counselor explained, "and that's why Satan is constantly trying to pervert it. The way He designed man and woman to fit together, physically, and to work together, in their own separate roles, as a family, is Satan's favorite thing to turn upside down. He loves to feminize men, to masculinize women, to fill our heads with unnatural lusts for the same gender."

Sin and salvation were mysterious concepts to me, but the path to righteousness in purity culture was straightforward: never deviate from your assigned gender role, remain sexually pure (though if you stumbled it was likely a woman's fault), and the more aggressively you pursued your masculinity (dominance, ambition, sexual prowess) or femininity (chastity, domesticity, physical beauty, and submission to your husband), the more you were on God's path for your life.

I made a sincere effort to participate in the virile, militaristic activities of the evangelical world—paintball, marching drills, hunting—though I would often wind up bored or scared, and skip away to a quiet corner to look at the latest issue of *Alloy* or *Sassy*.

Evangelical institutions championing "conventional masculinity," like Focus on the Family, the Family Research Council, and Strike Force (the bodybuilder exhibitionists I watched smash flaming bricks as a kid) had been around since the seventies, but in the late nineties and early aughts they became pillars of the culture wars. Christian Mixed Martial Arts (MMA) fight clubs and pro wrestling matches drew large audiences, and men's retreats amped up the misogynistic rhetoric of male dominance and female submission.

In the traditional world of working-class Midwesterners, not until the last decade or two had it become acceptable for a woman to want to "be like a man" (i.e., own a home, run a business, live alone, wear pants, and have short hair). It wasn't universally agreed that a woman *should get those things*—especially not at the expense of a man—but it was at least understandable that she'd want those things. Just as it's understandable that poor people would *want* entrance to the country club, but not that they'd be welcomed in.

But for a *man* to want to degrade himself to the level of a *woman*?

Well, that was viewed as a demotion, an intentional downgrade of your birthright.

For a man to forgo sports in favor of cleaning and decorating a home, to prefer shopping and beauty products to giant trucks and smoked barbecue, to want to gossip about crushes at high tea instead of harass waitresses at Hooters—it was baffling enough to make a good ole boy want to punch something.

The camp counselors' giving me wedgies and forcing boys to lift a picnic table while being feasted upon by mosquitoes was viewed by the older generation as good-natured hazing designed to toughen us up, a kind of alpha-bro boot camp that would make us into strong, obedient foot soldiers in God's army.

Rarely did we ever stop to explore the dark implications of this rhetoric: that encouraging men to be mindlessly aggressive toward women, to view sex as a transactional conquest, to haze and bully those younger and weaker, while discouraging empathy, emotional awareness, or temperance of one's impulses for dominance and consumption, could lead to some profoundly destructive behavior.

Especially when preached to children.

But we were being trained to fight the culture wars, the wars of the spirit realm, and, one day, the wars of the Apocalypse. There was no time for sensitivity training or mindfulness workshops, because Christianity was under attack in America, and God needed us to defend it.

CHAPTER TWENTY

Martyr Me, Manson

1999

In the spring of 1999, two teenage boys murdered twelve of their classmates and one teacher—followed by themselves—in a suburb of Denver, Colorado. And when the Assemblies of God church camp rolled around the following summer, our guest speaker had *a lot* to say about it.

A man in his twenties with short, gelled hair and horn-rimmed glasses, pacing the stage with anger and purpose, told us that Christianity was "under *attack*" in America! Bill Clinton had turned the White House into a swingers' club, gay couples were trying to get married, and Marilyn Manson's music held the power to convince teenagers to murder their fellow students.

He then told us the story of Cassie Bernall, a student at Columbine High School who was hiding under a table during the massacre. When the shooter Dylan Klebold crouched down and spotted her, he is said to have asked, "Do you believe in God?," grinning while sticking a gun inches from her face.

"Yes," she tearfully replied.

And that's when he pulled the trigger.[*]

---

[*] Later reporting revealed that this probably never happened: The killings were mostly indiscriminate and had nothing to do with Christianity. Moreover, Dylan Klebold and Eric Harris weren't even fans of Marilyn Manson's music, preferring the industrial sounds of KMFDM. And there are conflicting reports on which of the two shooters killed Bernall.

The camp speaker then clicked a button, turning the lights off and the video projector on, and played us a video called "She Said Yes: The Unlikely Martyrdom of Cassie Bernall." It was an adaptation of the book of the same name by Cassie's mother, a sentimental tribute to a brave life cut short by hatred of Christians.

Mass shootings would eventually become routine for America, but in 1999 this event was the biggest media sensation since O. J. Simpson's trial. Evangelicals cited their typical grievances with public schools as the culprit—evolution, banning prayer in school—while also rallying around the idea that Marilyn Manson was somehow responsible. It was the last gasp of the Satanic Panic era, when bands like AC/DC, Judas Priest, and Ozzy Osbourne were also blamed for teen murders and suicides.

Columbine also tapped into the fever among evangelical teens who craved to be martyred by the forces of evil infecting America.

In the fall of 1999, the CCM megastar Michael W. Smith released the song "This Is Your Time," which functioned as both a tribute to Cassie Bernall, and a manipulative confrontation to Christian teens of the time, asking how they would perform under a similar "test." Listening to the song, I felt Smith singing directly to my heart, clearly seeing that I was a coward who would probably deny God to avoid a bullet to the face.

Smith wrote a book of the same name, which links Bernall's story with the history of Christian martyrs, going as far back as the second century, when Christians were being fed to lions in the Roman Colosseum. Around the same time, DC Talk released a similar book as an accompaniment to their bestselling album, *Jesus Freaks: Stories of Those Who Stood for Jesus, the Ultimate Jesus Freaks.* This came out a few months before the Columbine shootings, but still inspired my generation to fetishize Christian martyrdom, leading us all to actively pursue being bullied, beaten, and ostracized for our faith.

By the summer of 1999, the *Jesus Freak* song and album had quickly become the biggest phenomenon in the history of CCM. The album sold two million copies (though none of this registered on the Billboard Hot 100, because, for the first few years of its life, *Jesus Freak,* just like every other CCM album, was sold strictly at Christian bookstores). DC Talk's record company, ForeFront, sent out four thousand copies of the album to youth pastors around the country, who blasted it before and after every youth group service for years to come, till it became an anthem for young evangelicals eager to spread the word of Christ before the coming rapture.

In the Gospel of Matthew, we are told, "Blessed are those who are persecuted for righteousness' sake, for theirs is the kingdom of Heaven." Throughout the late 1990s, we were reminded of this verse at church camps, youth groups, and conventions, instructed to actively pursue being mocked for expressing our Christian faith in school or, even better, for witnessing to our classmates. For each persecution (the more painful the better), a deposit would be made in a spiritual bank account that we would draw from throughout eternity in Heaven, like a celestial 401(k). We were constantly told we would be the generation to usher in the second coming of Christ, often by people who'd gotten saved during the Jesus Movement, who had been just as certain that the world would end by 1988. I knew adults from that generation who never saved for retirement, so certain were they it wouldn't be necessary.

"It's quite likely that most of you will never grow up to be adults" was a common refrain from youth leaders. And with that in mind, were we willing to let our fellow students burn in Hell, or suffer the torments of the Tribulation, simply because we were too embarrassed to witness to them? What was the worst that could happen? We'd become persecuted? Well, we knew there would be a radical reward for that in Heaven.

We were told it was our "duty" to pray at our lockers *every day*, loud, so everyone could hear us. We would be "extreme, in their faces"! This was always couched as an act of rebellion against the tide of peers, with drugs, sex, and secular music framed as the ultimate conformity.

Also, any hesitancy to make a public display of our faith was greeted by scriptures like Luke 9:26: "Whoever is ashamed of me and my words, the Son of Man will be ashamed of them when he comes in his glory."

Or Revelation 13:16: "Because you are lukewarm and neither hot nor cold, I will vomit you out of My mouth."

We had to be "on fire for God!" At all times! Or else there would be consequences.

Each fall, I participated in See You at the Pole, an event in which Christian students gathered at public-school flagpoles and prayed (loudly) for a surge of revival in our government-run education, as our fellow students filed past us into the school buildings. (Similar to words like "freedom" or "family values," rhetoric about "revival in government" was often vague, basically implying that public schools should operate just like Christian schools, and that all military or legislative action should be viewed through the lens of Protestant Christianity.)

Ever since teacher-led prayer in school was banned by the Supreme Court in 1962, evangelicals have claimed censorship of their religious liberties and free speech in public education (reflected in the Christian-rock band Audio Adrenaline's album *Don't Censor Me*). See You at the Pole was an attempt to test these boundaries, relying on a court ruling that allowed anti-Vietnam student protests in Des Moines, Iowa; both were permitted as long as they were student-run operations. The movement was not only a religious-liberties test case, or simply evangelical exhibitionism. It was an aggressive advertisement for the young Christian lifestyle, intended to provoke other students into asking us about our faith, which gave us the opportunity to witness to them.

In those moments, their eternal souls were in our hands.

They would burn forever if we failed to persuade them.

In addition to video clips of sports games (set to a Jock Jams soundtrack) and faux-MTV Christian-music videos, popular movies were a common tool for evangelical sermons. At another Assemblies of God convention, we were shown the climactic scene in *Schindler's List*, where the industrialist realizes he could've saved so many more Jews from the horrors of the Holocaust if only he'd sold more possessions and doubled his efforts. "I didn't do enough," Liam Neeson says, weeping. "I could've got more out."

When the clip was over, we were told that on Judgment Day we would have to account for the number of souls we'd failed to save. And in that moment, we'd ask ourselves, *If I'd just witnessed to a few more, if*

I'd given more to the church, if I'd gone on that missions trip, if I'd turned to the gay man, lost in sin, a few lockers down, and talked about the saving grace of Jesus Christ . . . how many more could've been saved from the torment of Hell?

There was so little time left for us to become the martyrs we were born to be.

CHAPTER TWENTY-ONE

The Boys in the Band

December 31, 1999

"Three . . . two . . . one . . . Happy New Year!"

Everyone cheered, and I held my breath, but nothing happened.

The lights didn't go dark.

There were no explosions in the distance, no police sirens, no gunfire, no screams, no curfew announced on the loudspeaker of a tank rolling down Main Street.

No Y2K.

Just pizza and pop at the Evangelical Free Church Youth Center.

I'd been a nervous wreck leading up to Y2K. Sleeping had become even worse during my teenage years, averaging only a few hours a night (and never voluntarily). I'd been feeling this enormous pressure in my lower gut, like a clogged vacuum-cleaner hose, which hurt in a way that transcended the word "pain." (Years later, I would be diagnosed with irritable bowel syndrome, common among those with anxiety disorders.) I'd found that movement helped, and would often wander the streets of Clear Lake at two or three in the morning, in my pajamas, holding my lower belly like a pregnant woman. Once, the pain was so bad I passed out on someone's lawn; they woke me up the next morning by poking me with a golf club.

As with my swollen testicle, I never thought to consult my parents about this. Explaining my terror to them—or my secret curse—could have led to questions that I might not have answers for, questions about the strength of my faith or the purity of my body.

The absence of a Y2K blackout wasn't as anticlimactic for me as it could've been, since I'd been glued to the news all afternoon, watching reports from Australia, Japan, China, and Russia, all of which were ringing in January 1, 2000, without descending into powerless chaos. News anchors were making Y2K jokes throughout their coverage of the holiday, treating the subject as a goofy pop-culture novelty instead of a global crisis, like a war or hurricane.

The world is laughing at you, Caldonia told me. *You're a joke to them, and a weak sinner to your community. No one has any use for you, or ever has.*

I was there with my best friend, Thad.

I first met Thad at North Iowa Christian School, when I was in first grade and he was in second, but neither of us recalls much about this. We were reunited in the mosh pit of a Philmore* concert in Mason City years later, both of us now fumbling through our early teenage years, him in a Superman T-shirt and me in JNCO jeans with a fifty-six-inch hem around the opening at the feet.

Still freckled with screaming red hair, he'd shed his baby fat since we met on the playground at NICS. Thad wasn't very tall, but years of farm work had swelled his arms and legs with rock-hard muscle, and somehow his pale complexion tanned in the summer instead of burning like that of most ginger boys; his hair would turn a light strawberry blond, which contrasted brilliantly with his deep brown eyes.

"Wanna drive to Walmart and buy the new MxPx CD?" he asked me; most of the cool kids had already left the New Year's Eve party.

"Heck yeah!" I said: This offer was just about as good as life got for a couple of teenage Christian boys in a small town.

Thad and I saw each other at a lot of local Christian-rock shows that year, and often bonded in the parking lot over the fact that neither of us knew how to talk to people. He'd had an isolated childhood on his

---

* Philmore was a Christian pop-punk/metal band that formed out of the Agapé youth-group scene. I absolutely adored this band, shyly asking the drummer, Brett Schoneman, if I could carry his drums to the van after each show. Years later, long after I'd lost my faith, I was tickled to see Philmore gain a national following.

family farm north of Mason City, and though I didn't know it at the time, he'd only begun exploring the world outside his farm that year, after he got his driver's license. We also bonded over our passion for analyzing music, our silent crushes on girls, and an arsenal of lewd jokes that made each other hyperventilate with laughter, sometimes for up to twenty minutes on a single punch line.

We'd both played demons in the Hell House Agapé put on earlier that year, excited to paint our faces like Brandon Lee in *The Crow* (I always loved playing demons in our plays; I had a wealth of imagination to pull from).

We left the E-Free church and hopped into a black 1971 Dodge Challenger, which Thad had restored by himself after finding it in a junkyard the year before. Unlike me, Thad was a *real* farm boy. The kind who had been working on his parents' farm since he could walk, rising before dawn to put in a few hours before school, then putting in a few more after he got home, and working round the clock all summer long.

His parents had come to Agapé off and on throughout the eighties, but though they were on board with the antigovernment politics and end-times prophecies (there were many reasons Thad's family lived on a farm, not just agriculture), they were put off by what they viewed as our foolish and Biblically inaccurate Pentecostal rituals.

Meeting his isolated rural family was the first time I began to see a difference between evangelicals who wanted to dress in modern clothes, listen to cool music, and connect with a national culture, versus those who wanted to retreat from society, cling to traditions of the past, and prepare for war with the government.

Thad's parents did *not* like me hanging out with him.

At the age of seventeen, aside from attending Forest City Christian School each year, Thad had only been away from the farm a handful of times, because his father believed that the Satanic, drug-dealing gang-bangers of downtown Mason City would leave him robbed, raped, and/or dead. They thought my influence on his fashion and taste in music made him "worldly," a term that more or less meant "pretentious sinner" in the eyes of evangelicals.

I likely spent more time thinking about scripture and sin—and evangelizing to the lost souls at public school—than anyone around me. But to rural fundamentalists like Thad's parents, my weird clothes and colored hair were all they needed to peg me as a "bad influence."

As Thad and I walked through Walmart, we randomly shoved each other into displays of toilet paper or energy drinks, knocking every-thing to the ground and running away, giggling. Despite our identities as born-again Christians, we were always hungering for small rebel-lions, like hitting people's trash cans with his car, or getting completely naked and driving as fast as we could around the lake (the logic of which is still a bit lost on me now, so many years later).

But most of the time we just wound up at Walmart.

As we were flipping through the CD racks, Thad asked, "Do you think you could teach me how to dance?"

I looked over at him and saw his freckled face flush bright red.

There were no proms or homecoming events at Forest City Chris-tian School, only "banquets"—with no dancing allowed. I'd been dancing in church and at Christian-rock concerts since I could walk, but Thad's church wasn't Pentecostal like ours, and he'd never dared to move his body to any kind of rhythm, despite being an excellent guitar player and songwriter.

"Sure," I told him, "but since I'm flunking my way through school, I don't know if I'm in a position to be teaching anybody *anything.*"

Thad wanted to go to clubs in Iowa City or Des Moines but was sure he'd make a giant fool of himself if placed on a dance floor. I often tried to make plans for these road trips (a club in Des Moines called Bugsy's had an all-ages night on Fridays), but he'd always find some way to back out at the last minute.

Like so many Iowans I knew, Thad often became embarrassed when he revealed any sort of passion or ambition. He was constantly on the lookout for land mines of humiliation, always paranoid that everyone was laughing at him. We'd talked about hosting a comedy show on the radio together, or starting a band and moving to a big city. But whenever I mentioned this in front of other people, he'd either deny it or say it was just some stupid idea I'd come up with.

"Oh, heck, yeah!" Thad said, changing the subject and sprinting into the CD aisle. "There's a new Plankeye album out!"

We used to go to the Christian bookstore for all of our music, but once Walmart started carrying Christian music (thanks to the overwhelming popularity of DC Talk), our Christian bookstore went out of business. For decades leading up to this, retailers under the Christian Bookstore Association were the epicenter of the Christian-music industry, where people like Thad and me discovered our new favorite bands, and parents could purchase albums for their kids with the confidence that no cursing, sex, or drug or alcohol use would be referenced in the music (except as a negative).

But Christian-music labels wanted the larger distribution of Sam Goodys, Virgin Megastores, or the ubiquitous Targets and Walmarts of America, and this led, eventually, to a slow shuttering of the indie Christian bookstores that had built the industry.

Now there was nothing keeping boys like Thad and me safe from the mainstream hits of 1999: the libidinous provocations of Britney Spears and NSYNC; the foul desires of Eminem; and, naturally, the demonic forces lurking within every Marilyn Manson CD.

Though I used to love dancing to INXS videos at my grandma's house, and went through periods of buying secular CDs (only to burn them ritualistically at youth-group bonfires), for most of the mid-to-late nineties I strove to keep my eyes and ears pure with exclusively Christian music. But now, flipping through CDs at Walmart with Thad, my breath quickened, my heartbeat doubled, and my hormones pulsed as my fingers caressed the faces of Ricky Martin, Sugar Ray, and the Goo Goo Dolls' Johnny Rzeznik.

"What are you looking at?" Thad asked.

"Nothing!"

Thad reached over and pulled out the Goo Goo Dolls CD I had in my hand. "Oh, man, I love this record! Don't you think he has the coolest hair? I wish I could look like that."

With misplaced confidence, I told Thad I could dye his hair with Johnny Rzeznik's blond streaks, and all the materials we'd need could be purchased right here at Walmart.

His hair wound up looking like something a sick dog would vomit up, but I vigorously defended it as "So punk rock!" as if this explained everything.

He looked absolutely nothing like Johnny Rzeznik.

Earlier that year, I'd enrolled in Forest City Christian School for my junior year of high school.

This was partly so I could hang with Thad all day, but also because of my (misguided) impression that I'd find acceptance and belonging from students who were surely just like him (sensitive, artistic, owning every CD released by Tooth & Nail Records), while being freed from the confusions, temptations, and trials of life in public school. All of these kids would be saved already, I assumed, and would embrace my punk-rock fashion as the extension of Christianity I believed it to be.

I was desperate to strengthen my faith enough to be healed from my swollen testicle, or to feel worthy of God's salvation. If I prayed enough, if I fasted enough, if I knew the Bible front to back, at some point I would feel reassured that I was, to quote DC Talk's first single, "Heavenbound."

I yearned to be isolated from the secular world, while feeling increasingly pulled away from evangelicalism by my itchy curiosity and love of rock music.

At the time I was unaware that the small rebellions Thad and I encouraged in each other (lewd jokes, secular music, engaging in conventionally feminine activities like dyeing each other's hair) would only grow in the years ahead, until we were both engrossed in heavy drug and alcohol addictions. And that the intellectual and cultural grounding I was searching for at a Christian school would never arrive.

My time at Forest City Christian School would leave me with even more unanswered questions than I'd had at the public school.

A Is for Apologetics

2000

"Satan is using the evolution theory to make kids go to Hell," a man in a tan suit with neatly parted hair explained to us, via an old VHS tape played on a console television. "The evolution theory removes all morality and all ways to discover how to have morality. It is the foundation for humanism, racism, Nazism, communism, and the New World Order."

The man's name was Kent Hovind,[*] one of the leading educators of "intelligent design" or "young Earth creationism," a field of Christian education that used the Bible as a guidepost for all scientific and historical inquiry. Belief in a six-thousand-year-old Earth had been around for centuries—even cited in one of Shakespeare's plays. It was the birth of the fundamentalist movement, bolstered by the Scopes Monkey Trial, that galvanized Christians into solidifying their beliefs with "scientific" explanations.

Basically, they took the genealogy of the Old Testament—Methuselah begat Lamech, who begat Noah, and so on—spanning from Adam in the Garden to Jesus on the cross, estimating each individual's life span (the Bible says Noah lived to the age of 950), thereby calculating the Earth to be somewhere around six thousand years old.

---

[*] While this and the following are all documented quotes of Hovind's, I cannot say for sure these were the quotes we absorbed in science class at FCC, since I do not have access to the curriculum from that time.

(Some creationists believe that it's as old as ten thousand years.) There have been many geological, botanical, and hydrological arguments offered to reinforce creationist teaching, but the nucleus of the theory is the infallibility of Biblical genealogy.

As strange as creationism may appear to those unfamiliar, its basic tenets are widely accepted even beyond evangelical Christian schools like mine. A 2017 Gallup poll found that 38 percent of American adults believed that "God created humans in their present form at one time within the last 10,000 years."

In the video on that day in science class, Kent Hovind was lecturing on the meteorology of the Earth in the time of Genesis, before Noah's flood, when the Earth was surrounded by a thick layer of water just beyond our atmosphere, and filled with water at its core. God's release of both of these created Noah's flood, he explained. Before this, the Garden of Eden was a biologically harmonious paradise where humans lived to be nine hundred years old, largely thanks to a lack of UV rays from the sun, which were filtered by the water above the planet.*

Watching Hovind's lecture, I thought of the flood myths I'd learned about in public school—the *Epic of Gilgamesh* was written in 2100 B.C., hundreds of years before the story of Noah, yet is nearly the same story—then bit down hard on my tongue, till the pain shut down all thoughts.

It's too late, there's no time to change your mind, Caldonia said.

Hovind was one of the most celebrated creationist lecturers of the time—along with Ken Ham, the Australian guy with the neck beard who rebuilt Noah's Ark in Kentucky—and was once even immortalized in a Chick Tract. (Hovind would later be martyred in the eyes of his followers when he was sentenced to ten years in prison for refusing

---

* Two decades later, as a journalist in Denver, I would cover a Flat Earth Conference and discover that the conspiracy theorists who believed the world to be shaped like a pancake—who numbered in the millions on social media and YouTube, and in the thousands at this conference—were getting most of their "evidence" from the book of Genesis and the teachings of creationists like Hovind.

to pay income tax, which he believed was an unconstitutional creation of Karl Marx.)

His lectures could be somewhat dense in detail and complex in argument, inspiring our teachers to nod with a furrowed brow while watching these videos.

I wondered if perhaps I'd been so brainwashed by the liberal education at public schools that I couldn't comprehend the righteous education I was being given at FCC—because, even though I'd never admit it, Kent Hovind appeared a bit unhinged to me. As I looked around the classroom, I wondered if any of my new classmates were as baffled by these ideas as I was, but instead I only got some dirty looks.

Often when people hear "private school" they think of upper-class boarding schools, or at least middle-class Catholic schools—but few students at FCC came from financially secure families. Nearly all of them shopped at thrift stores, were secretly on welfare, and were often behind on tuition payments. (FCC would go out of business a few years later.)

Most of the students were farm kids who viewed my flamboyant fashion choices and obsession with rock bands derisively. These things were associated with city folk in their minds, and cities were associated with bankers who stole land that had been family-owned for generations during the farm crisis.

Suffice it to say I did not find the belonging I was searching for at this school.

"Hey, faggot!" I heard on my first day.

"You are such a freak," another kid said, and not in the complimentary, DC Talk way.

I quickly deduced that Thad (with his hipster-punk clothes, guitar chops, and robust music collection) was an anomaly at FCC. Most of the students drove pickup trucks, sometimes with rifles in the back seat for some deer huntin' before or after school. It wasn't uncommon for students to be let out early because their cows got out of the pasture, or because it was harvest season and their families were falling behind. Many of them got married when they were still in high school, since starting a family early was a necessity of farm life.

The school taught fourth to twelfth grade, around thirty-five students all together, and we all met in the lunchroom each morning to pledge allegiance to the Christian flag: "I pledge allegiance to the Christian flag, and to the Savior for whose Kingdom it stands; one Savior, crucified, risen, and coming again with life and liberty to all who believe."

Only a handful of the kids were really into it; many of them would have preferred to be out in the woods, smoking pot and drinking Natural Light while shooting guns and listening to Kid Rock. About half of them were rebelling against Christianity, but they were all political and social conservatives and had zero patience for the effeminate "city boy" who showed up in junior year.

You don't belong here, Caldonia said, pecking her way into my thoughts every few minutes. *They all know who you really are.*

One November afternoon, we were shown a video about the fight for gay rights in San Francisco. It wasn't a Christian video—or, at least, not *our* brand of Christian—but one that was shown in public schools in California, where gay men and lesbians talked to children about the difficulties of being "in the closet," and why we should "accept all people for who they are."

"So you see how these people are trying not only to indoctrinate children into their worldview," our teacher explained, pausing the video, "but to *recruit* them as new members of their sinful lifestyle?"

A pool table in your community!

I squirmed in my seat and scratched my upper thigh, which was itchy from knife wounds that were beginning to heal, as Caldonia cackled with laughter in my head.

During the video, several kids turned to look at me, pointing and snickering. Afterward, I was approached by a gaggle of sixth graders, all of them hyper and giggling. "Are you *gay?*" one of them asked me, and they all ran away, laughing hysterically.

This routine would continue *every day* for the rest of the school year.

The question was obviously a rhetorical joke: just being asked it was the mother of all insults.

What I really wanted to say was "I don't know, but I'm trying hard not to be."

At the public school, I'd worked very hard to keep Phin and Faith from ever witnessing the way I was bullied, often letting my tormentors chase me so I could direct the scene away from my siblings. When I wasn't able to run away, I'd laugh loudly while being punched, choked, or pushed to the ground, hoping anyone within earshot would think that we were just playing around and that I was in on the joke.

I tried to mask my bullying from Thad as well, until I noticed that he was getting it, too.

"Hey, gay boy," they'd say to him, "nice hair color; your boyfriend do that?"

His girlfriend had just broken up with him, and while he was hanging with me in his living room, depressed and a little tearful, I heard his dad say, "What do you expect her to do when your hair looks like *that*?"

For a while, Thad carried a briefcase to school covered with band-logo stickers, like MxPx and The Supertones. But this eccentricity drew too much attention, and it was often knocked out of his hand when he was walking down the hall, or kicked off his desk and onto the floor, making papers spill everywhere. His sister was the worst at this, encouraging his tormentors at school and delivering the special kind of poisonous insults that only a family member can conjure.

My arrival at FCC did little to improve Thad's situation, and after a few weeks I avoided sitting with him at lunch or hanging with him in the parking lot after school, so as not to cause him any more trouble than I already had.

It was hard for me to think of this bullying as earning me martyrdom points in Heaven, since they were making fun of me for my sinful, effeminate demeanor and worldly fashion. But despite the bullying, I was excited to be attending classes at FCC.

I was determined to make sense of the creationism I was taught in science class, convinced it would only be a matter of time before I understood it all. And even though he wore a horrible tan suit and jumped from topic to topic, I felt soothed by Kent Hovind's lectures, for he seemed to have an answer to any question a skeptic could throw at him.

How did people live to the age of nine hundred in the book of Genesis? *Simple: more oxygen under the dome, better nutrition, and perfect genes.* How did large animals like elephants and giraffes fit on Noah's ark? *Easy: bring them on as babies.* How did all 7.7 million animal species get to, and fit in, Noah's Ark? *Answer: they didn't.* "The Bible says only two of every *kind*, not every *species*," Hovind explained. "Only those with nostrils. Insects can survive floods without land."

In the Gospel of Luke, when Jesus is fasting in the wilderness for thirty days, he is visited by Satan, who asks him to prove he is truly the Son of God by jumping off the roof of the Jewish Temple. "Do not put the Lord your God to the test!" Jesus angrily replies.

This passage is often used when fundamentalists are asked to apply scientific inquiry to Christian beliefs. However, that rule was suspended when it came to proving creationism over evolution; there was a bevy of data and scientific lingo to arm Christians whenever they found themselves debating an atheist.

Even if I didn't understand everything, it was enough to know that there were people like Hovind, who were so confident in their own understanding of our God-made world.

Suddenly I felt granted permission to widen the aperture of my curiosity.

I felt empowered to use my logic to reinforce the ideas of the Bible and my church, instead of just hiding from problematic information. If I was going to be able to debate liberal intellectuals into turning away from atheism and toward the bosom of Christ—as I was tasked with doing by church leaders—I needed to be able first to confront all the unanswered questions that had been pinballing around the back of my mind for the last decade or so.

Back at my dad's house, I booted up the family computer, wincing at the squealing of our dial-up modem.

As soon as I got to the WebCrawler search-engine page, I typed in: "How many religions are there in the world?"

Ever since my public-school teacher assaulted me with all that religious history in the eighth grade, I'd been obsessed with this question. Up until then, the only religion I knew other than Christianity was the Church of Satan (which was still technically within the Christian wheelhouse). The knowledge of *other* holy books similar to the Bible, other Jesus-like gods, other trinities and crucifixions and miracles and floods and apocalyptic prophecies—there was no way I was gonna let myself think about all that.

Until now.

I wanted to be able to confront atheist rhetoric head on, just like Kent Hovind.

I wanted to be able to take whatever information came my way, knowing my faith was strong enough to navigate it. But after five minutes passed and the page loaded, my skin turned cold.

"There are an estimated 10,000 distinct religions in the world," a web page explained to me.

How could that be?

So many of them were similar to Christianity, yet many predated Christianity.

This is all just liberal propaganda, Caldonia said. *It's the Antichrist's campaign to turn people away from Jesus and toward the communist humanism of his coming regime.*

Still, I couldn't stop myself, and moved along to scratch my next itch of curiosity: "How many different types of Christianity are there?"

I thought of my grandma Marilyn's Methodist church and how different it was from Agapé. I'd also recently attended a Catholic funeral, and was wide-eyed with wonder throughout the whole service, having never been exposed to Catholicism before and finding it as unfamiliar to my view of Christianity as Hinduism or Buddhism.

"There are 45,000 different Christian denominations in the world," I read.

In Mason City and Clear Lake alone, there were scores of Christian churches, each of them a bit different: Presbyterian, Episcopalian, Christian Science. At least a dozen evangelical churches like ours functioned in the area, and many of them argued with one another about which was following Biblical teachings correctly, which were corrupt, and which should be run out of town (if you got down to it, the universal answer to this question was: All of them except ours).

Careful, Josiah, Caldonia warned me, *you're sowing seeds of doubt. Blaspheming the Holy Spirit.*

If it was true that there were forty-five thousand different types of

Christianity, and they varied greatly with time and geography, how could I reasonably assume that *our* church was the "correct one," that I was born in *just the right time AND location,* to the *right* parents with the *right* beliefs, to land in the *one true church*?

After nearly three hours of research—probably more time than I'd spent doing homework in all my life—I turned off the computer and stared into space.

You've done it now, Caldonia told me. *You've blasphemed the Holy Spirit, and your belief will never, ever recover.*

"I think you're right," I said aloud to myself, slowly nodding, with wide, unblinking eyes.

CHAPTER TWENTY-THREE

Tuning In, Flunking Out

On the final day of my junior year, I was pulled aside by one of the school administrators and told that I could not return to Forest City Christian School next year until I paid off my tuition debt.

My parents had said I could transfer from public school to FCC as long as I paid my own tuition with the part-time job I had making sandwiches at Subway, though I don't think any of us did the math on this. Mom was still a year away from landing a job that would earn her serious (i.e., middle-class) money, and Dad was struggling to hold on to his job at KAAL while taking care of Faith and Phin. (He was allowed to work from home and was spending ever more time stoned in his bedroom.) I hadn't been doing great at managing my paychecks from Subway, and often blew them on clothes, CDs, and Christian-rock festival tickets before paying off my FCC tuition.

As careless as this sounds, I wasn't avoiding paying my debt. I was just having a difficult time concentrating on anything long enough even to make a plan, let alone consistently follow through with it. Most of my homework was forgotten as soon as I got home. I often showed up to work on my off-days and was absent when I'd been scheduled.

You were like a weed left to grow at the back of the yard, totally unnoticed.

Between enduring incessant doses of fear and shame from Caldonia, keeping my theological curiosity in check, and being constantly ready for the horn of Gabriel to signal the Apocalypse, I rarely had much bandwidth for things like homework, sandwich orders, or maintaining a schedule. I was fired from Subway after only a few months, then made it a bit longer as a host at Bennigan's before they gave me the boot as well.

After putting up with me for eight years, Clear Lake Public School didn't want me back, either. (My terrible grades and apparent lack of job ambition likely had something to do with that.) They suggested I attend the "alternative school" in nearby Garner. I didn't think any school could possibly be smaller than FCC, but this was just a single room with eight teenagers, most of them either pregnant, recently out of juvenile hall or drug rehab, or all of the above.

I was a virgin (at least heterosexually) who'd never tried drugs or voluntarily fought with anyone. I'd never skipped school a day in my life, though I might as well have: my grades were just as poor as they would have been if I'd never shown up.

And yet, for me, the alternative school was a perfect fit.

Some might have looked at these kids smoking cigarettes and weed outside the school each morning, kids who had violent histories and few job prospects, and thought, *There's no way my child would be safe and get a decent education there.* But I actually thrived at the alternative school. After all, it was free of the rich kids who typically bullied me at the public school, the ones with vacation homes and private planes, who drove sports cars and carried cellphones as early as 1996.

At the alternative school, though we had some group projects (and guest speakers, who taught us about the dangers of drugs, alcohol, and teen pregnancy), mostly they just gave us textbooks and some homework and pointed us toward our cubicles. This was the first time I'd ever done schoolwork in complete silence and safety, and suddenly my mind could focus long enough so I could not only *learn* something, but actually *enjoy* learning—and want more of it.

Somehow, even Caldonia would quiet down when I was there.

My grades improved dramatically in the first quarter, and I thought: *I may have a shot at this school thing.* Then my teacher pulled me into her office one afternoon and told me, "Josiah, you may technically be a senior, but you only have the credits of a sophomore."

I had hardly been acing my classes at Forest City Christian School, but I did better there than at the public school and got at least *passing* grades (most of the time). Apparently, however, that didn't matter, because, unbeknownst to me, FCC was not an "accredited educator" (a term I was unfamiliar with), and the credits I earned there were meaningless in the public-school system. I'd given a year of my life to that school without having anyone explain this to me. My parents were aware of it, but since they had enrolled me in a Christian school for kindergarten and first grade, and my mom had attended Open Bible College (also not an "accredited school") and my dad thought little of formal education, they didn't consider this as the same issue it would've been for parents in secular households.

"Actually," the teacher said, flipping through some papers, "that's not right."

I sat up, relieved that this might all just be some bureaucratic error. I would walk across that graduation stage after all. I would get the cap and gown, the diploma, the pats on my back at the reception.

I would, for once in my life, finish and succeed at something.

"Yes, here it is," she said. "You don't have the credits of a sophomore. Looks like you flunked algebra and biology sophomore year at Clear Lake. You have the credits of a freshman."

My heart sank, and I felt nauseated.

"So . . . what should I do?"

As soon as this question left my mouth, it felt much bigger than I intended. I could feel panic circling me like a pack of wolves, and that made me think of my mother.

I knew Mom suffered from an obsessive fear that she was a bad parent, and was often embarrassed during parent-teacher conferences whenever my long list of failures was read aloud in an accusatory tone.

I wanted to graduate, if for no other reason than to make my mother smile. My flunking out of school would be a tremendous humiliation for her, considering how important education (and the appearance of success) was to Mom. I could feel her embarrassment at having me for a son. I could feel how shamed she felt by our church, the teachers, the other parents, her bosses, and the pediatrician who read my report cards and decided to prescribe me Ritalin. I knew she felt like a failed mother, and that I was responsible for it.

I wanted to do better. I just didn't know how.

"So . . . do I have to stay in school for another three years?" I asked my teacher.

She shook her head. "You could try that, but I'm not sure if even that would be a good idea. I think getting your GED is the best route for you."

She laid out my options in detail, and I went back to my seat and sat quietly for a moment. Then I realized something and walked back to her desk.

"So . . . if I want to do the GED thing, does that mean I can just go home? Like, now?"

She confirmed that it did.

I picked up my stuff and walked out the door.

"I think I just dropped out of school," I said aloud to myself in the car.

I was finished with formal education forever and wasn't sure how to feel about it. Though I was certainly excited, it wasn't like the hyperventilating joy I got when a blizzard forced school to close for the day. I put a mixed CD into the car stereo, rolled down the window, and lit a cigarette.

The February air was violently cold, but I hardly noticed.

I had picked up smoking during a recent visit to my sister at Evangel University, a private Christian college in Missouri. While there, I also met a handful of "intellectual Christians," who not only educated me on all sorts of theological fun-facts (such as the existence of the Gospel According to Mary Magdalene, and According to Judas, which were excluded from the canon), but also introduced me to secular bands like Radiohead, The Velvet Underground, R.E.M., David Bowie, and Björk.

It was a revelation not unlike the scene in *Almost Famous* in which the budding music journalist inherits his sister's record collection. Discovering effeminate peacocks like Morrissey, Beck, and Michael Stipe led to some mysterious click of recognition inside me, like a border collie's instant knowledge of how to herd sheep. It wasn't that I was as talented as they were, or even a capable musician, but I had some of the same pixie dust inside of me that they did, and it needed to come out.

One night, while all these young college students were out partying, I made a mixed CD from their computer's MP3 catalogue.

And now, back in Iowa, this CD became the soundtrack to the day I dropped (flunked?) out of high school.

Pink Floyd radiated out of the cracked speakers of my Chevrolet Celebrity, as I looked at my unfinished homework in the passenger seat. Without thinking, I cracked my window and slowly fed those pages into the gray afternoon air, watching in my rear view mirror as they flapped around like rabid doves. David Gilmour sang about being aimless in your hometown, waiting for someone to come along and "show you the way." I needed someone to show me a path forward, because I seemed destined to fail at every turn, despite my best efforts.

I couldn't maintain my faith.

I couldn't maintain my grades.

I couldn't hold down a job.

I had no friends other than Thad, rarely spoke to anyone in my family, and had no idea what I was going to do with my life.

I'd even lost the urgency I once felt to know and preach the will of God. The lack of a Y2K Armageddon had put a significant crack in the faith of many evangelicals of my generation, and for me it would never heal. An existential despair, a theological malaise, an Apocalypse fatigue had set in for me after that, though maybe I was only just now realizing it.

I turned onto a random gravel road, heading in the opposite direction of home, not knowing where I was going, just reacting. I suddenly had no obligations. No one expected me to be anywhere or do anything. Endless blizzards had suffocated the earth in a layer of old snow and single-digit temperatures for months. The sun remained hidden behind a dead-gray sky most of the winter, the color matching the ground beneath it. Since the Iowa landscape was so perfectly flat you could see for miles in every direction, on days like this it was easy to lose track of where the ground ended and the sky began, just as a pilot's sense of the horizon can waver when his plane is lost in a fog.

I turned down another gravel road, then another, having no idea where I was.

It felt like I was driving this car through an infinite abyss of dirty-white clouds, floating helplessly, with no use for the pedals or brakes. Filled with a sudden balloon of fear and rage, I slammed my foot on the accelerator. The speedometer climbed to forty, fifty, seventy miles per hour on the snowy gravel road. Tears spilled down my cheeks, and I screamed through gritted teeth, banging my palm on the steering wheel.

The car began to fishtail to the left, then right.

I passed over a bridge, the ass end of my car swerving from side to side.

I slammed on the brakes (when I should've downshifted), and the car skidded sideways, then went airborne and flew off into a ditch just past the bridge, slamming headfirst into the frozen ground.

I sat there for a moment, in shock, slowly checking myself for injuries.

The car was pointed straight down, like a rocket that just plunged into the Earth.

I climbed out the window and onto the empty road, bruised and scraped but mostly okay.

I looked in one direction, then another, until I'd turned a full 360.

I was surrounded by a thick fog in all directions. Then I saw an abandoned farmhouse I recognized as only a few miles from Thad's house, on the north end of Mason City. I began walking in what I thought was the direction of his house, though it was difficult to see through the gray air. Feeling the dark panic return in my belly, thinking about flunking school, crashing my car, and being forced to enter an adulthood I was told would never arrive, I started to run.

I hadn't really *run* since I was a little kid, because I always forgot to bring the proper workout clothes and shoes to gym class (which was how I earned that particular failing grade). But I was sprinting like a leopard that day, feeling the urgency surge through my body as my feet punched the gravel road.

Then I ran out of steam, after just a few minutes, and was panting for breath as I went from a run, to a jog, to a walk, to putting my hands on my knees, still panting, realizing I wasn't actually anywhere near Thad's house.

I had no idea where I was, or where I should go.

Interlude: Highway to Hegemony

2023

Over the last few decades, commerce for much of North Central Iowa has gravitated toward a small strip of highway on the far-west end of Mason City, all composed of the same corporate chain stores that can be found anywhere in America. "We call this the franchise capital of Iowa, because we've got every restaurant franchise in town," the executive director of the North Iowa Area Council of Governments, Joe Myhre, said to *The Des Moines Register* in 2016.

As a young man, I pinballed my way down this highway, working for familiar restaurants like Subway, Perkins, Bennigan's, and Red Lobster. I spent a year in the (relatively) big city of Des Moines and felt like king of the hipsters while working at the Gap. If you had a more cultured childhood, this may be difficult to understand, but there was rarely news as exciting to a small Midwestern community as a universally recognized chain store arriving in town.

In the 1993 Johnny Depp film *What's Eating Gilbert Grape,* the tiny hamlet of Endora, Iowa, is under economic threat by a new supermarket and fast-food chain, and yet all John C. Reilly's character can talk about is how amazing everything will be once Burger Barn comes to town.

"There were two big promises made with the arrival of chain stores in small towns," Bethany Moreton, a professor at Dartmouth University who specializes in the history of capitalism, tells me over the phone as I'm driving down the Mason City highway, with brightly lit signs for Pizza Hut, Burger King, and Starbucks on all sides of me. "One was entry-level jobs for young people, so they wouldn't have to leave town and go to the big, wicked city. The other was that you will join the national mainstream by having access to the same consumer goods or dining experience as everyone else, which confers legitimacy to your town . . . There were efforts to create a national culture of consumption, and an idea that that would unite us nationally."

This was Burroughs Waltrip's strategy when convincing the farmers of Mason City to invest in his Radio Chapel, with its modern design, air-conditioning, hymns projected onto the wall, and sermons broadcast on the radio.

The same thing can also be found in *The Music Man,* when everyone goes apeshit as the Wells Fargo Wagon rolls into town, bringing salmon from Seattle, grapefruit from Tampa, maple sugar, a rocking chair, curtains, dishes, and tools from all over the nation.

After so many families lost their farms throughout the eighties and nineties, many North Iowans were searching for some kind of identity they could latch on to. And chain stores—or a retail waterbed store like Sleepy Hollow—acted as a temporary salve, proof that, as Americans, North Iowans hadn't been left behind, culturally or economically.

"The original purpose for these small towns was to provide service to the farming communities," says Don Hofstrand, an agriculture-business specialist with Iowa State University for thirty-five years, with whom I also spoke during my time in Iowa. "And the fewer farmers there are, the less reason these towns have for existing. And that's why small towns all over the Midwest are dying."

The proliferation of these box stores and restaurants along Highway 18 has pulled business away from downtown Mason City, which was designed to concentrate pedestrian traffic throughout its retail stores, bars, hotels, theaters, and ice-cream shops, so that people would randomly bump into one another, creating community as well as commerce. My grandma Marilyn often told stories of having a night out in downtown Mason City in the 1950s and '60s, when "you couldn't hardly walk down the sidewalk, it was so packed with people."

Today, downtown Mason City is eerily quiet, with vacancy signs in every other window. Yet it's still far more aesthetically pleasing, with its lampposts and Frank Lloyd Wright architecture, than the cheap, lifeless structures off the highway.

The economic collapse of the 1980s farm crisis rippled out to many of the restaurants and retail stores in the area, creating ideal conditions for national chains to swoop in (not unlike the intrusion of corporate agriculture), offering a comforting, nostalgic, low-price escape from all the changes in society.

No one perfected this idea quite like Walmart.

Beyond the (as Midwesterners would put it) "reasonable" prices, Walmart offered a kind of time-travel experience, back to a cartoonish version of a 1950s that had never really existed—a time before civil rights, feminists, and gays made everything so darn complicated. It was an experience no longer offered on television, or walking through downtown, where kids refused to respect their elders or pull their pants up.

Employees' dress code at Walmart consists of twill pants, a royal-blue vest, and a polo shirt (which employees must purchase); only ear piercings are allowed. Men are favored over women for positions of authority. No offensive music is ever on the shelves, but you can find plenty of Focus on the Family materials, and an abundance of basic, unprovocative clothing.

One Princeton study found that Walmart has an exceptionally devoted fanbase in the evangelical community. Those with a college degree (B.A. or higher) are 33 percent less likely to shop at Walmart than those with a high-school education. The same holds for those who make more than seventy-five thousand dollars a year, but not if they're evangelicals, among whom the figures remain steady across income and education levels.

And evangelicals are found to be twice as likely to have a favorable view of Walmart as those in all other religious sects surveyed.

Despite Walmart's deep nostalgia for the Eisenhower era, it has no love for the labor policies of that time. Unlike the single-breadwinner model of the 1950s—whereby a man working in a factory or an office could provide enough wealth to support the whole family—Walmart strategically built its empire in rural, Christian areas more accustomed to an agrarian model of work, whereby labor was distributed among the entire family. The man was always viewed as the head of the farm, but the women and children pulled their weight, too—even if there wasn't direct monetary compensation for their individual efforts.

And, perhaps most important, when farm families were poor, they blamed themselves, not outside forces, and so would be far less likely to complain about low wages or lack of opportunities when working these disposable jobs.

As employees of Walmart, we were often referred to as a part of "a family," as though we were all in this together, just as on a family farm. Thus, you labored not for your own selfish ends (like a paycheck) but for the good of the whole, which would eventually benefit (i.e., trickle down to) each individual.

The Think System.

I saw a lot of people I recognized from church sporting those royal-blue vests. Plenty of husbands and dads were employed by Walmart, but working there seemed to impose a silent emasculation on a man. The generations of farmers before them had found their pride and identity in the autonomy of running their own farms, and now they were wearing a uniform with a yellow smiley face, earning less than they would've paid a kid to pull weeds in their bean fields a short time ago.

Most of these jobs didn't even offer a respite from the shame of welfare. Research shows that Walmart employees cost the U.S. government $6.2 billion annually in public assistance, essentially supplementing the low wages provided by that corporation. (In 2023, Walmart earned $11.6 billion in profits.)

Management positions offered some small relief from this, but the patriarchal model continued there, too. A few years after my time as a Walmart employee in 2003, the company was sued for overlooking women in distributing pay raises and management positions.[*]

---

[*] The Supreme Court ultimately ruled against the class-action lawsuit in a five-to-four decision.

Walmart has been notoriously aggressive about crushing any attempts at unionizing among their employees. During my orientation process to work there, I was shown a lengthy video about why unions are bad for employees, instructing me, if I was ever approached by anyone attempting to form a union, to avoid responding in any way.

Bethany Moreton has written about Walmart's all-too-familiar trend of entering a community and bankrupting the small local businesses, which leads to a shrinking of the economy and the flight of local people to the nearest big city. Then, when there are too few people with too little money left to support the big box store, "the people who know Walmart destroyed their town are put in the position of begging them not to leave, because it's the last productive entity left," she explains.

Moreton is critical of the subsidies small towns offer businesses like Walmart to set up shop—under the promise of economic stimulation. She argues that giving such subsidies to a town's own small proprietors would stimulate the local economy much more effectively, and truly keep its sons and daughters from leaving.

Iowa is just behind North Dakota, with the second-highest "brain drain" in the nation: young people with college degrees moving out of state in pursuit of better jobs. "My kids left for Des Moines and New York City," Don Hofstrand tells me. "You can talk to almost anybody in town, and their kids aren't here, either . . . Mason City is getting to be like an old folks' home."

Following a generation of brain drain—and corporate dominance of the economy—North Iowa was left with people like Thad and me, lost, with no identity, direction, or passion to latch on to.

Thad had graduated from Forest City Christian School, but was just as adrift as I was.

Everywhere we went, Green Day's "Good Riddance" was on the radio, with Billie Joe Armstrong singing "Another turning point, a fork stuck in the road, / Time grabs you by the wrist, directs you where to go." I'd heard this song at countless graduation ceremonies at that time—watching friends and siblings pass through the turnstiles of life, toward a glittering horizon of domestic and economic bliss, leaving North Iowa behind—and each time I heard it I wondered: *When is time going to grab me by the wrist and direct me where to go?*

Of all the socioeconomic setbacks a young adult may be burdened with—belonging to a racial, gender, or sexual minority; poverty; childhood trauma; a criminal record—dropping out of high school is certainly high up on the list. On average, a high-school dropout earns only around twenty thousand dollars a year, and that's assuming he or she can even find a job, because the unemployment rate is nearly two times higher for those without a diploma. Dropouts are around sixty-three times more likely to wind up in prison than graduates, and are far more susceptible to addiction and suicidal ideation. On average, failing to get a high-school diploma knocks nine years off your life.

Low-wage, disposable jobs became the only option for dropouts like me living in North Iowa. Standardized gigs designed by people on the other side of the country, created with fast training and high turnover in mind. Jobs that offer little incentive to work hard, since the wages and opportunities for advancement typically remain low.

In her book *To Serve God and Wal-Mart: The Making of Christian Free Enterprise,* Bethany Moreton traces the outsized role the Christian right has played in turning small-town economies into profit machines for faraway corporations, stripping them of not only their economic momentum but their regional cultures, while making heroes out of robber barons.

By shifting the image of the leadership of big business from singular tycoons like J. P. Morgan to families like the Waltons or the Sacklers, industrialists appealed to the "family values" evangelicals had been espousing since the days of the Klan. This allowed the Reagan administration to dismantle antitrust laws set in place in the aftermath of the Gilded Age, allowing corporations to merge, grow, and dominate the U.S. economy, while assuring voters and consumers that good, wholesome people were running the show.

Reagan also reformed the banks to generate a massive amount of economic activity on Wall Street, creating, as Moreton puts it in our interview, a "canopy of finance," which buzzed high above the heads of working- and middle-class Americans but promised that it would eventually "trickle down" to them.

It did not.

During the prosperity of mid-twentieth-century America, the income of the average CEO was around twenty-one times the pay of the typical worker; today, a CEO is likely to take home 340 times what his or her average employee makes. When the libertarians and evangelicals first began campaigning for a deregulated market in the 1960s, the top income-tax rate was 91 percent; it fell to around 70 in the following decade, the Reagan revolution dropped it to 50, and it eventually fell to 31 percent by 1992 (it hasn't changed much since).

When the amounts are adjusted for inflation, most working-class employees have not seen a pay raise in my lifetime—while productivity and work hours have steadily climbed. Federal minimum-wage increases ceased throughout most of the 1980s, and the minimum rate was only bumped up a few times before stopping again in 2009 at a level where it remains today: $7.25 an hour.

Today, a million hourly workers in America are living off the minimum wage (or less, since many jobs aren't subject to the federal wage law), and a third of the workforce in this country are earning less than fifteen dollars an hour.

After hopping off the phone with Bethany Moreton, I walk into the Walmart that once employed me, with its toxic buzz of the fluorescent lights and smell of cheap, thin fabrics. The sound of nineties Top 40 sizzling down from cracked speakers high above takes me back to the year 2002. I recall the heavy dissociation that washed over me when I'd enter these doors, as it had at school. I can easily recall chain-smoking cigarettes in a break room with yellowing walls amid exhausted ex-farmers, the nauseating vertigo of nicotine the only feeling left in my body.

I drive back to the Mason City Library, where I've more or less set up an office in one of the study rooms. It's next door to the Mac-Nider Museum downtown, and through a picture window I can see a lazy river running behind the library, above which sits the Music Man Footbridge (a block away from Meredith Willson's childhood home). Across the street is the old Methodist church where my parents were married, in whose chapel my grandfather installed the stained-glass window.

I'm doing a Zoom interview with Oscar Jiménez-Solomon, who researches the intersection of mental health and poverty at Columbia University's Center on Poverty and Social Policy. His work is largely centered on the cyclical, generational impacts of poverty on various aspects of a family or community, such as reshaping DNA; impairing cognitive functions, emotional regulation, and social abilities; reducing educational achievement; and lowering people's overall level of happiness with their lives.

Beyond the stagnant wages, there has been a serious psychological impact from the proliferation of disposable jobs throughout the small-town job market.

"There is a lot of research around the positive, nonmonetary impact of employment," he explains to me. "There is a sense of purpose and meaning, there are social connections that come from work. And there are benefits of security, such as with health insurance, or paid time off for emergencies . . . When people can't find work or are employed at jobs that don't offer any [of these benefits], the absence of these attributes will likely have a detrimental impact on their mental health."

According to one study, only around 40 percent of workers earning less than ten dollars an hour received health insurance through their employer. And as for a sense of purpose and social connection, most of the disposable jobs are designed to reduce or eliminate these attributes: co-workers and bosses are hired and fired (or quit) regularly. More than once, I got the boot from one chain store only to cross the street and be hired by another in the same afternoon.

When workers have little influence over the work they do, aren't paid a livable wage, receive little respect from their community for the position, have no security or health insurance, and work in a field with such a high turnover rate that social connections are brief to nonexistent, it's difficult to view the promises these industries claim when they come to town as anything but a *Music Man* grift.

It's little wonder that Thad and I would eventually embrace drugs—and drug dealing—at around this time. We'd been told our whole lives that the rapture was coming any minute, that we'd likely never live to see adulthood. And now that we were adults, we had no idea what to do with ourselves. We no longer felt the drive to "reclaim America for Christ," and our post-agriculture small towns offered no sense of purpose to replace it with.

I was desperate to leave Iowa but wasn't sure where to go, or able to save up enough money to get there. I would be twenty-two before I met a girl in a bar who offered to take me to Denver, a move that most likely saved me from incarceration, suicide, or opioid addiction.

Sitting in the Mason City Library in 2023, after finishing my interview with Oscar Jiménez-Solomon, I lean back in my chair and recall the faces of dozens of people I knew in those years who are now dead from overdoses, in prison, or continuing to live lives of quiet desperation, void of meaning or respect.

Then I think about the work I'm here to do and how that sense of purpose has kept me from going down the same path.

CHAPTER TWENTY-FOUR

Children of the Industrialized Corn

"If you hump away at menial jobs 360-plus days a year,
does some kind of repetitive injury of the spirit set in?"

—BARBARA EHRENREICH, *NICKEL AND DIMED*

2002

"You've worked here for six weeks; I shouldn't have to tell you how to make a fucking rum-and-Coke," my boss at Red Lobster shouted at me during one busy Saturday night. "The recipe is in the fucking name!"

I told myself I should care that I was about to be fired from my sixth job, but I just couldn't muster the energy.

I knew that this man yelling at me had said a great many things during my weekend of training, but I hadn't paid attention to anything other than the free cheese biscuits, just as I could now only stare at the sea-life pattern on his shirt as he roared at me.

I had yet to try drugs, but I might as well have been on heroin all day for all the cognitive engagement I had with the world. A couple years later, I would see the indie comedy *Napoleon Dynamite,* made by two Mormons about low-class life in semirural Idaho. I would instantly recognize the existential deflation in Jon Heder's pathetic sigh and empty expression as his gaze fell to the ground.

Thad was living with me at my dad's house, both of us wandering through low-wage jobs in Mason City and Clear Lake. He'd signed me up to enlist in the navy as a joke (inspired by the sexual connotations of a certain Village People song), and when a recruiter showed up at my door, he successfully seduced me into this branch of the military—which happened to be the only one that admitted high-school dropouts.

Though, given my lack of a diploma, I'd have to pass an aptitude test.

I'd always hated tests, struggling to stay focused long enough to get through them. Any attention I had in those days was devoted to Caldonia, and the constant pain between my legs. *You are such a waste of life, even the bottom rung of society has no use for you,* she reminded me throughout the day. Her words made me feel so self-conscious that I would fold my body into itself to make myself small, as if to apologize to the world for my own existence. I mentally checked out during the navy's aptitude test—breath shallow, eyes locked on the pattern of the carpet for ten minutes at a time—and flunked it.

Twice.

There was no way I was even going to *think* about taking the GED test after that.

I'd been fired from Perkins, Subway, Walmart, the Gap, and Bennigan's, and could now add Red Lobster to that list. Despite being nineteen and never having tasted a drop of alcohol, I was allowed to bartend at Red Lobster under Iowa labor laws. During my training, I'd failed to retain that the word "virgin" meant "no alcohol," and on more than one occasion introduced children to the taste of rum in their daiquiris.

Speaking of virgins, I no longer was one.

Despite having fooled around with a lot of boys over the years, I was still profoundly disappointed in myself the first time I had sex with a woman, giving it up in a flash to a Bennigan's server. I'd been taught that my virginity was my greatest asset to a future wife, so I'd just robbed myself of another essential touchstone of a happy life. No education, no career, no wife, no family—why even bother, I asked myself.

I stayed in bed for three days after losing my virginity, which lost me another job.

Who is going to want you now? Caldonia asked.

I was allowing myself to sink to the bottom of the water, not caring if my feet ever reached the ground.

By my age, my parents were married with kids. Phin and Faith waited until their mid-twenties to start their own families, but still seemed to have no trouble maintaining careers and raising kids (and would do quite well for themselves in the years ahead). Whereas I couldn't hold down minimum-wage jobs long enough to pay my rent. Asking whether or not I was ready to care for children . . . you might as well have asked if I was ready to compete in the Olympics, or navigate a trip into deep space.

Eventually, I accepted the inevitable and got a job at the Winnebago factory, as so many of my friends and family had done before me. This was my first full-time gig that offered health insurance, and I considered seeing a doctor for my swollen testicle, toying with the idea that it might actually be a medical issue rather than a punishment from God for fooling around with boys.

I had kept it a secret for three years.

In my first week on the job, a guy working next to me on the assembly line approached me on our lunch break, shoving what looked like a hand-rolled cigarette into the pocket of my shirt. "Welcome to the team," he said, and walked away.

I held it up to my nose and thought, *This smells like my dad.*

It was a joint.

Throughout my whole life, the narrative from my mom and my sister had been that marijuana had broken up my parents' marriage, destroyed my dad's ambition, and held the power to open your body to demonic possession. At both public and Christian schools, I'd been terrorized by the vague but ominous specter of DRUGS in the world, with little understanding of the what or why of the equation. Drug gangs had turned cities into lawless battlegrounds, I'd been told, picturing the Detroit of *RoboCop* or the violent world of *Mad Max.*

Intoxicants of any kind were taboo on my maternal, Methodist side of the family. Methodists were leaders in the temperance movement, and we were often told stories of our grandfather Josiah (for whom I was named) hiding under the corn cribs when his father drank, hoping to escape a merciless beating. My grandmother Marilyn was so opposed to alcohol that she refused to ever let so much as a beer into the house, and never fully trusted my dad after rumors of his pot smoking surfaced.

Alcohol, marijuana, heroin—they were all the same according to Midwestern evangelicals. And yet, without hesitation, the second I got home that day, I exclaimed to Thad: "I have a joint, wanna smoke it?!"

I wasn't sure exactly when Thad started living with us.

It was after a brief stint in Des Moines that I ran out of money and moved into my dad's house in Clear Lake. At first, Thad stayed over most weekends. Then we pooled our money and bought a two-hundred-dollar car from a junkyard to get us around. After that, he just never left. Like every other farm in the Midwest, his family's had slowly phased out all livestock when industrial farming took over the industry, and shrank their crop production until there was almost nothing left for Thad to inherit.

Three boys in a lakeside house, shrugging at the future.

I didn't know it at the time, but Dad had just been fired from his job at the TV station. For the first two months I was home, he rarely came out of his bedroom. Once Thad started sleeping over, Dad decided to charge us rent, and he moved in with his girlfriend in Mason City. Another detail Dad neglected to mention was that he hadn't paid his mortgage in months, and the house was about to be foreclosed upon at the end of the summer.

"Fuck, yeah!" Thad said, searching his pocket for a lighter.

The smell of the burning cannabis made the connection to my father even more visceral. I'd been inhaling that scent off him as far back as I could remember, and now that I finally knew what it was, Dad wasn't here. He'd had that house for more than a decade, the greatest symbol of material success he'd ever know. To me it was the clean home with good food, where my older, cooler brother and sister lived. Now they were all gone, and I was on drugs.

"Turn it up," Thad said, as we listened to the Smashing Pumpkins' *Mellon Collie and the Infinite Sadness* on a cheap boom box.

Thad and I had recently been getting a low-grade thrill from exploring all the classic nineties albums we'd missed out on while restricting ourselves to exclusively Christian music. By the time we'd finished that joint, we'd gone through all the CDs by Oasis, Beck, Nirvana, and Fiona Apple (my choice) that we'd purchased at the pawn shop the day before. We sat silently through each album, disappearing into the guitar solos, the harmonies, the production tricks of the recording, our minds hungrily clamoring after every detail.

After that, our lives more or less revolved around getting stoned and listening to music. Thad was hungry to pursue the outer limits of pleasure and rebellion, drunk on newfound freedom after a childhood of domineering control by his family. I just really enjoyed getting high and listening to Belle and Sebastian albums.

The term "inner child" may inspire eyerolls from most conservatives, but nothing soothed the frightened boy inside me, made him feel safe enough to be playful with thoughts, fashion, and dance, quite like pot. It also quelled my nightmares and sleepwalking, facilitating a greater level of trust between myself and the act of sleep.

"If we start buying our weed an ounce at a time, we could sell half of it and smoke the other half for free," Thad proposed one night, and I called him a genius.

We'd been buying weed from an old friend from youth group (we weren't the only evangelical boys in a state of rebellion) who later introduced us to his connection in Des Moines, where we got better deals when buying large quantities. Soon an ounce turned into a half-pound, and we became less reliant on our ever-changing minimum-wage jobs.

Dealing drugs was the first work I ever felt any sense of pride in; I genuinely believed in the service and product I was providing to my community. This became all the more true when Thad and I entered the Iowa rave scene (mostly on abandoned farms, several years after raves stopped being cool in L.A. and New York), and I became as big an evangelical for ecstasy as I once was for Jesus.

I made friends, got into adventures, and watched a thousand sunrises.

My posture improved as I became more confident.

We hosted days-long parties at my dad's house, turning each room into a diorama of immersive art, utilizing skills we'd gleaned creating Hell Houses as teens. We befriended DJs who would spin house music all day and night, as rave kids either danced under strobe and black-lights in the living room, or cuddled like puppies in the chill room upstairs, decorated with a mix of fifties suburbia and Victorian opium-den aesthetics.

The house welcomed an eclectic mix of rednecks, punks, ravers, drug dealers, and even a few jocks. Some of them were educated professionals slumming it for the drugs, but most of our new roommates either were high-school dropouts or had a diploma but no plans for higher education. One guy took his student-loan financing, cashed the check, and bought a Suzuki motorcycle instead of enrolling in college.

We were the townies of a community-college town.

Another friend was constantly ordering furniture, stereos, and TVs on credit, then stiffing the stores. Many had warrants out for their arrest; others had just gotten out of prison and were violating their parole by being around all these drugs. They'd overdraw checking accounts by hundreds of dollars, then abandon them. No one knew how to write a résumé, or what a credit score was, or could even tell you their Social Security number. Like the Latchkey Boys in the trailer park, most of us were raised by parents in constant emergency mode. All we knew was what was in front of us at that moment.

And, if we were honest with ourselves, we saw that all there was in front of us was depression, shame, and denial.

None of us talked about it, but it was clear that, by indulging in constant drug use and parties, buying shit we didn't need, and sleeping away most of the daylight hours, we were attempting to push away existential anxiety over our uncertain futures. Everyone was working, but none of us were very invested in our jobs, or even ourselves. Most would go on to have numerous children with different partners, keeping the wheel of poverty and generational trauma spinning.

I welcomed the disposable jobs in those days, because I had no confidence in my ability to handle responsibility; I was certain that I'd fuck it all up.

Thad and I enrolled with several day-labor and temp agencies, a place for businesses to hire a set of hands for a week or two for fifteen dollars an hour (of which we'd only get 40 percent). Over the course of that summer, we swung 150 feet in the air assembling windmills, installed dropped ceilings for a new Dollar Store, and loaded giant bags in a powdered-milk factory, all for minimum wage.

"The trick is not to look at the clock," one of my co-workers told me when working the twelve-hour graveyard shift at a paper factory (not a factory that *makes* paper, mind you, just a lot of machines that fold and staple it into brochures and Chinese-food menus). "Or, when you do, and, say, it's only eight p.m., don't think, *Aw, man, I got eleven more hours to go!* You have to think of it like *Hey, we're almost halfway to our first break.* And if your first break just got over, you must think, *It's only two more hours until we're halfway done with the night!*"

"You only do two days," I replied to him, impersonating Avon Barksdale from *The Wire*, who was talking about facing a long prison sentence. "The day you go in, and the day you come out."

My co-worker—with his thick glasses and broken teeth, smelling of Old Crow whiskey, cheap cigarettes, and stale coffee—looked at me blankly; he was obviously not a fan of *The Wire*. I stared back at him, wondering what TV shows he *did* watch, what concerts he went to, what was left of his life after sleeping and working here twelve hours a night for minimum wage. Perhaps he was fine with it, but, to me, getting drunk and feeding glossy paper into loud machines for twelve hours all night, sleeping all day, and doing it over again the next evening, for years to come, felt like a gentle kind of suicide.

What choice do you think you have? Caldonia asked. *You don't even have the guts to take the GED test.*

Years later, I would watch a Chris Rock stand-up bit about jobs versus careers, and would think of my Old Crow friend at the paper factory. Recounting his life as a high-school dropout washing dishes for minimum wage at Red Lobster, Rock says, "When you have a job, there's too much time . . . You play the game of not looking at your watch, or just sitting on the toilet . . . But when you have a career, time just flies, there's never enough time. You think, *I gotta get to bed early so I can get up and work on my project.*"

These jobs felt like an endless purgatory, with no clear way out. I felt hungry for something more, but couldn't put my finger on what.

For years, I'd heard conservatives like Jerry Falwell talk about "the dignity of work," the pride that comes from earning a paycheck by a hard day's labor. We were all employed, but it was clear that we lacked self-respect or any sense of agency in this world.

It was becoming clear to me that these disposable jobs offered us no dignity.

Or perhaps that none of us felt worthy of such a thing.

When Thad and I became employed by the local debt-collection agency, we would find out some jobs sucked the dignity out of more than just the employee.

CHAPTER TWENTY-FIVE

God's Pyramid of Debt

"Come on, sir, it's time to be a man and pay your bills," I said into my headset, sitting in one of dozens of cubicles in an enormous room, all of us belittling strangers over their financial decisions. "Your refusal to pay your debt is no different than stealing, which makes you a common thief. How would you like it if your friends and neighbors knew what a pathetic thief you were? Maybe I should give them a call?" I said, listing off the names of families on his street (easily found in our library of phone books from around the country).

The man hung up on me, and instantly another debtor came up on my headset, and I recited the opening monologue given to me at the debt-collection call center.

We made a lot of calls over medical or student-loan debt, or the funeral costs of a relative, but mainly it was overdue credit-card debt. Often, people would have no idea what the debt was or where it came from, not recognizing the name of the person or company they were indebted to, and I didn't have any answers for them other than "It's time to grow up and pay your bills." Many of the debtors cried or became profoundly angry with me. I was encouraged to lean on them with shame and threats until they handed over their debit-card information.

After years of being shamed for my own poverty by Christian conservatives—told it was evidence of laziness, lack of moral fiber, and a desire to mooch off the system—I had an arsenal of hateful zingers to fire at these debtors, knowing exactly what would shrink them down to size. Really, I was just repeating the incessant voice of Caldonia in my own head, reminding me what a weak, lazy, sinful disappointment I'd turned out to be. When I told Dad where I was working, he went pale and silent, likely remembering the years of threatening calls he'd received when the waterbed store failed.

"I hope you look good in stripes," one debt collector had told him over the phone in the eighties. When asked what he meant by that, the man said, "Because we're gonna put you in jail."

I discovered my parents' names in the database (and I myself would end up there soon enough), as well as some familiar names from church. Most of these people were involved in multilevel marketing (MLM) businesses like Amway, AdvoCare, or Nutrilite, selling everything from household cleaners to makeup to nutrition supplements, in an industry dominated by evangelicals.

There's no better term than "pyramid schemes" to describe these operations. The 1980s MLMs have rarely been prosecuted under the laws banning these operations, which are characterized as deriving their profits not from sales but by recruiting new members.

The idea sold to new recruits is that you will run your own business, buying the inventory with your own cash and selling it to your social network. In reality, you're operating within the context of a larger company that has outsourced all of the risk onto you. Most participants are encouraged to go into debt to launch their business, viewing it as a leap of faith, a sign of commitment. They then recruit friends and family, not only to buy these products, but to start a business of their own, thereby becoming part of the original participant's "downline."

The Think System.

The pitch usually goes: "If you only recruit five of your friends or family, and they recruit five people, and so on, then you'll have a downline that will make you a millionaire inside a year!" Rarely does any math student raise a hand and point out this can only happen fifteen times before you literally run out of people on the planet.

Years later, I would interview Robert L. FitzPatrick, author of the book *Ponzinomics: The Untold Story of Multi-Level Marketing,* who told me that poor evangelicals were the most common target of pyramid schemes. He says churches are the ideal environments for recruitment, not only because of MLMs' "pro-family" rhetoric, but because their theatrics, morality, and outrageous promises of material wealth fit like a hand in glove with prosperity gospel.

"It's very much a religious, authoritative institution that says, 'This works 100 percent of the time for 100 percent of the people,' and if you fail it is *always* your fault," FitzPatrick says of MLMs, underscoring the similarities to prosperity gospel, which says, "God *wants* you to be prosperous, God *wants* you to be rich, and if you fail it's only because you didn't believe enough, you were weak, you're a sinner."

FitzPatrick pointed out to me that, for most of its history, Amway has been widely considered an exclusively evangelical institution.

"It's a viral financial fraud spread through churches," says FitzPatrick. "They use very cultlike tactics. You are told not to argue with anybody who criticizes it, they are no-believers. You make money off getting people into it, not selling the actual stuff. You become a predator among your friends, family, colleagues . . . And in the end, less than *one percent* of people who get into multilevel marketing ever so much as turn a profit."

MLM events often mirror those of a megachurch worship service, with a lot of high-energy speakers, pyrotechnics, and promises of enormous wealth waiting for you to reach out and grab it—just as soon as you've filled out that downline.

Shortly after dropping out of school—when feeling my absolute lowest—I was, briefly, a link on another man's downline, selling AdvoCare nutritional supplements. He introduced me to well-dressed people at AdvoCare conferences, bought me dinners in nice restaurants, laughed at my jokes, and charmed me with the notion that I was a brilliant salesman who could be a millionaire in a year's time if I stuck with it.

The whole thing reminded me of the navy recruiter, or the evangelical youth leaders who told me they'd been given a vision of me as a mighty leader in God's army, overseeing the conversion of millions of my fellow high-school students, reclaiming America for (white Protestant) Christianity. It was the same rap I'd recognize years later when interviewing Marsha Stevens-Pino of the 1970s Jesus Movement, reflecting how "we were made to feel special" when being courted by the Christian right.

Or as in *The Music Man,* when Professor Harold Hill is recruiting a pair of twin redneck boys in overalls for his marching band and asks them to sing a single line each: "I love music, Moooommeeeee!" Both sound as lifeless and tone-deaf as a wheezing coyote, but Professor Hill announces to their mother, "It's a miracle! Two members of the same family with absolutely perfect pitch! Sign here!"

The MLM promise of enormous wealth earned by being your own boss and working from home alongside your family captivated my parents' generation, particularly the Iowans who'd recently lost their family farms. My dad was seduced not only by Amway, but also by MLMs selling alkaline-water machines, phone cards, gold coins, and nutritional supplements whose primary ingredient was "prayer." Sometimes he'd purchase an enormous inventory of unassembled crafts like wind socks, or circuit boards that needed soldering, encouraging us kids to work together as a family to become rich. Often these investments wound up half assembled in boxes in a basement corner, a constant reminder of our failure to come together as a family.

Working at the debt-collection center, I was surprised to learn of families who owned lakeside houses, equipped with jet skis and tennis courts, but were actually delinquent on several accounts. These were all MLM families, who'd apparently been living the "fake it till you make it" lifestyle they'd been encouraged to indulge in as a sign of faith in their business's future. In the same way we had to project an almost violent cheerfulness as an advertisement for the bliss of evangelical Christianity, they had to flash their (supposed) wealth as often as possible, making their lives a walking advertisement for Amway.

But now I could see they'd built a castle on the sinking sands of credit.

And, somehow, I found myself the reaper coming to collect an unpayable debt.

All of us working at the call center were just as broke as the debtors we were harassing, repeating the age-old trend of the poor attacking the poor. This was a common tactic of union busting throughout the Gilded Age, articulated best by the most ruthless robber baron of the era, the railroad tycoon Jay Gould, when proclaiming his violent plan to "hire half the working class to kill the other half."

Many of us were profoundly high while working the phones.

Cannabis didn't help me in this scenario, but cocaine and meth (the drug of choice for many of my co-workers) helped fuel the witty rejoinders and tamp down the empathy. Sometimes I'd sneak earbuds into my headset while calling debtors, so I could listen to Mozart's *Requiem* or Scott Walker's "Farmer in the City," the darkest music I could find to score our ominous dialogue.

I never used my real name on the phone, always introducing myself as Liam Greenwood (a combination of names from members of Oasis and Radiohead).

After work was over at ten p.m. (the last hour we were legally allowed to hassle people about their debts) and we all filed out to our cars in the parking lot, there was no amount of any drug that could numb the deep conviction in me that we were doing something wrong. I knew how awful it felt to be bullied for being poor, and yet I'd somehow found myself getting paid minimum wage to bully others over their poverty.

You were never man enough for this job, anyway, Caldonia said, her voice like a snake's tongue flicking inside my skull.

CHAPTER TWENTY-SIX

Hydrocele and Hydrocodone

The doctor literally gasped when I dropped my pants and showed it to him.

"You have a hydrocele," he said, once he'd collected himself. "It's actually very common. There's a blockage creating a large amount of fluid around the testicle, likely caused by some physical trauma."

Flipping back a few years, I could think of at least a dozen instances of getting flicked, punched, or kicked in the groin (once thrown crotch-first into a flagpole). Though it was those nights in the basement, repeatedly punching myself in the groin, that were likely the culprit of my comically large left testicle. That all felt like an eternity ago, and the idea that this deformity in my underpants was some cosmic punishment seemed tragically ridiculous to me now.

"So . . . what do I do?" I asked the doctor, feeling as helpless as when I asked my alternative-school teacher about my failing grades.

"Well, technically, there's nothing *wrong* with the testicle. It's still functioning, still creating sperm. We can perform surgery to drain the fluid, though."

I was later told that, since my hydrocele didn't diminish my fertility, the surgery would be considered "cosmetic," no different from liposuction or a face-lift. And since I'd kept it a secret for three years, it qualified as a "pre-existing condition," so my health insurance wouldn't cover it. I'd taken a factory job specially for the health insurance so I could get this addressed, but I didn't know how to advocate for myself and never thought to make a point to my doctors or the insurance company of the constant pain this "hydrocele" left me in.

I got the surgery anyway, which cost around seven thousand dollars.

There was no way I was going to recover from surgery in the twenty-four-hour party that was the lakeside house, so I moved in with my grandma Marilyn for two weeks.

Years later, I would hear stories about my grandma in the sixties and seventies, when she was an anxious and angry mother, criticizing and micromanaging her brood of ambitious children. But, like most parents becoming grandparents, she'd softened by the eighties, and became the warmest, most loving and validating force in my life as a child. When I was a kid, she lived in the enormous house they'd moved the family into after selling the farm in 1960, and we often stayed there for long stretches when Dad's explosive rage and Mom's crippled mind made home an unsafe place for us. Every wall was covered with pictures of ancestors, friends, and my sixteen cousins at every age, alongside religious paintings and children's drawings made by the dozens of kids she babysat.

Grandma Marilyn was a bona-fide Norwegian farm wife, using terms like "uff da" (the Scandinavian equivalent of "oy vey") and pronouncing her "a"s with an "r," such as "Warshington" or "warshing machine." This Midwestern accent (exaggerated for comic effect in the 1996 movie *Fargo*) was exported to southern Alaska during a mass migration from Minnesota in the 1930s, and is the source of the "you betcha" folksiness that made Alaska's Sarah Palin such a hit with Iowa conservatives in 2008.

When I was growing up, Grandma Marilyn's house was a refuge of tenderness, where I was accepted for the eccentric and effeminate boy I was. Here I was allowed to play with dolls—toy guns were banned at Grandma's—and enjoyed brushing out the hair of my plastic mermaids as I sang New Kids on the Block songs during my bubble bath. Though she never articulated it, Grandma Marilyn knew I was "different," and always made a point to say, "Never forget, Josiah, God loves you *just the way you are*. God *is* love, and anyone who says otherwise is full of it."

I shudder to think who I would've become without her.

Years later, when undergoing intense therapy, I'd be asked to conjure a place of ultimate refuge in my mind, and instantly thought of Grandma's house, Grandma's face, and Grandma's voice saying my name as I walked through her door. My grandpa Jack had died from an Alzheimer's-induced stroke in 1995, and so Grandma was happy to have me stay over on her fold-out couch as I recovered from surgery. She was no longer in the big house, which had been sold, thanks to the reverberations of the farming crisis years before, but the apartment where she now lived was still my closest definition of "home." The quiet ambience of Grandma's place was welcome after the incessant techno music at the lakeside house.

During those two weeks of recovery, I discovered a passion for reading.

Other than a few S. E. Hinton and *Goosebumps* books as a kid—and, naturally, the Bible—I'd never been much of a reader. We didn't have many books in the house, and I couldn't think of any family that did. Reading just wasn't a part of our culture.

But just before staying at Grandma's, I'd spent my last thirty dollars on a pair of British music magazines—*Mojo* and *NME*—which contained long essays on Britpop and glam-rock history. Before I knew it, I had read both of them cover to cover. As a teen, I'd had a feverish hunger to learn everything I could about Christian rock, and when I began listening to secular music with Thad, a whole new world of investigation had opened up to me. Learning about Oasis made me want to know more about the Beatles, so Mom got me a copy of the coffee-table book *The Beatles Anthology* to read while I recovered. (My mom has always been an amazing gift-giver.)

I consumed the massive volume in forty-eight hours, then began reading Nick Hornby's *High Fidelity,* which was the basis for a John Cusack movie I adored.

Anytime Grandma came into the living room and found me reading, she'd say, "Oh, I'm sorry to interrupt you. I'll leave you alone so you can finish your studies."

"My studies?" I'd reply with a laugh.

Beyond how antiquated the word was, I never considered what I was doing to be studious in any way. There was no ambition behind it, no plan or goal I was working toward. I was just incessantly hungry for more information about the things I loved. When I consider the path I would pursue years later, I see that my grandma Marilyn was the first person to recognize my curiosity for what it was: a mighty resource of zeal and productivity that could be harnessed into a writing career.

I began writing in a journal, and even though I had all the grammar skills of a fifth grader, the consequence-free experiment of blabbing my thoughts and passions into a little notebook was incredibly soothing.

I remembered I wrote a dozen *Friday the 13th* fan-fiction short stories when I was nine, exhilarated by the idea that I could create any world, conjure any scenario, merely by describing it with sentences. Now the desire to write my own stories—both fiction and journalism—was becoming as overwhelming as my pubescent desire for sex. It was like I'd struck oil, and I started to believe I might have some inherent talent for words, despite having flunked every English class I ever took.

But Caldonia was still there to set me straight.

You don't even know the difference between a comma and a period, and you think you can be a writer!? she sneered, laughing.

Thad visited me a week after my surgery. He looked pale and skinny, so much of his farm-boy muscle faded away.

After making some chitchat for a few minutes, bouncing his knee anxiously, he asked, "You gonna take those?," gesturing at my hydrocodone prescription. Though I'd eventually outgrow it, at that time I still had a fear of pills, remembering my days on Ritalin as a kid. So I endured a transcendent level of constant pain while recovering from my testicle surgery without any pharmaceutical intervention.

"Naw, you can have 'em," I said, thinking nothing of it.

After all, drugs were just a fun, whimsical novelty, right?

We were only using them to enhance experiences, to playfully manipulate our consciousness, to expand our minds via neuropsychopharmacology, weren't we? At this time, I knew little of the opioid epidemic simmering in Mason City. I was unaware that 80 percent of heroin addicts had initially gotten hooked on prescription pain medication. Thad and I had both snorted lines of crushed-up OxyContin at parties, but although the feeling was fantastic (smothering me in a maternal bliss I'd not felt since before my mother's breakdown), for me it was nothing compared with the communal love that ecstasy delivered, or the transporting romanticism of cannabis.

For Thad, however, opiates were a total game-changer.

They were the answer to every lingering question or discomfort life threw at him, soothing his insecurities and panicky sense of alienation. He consumed my prescription in a matter of days, then asked me to refill it twice (which was not difficult in 2002, years before doctors began cracking down on such things). I was unaware that, in addition to this, Thad was purchasing OxyContin from our retired neighbor with terminal cancer and a generous prescription, along with morphine from a nurse who lived in our basement. This nurse also had access to medical-grade liquid cocaine and regularly injected it into the webbing between his toes so he wouldn't have visible track marks.

As Thad was discovering pain pills, I got a job at a local record store called CDGB. (I was confident no one in Mason City but me understood the pun behind their name.) This independent record store had just relocated to Mason City from Arizona and carried over three hundred thousand titles—far more than even Sam Goody or Walmart. While I was organizing and stocking shelves, my brain was alive with curiosity and passion, committing to memory the entire discography of prolific artists like Frank Zappa, Miles Davis, and Sparks. I started budgeting my income, purely so I could afford box sets by The Beach Boys, Billie Holiday, or Bob Dylan; I hungrily devoured every CD and accompanying booklet, alone in my bedroom, with my headphones on.

Like drug dealing, working at the record store was one of the first occasions in my life when a job didn't feel like a job (though I was still only earning minimum wage). Unlike the hours I'd spent at factories, or the endless string of restaurants, and certainly the debt-collection center, time dissolved effortlessly for me at CDGB, and I was often told that my shift was over before I was ready to go home.

You're still just a pathetic little fag without a diploma, Caldonia often reminded me.

But a counter-narrative was slowly forming in my mind. One that acknowledged just how much information I'd absorbed from books, albums, and magazines, and could easily recall: not only memorize, but actually *understand* and articulate in my own writing.

I decided to take the GED test and was shocked to find I scored between 80 and 100 percent on each subject, easily receiving the High School Equivalency Certificate in a single weekend.

Behind every sentence I wrote and new song I fell in love with, a momentous craving for *more* was spiraling. More learning, more experiencing, more adventure. I was hungry to devour not only music but all kinds of information that I'd deprived myself of as a young evangelical: science, economics, history, crime, world religions. It was like assembling pieces of a puzzle in my mind, and I got a thrilling sense of satisfaction with each piece that clicked into place.

I'd never been on an airplane, had never even left the Midwest, rarely traveled more than fifty miles from my hometown. Now I was suddenly eager to travel, to visit all the pockets of America I'd been reading about in books.

Fortunately, Thad cooked up a new scheme for us.

"You wanna drive across the country delivering puppies to pet stores?" he said, handing me a lit joint as we sat in my dad's former living room.

As much as I loved working in the record store, I was determined to get out of Iowa, to be among the city folk I was so often associated with by my peers (usually with a derisive tone). I wanted to stop feeling stuck in Clear Lake, standing still as life moved past me.

"Yes," I said without hesitation. "Yes, I do."

CHAPTER TWENTY-SEVEN

Man's Dominion

"Animals are either for food or money," Dad said to me when I told him about my new job.

He wasn't a heartless monster; most of the people I knew in Iowa viewed all nonhuman life this way. When he was a teenager, Dad had worked as a farmhand in stressful, dangerous conditions with livestock, and was once attacked by a mother sow for getting too close to her babies. There was no room for any kind of emotional bond with the animals in that job, or you'd risk being driven to madness by the conditions these creatures had to endure. Eventually, most Iowa farms stopped dealing with livestock altogether, because industrial meat production drove prices far below what a small operation could compete with. In response to this, many farmers switched to puppy mills.

I'd learned early in life to keep the emotional bond I felt with farm animals to myself (my tender feelings seemed to be an anomaly amongst my peers), but I was sure this gig would be different. This would be puppies!

The offer to travel the country in a van with my best friend and a bunch of young dogs for weeks at a time, with no bosses breathing over our shoulders, felt like a winning lottery ticket. But I quickly realized this wasn't the Scooby-Doo adventure I'd anticipated.

We were hired through a local breeder, who had launched a side business collecting dogs from various other breeders around the state and transporting them to pet stores across the Midwest and East

Coast. I'd never heard the term "puppy mill" before, and was unprepared for what I saw.

The dozen or so mills from which we collected these eight-week-old canines were filthy and overcrowded. The dogs were kept in long aluminum warehouses lit by pulsing fluorescent lights that shone down on a seemingly endless corridor of wire kennels. The kennels were stacked six or seven high, with three or four dogs crammed into each one. Dachshunds, bulldogs, beagles, huskies, mastiffs, pugs, rottweilers—all babies separated from their mothers far too early.

They were everywhere, hundreds of them, stacked high above my head, all clamoring for attention with a frenetic urgency. These were not the playful barks of excitement we normally associate with puppies. There was no mistaking them as anything but cries of distress.

The smell of shit, disease, and decay (the dogs died regularly, and were buried in mass graves on the farms) made me vomit on the frozen ground. We were instructed to cram the puppies three to a crate, filling our small van with 130 panicking, confused baby dogs.

Thad appeared to be unaffected by this. Like my dad, he had been raised with the idea that animals were products to be bought and sold, no different from bicycles or computers. But years later he would confess to me that his soft heart had also been breaking in the face of all this horror—he'd just gotten used to hiding it.

Even though they would be sold as pets, these puppies were raised as livestock, just like chickens, cows, or any other product of modern agriculture, in conditions just as poor.

Whenever anyone dared to question the justification for, say, gestation crates that prevent pigs from being able to turn around, or filling warehouses with so much livestock that their waste pollutes the water and crops and fills the air with more carbon emissions than any other industry, the evangelicals I grew up with were fond of quoting the book of Genesis, where God says of His human creation, "Let them have dominion over the fish of the sea, and over the fowl of the air, and over the cattle, and over all the earth, and over every creeping thing that creepeth upon the earth."

It wasn't surprising, then, that I recognized people from my church running the puppy mills we visited. Breeding dogs became a way to make quick cash, since the practice required little infrastructure and was so under-regulated in the state of Iowa. (Most other states had banned puppy mills; hence our delivering them to stores across state lines.)

To make matters worse, this cargo van of horror needed to keep moving twenty-four hours a day. Thad and I were instructed to stop the van only to deliver our canine commodities, then get right back on the road. This was why it was a two-man job: one could sleep while the other drove through the night. Since they were paying us both minimum wage, it was cheaper to hire two dumb boys to do this than pay one professional a reasonable wage and let them sleep in a motel.

The owner of a pet store in Chicago helped us unload the dogs, then casually warned us not to get pulled over in Illinois with so many dogs in the van in such bad condition, or we'd be arrested for animal abuse. The idea of being charged with such a crime scared me even more than serving time; I don't think I could've lived down the shame of having animal abuse on my record.

A few years later, two boys doing the exact same job, for the exact same company, were, in fact, arrested in Illinois. Both were given ten years in prison.

Naturally, we were never informed by our employer that we would be risking jail time with this minimum-wage gig.

After ten days of little to no sleep in a van overflowing with puppy feces, Thad and I got sick with what felt like the flu (or possibly E. coli, though we were never tested), both of us feverish and vomiting. The van smelled horrible, but it was January, so we couldn't open the windows, lest more dogs become sick and die from the cold. We were delirious and driven to madness by the incessant howling of the dogs, and desperate for a shower and some clean sheets. We felt as trapped as they were, and wanted to do a bit of screaming ourselves. There were only half a dozen dogs left by the time we made it to New York City—the number I'd originally imagined us transporting—all of them rejected by pet stores for being sick and to be returned to the puppy mills they came from. But at this point I felt little momentum to explore the place I'd so often heard Lou Reed sing about. I just wanted to go home.

Driving home, we stopped at a park somewhere in Ohio and let the puppies out of their cages. It was an unseasonably warm afternoon, and I played with the dogs on a grassy hill. They jumped about ecstatically, experiencing grass and fresh air for the first (and possibly last) time in their tragically short lives. I ran, and they chased me. I tumbled to the ground, and the dogs leapt across me, licked my face, and tickled my skin with their sinewy, cotton-soft fur—never once understanding that I was the villain.

I was the one responsible for their misery.

You're being paid minimum wage to torture animals, Caldonia said. *That'll show them at the high-school reunion. Oh, wait, you'll never be invited to that, because you didn't graduate.*

But all the puppies seemed to understand was this one moment of happiness and love, a single instance of grace, quite likely the only one they'd ever know.

Lying on the grass in the sunshine, I looked up at Thad, who was sitting in the van with the door open. He was wrapping a rubber tube around his arm, pulling it tight, and injecting himself with heroin. I lifted my chin, looked directly at the sun, and lit my second joint of the morning, careful to keep the flame away from all the puppy fur. The Strokes' debut album was playing on the van radio, reminding me of my time at the Gap a few years earlier, when this song was on constant repeat.

"Can't you see I'm trying? / I don't even like it . . ." Julian Casablancas sang. "I can't think 'cause / I'm just way too tired. / Is this it? / Is this it? / Is this . . . it?"

Drugs were no longer playful fun; they just meant numbness, at best.

I thought of my dad, alone in his dark bedroom, detached from himself and his children.

Anhedonia: the inability to feel pleasure, the plateau of substance abuse.

Watching Thad drift in and out of consciousness, with a breeze pulling the smell of animal shit out of the van, I turned and looked at the puppies, many of them suffering kennel cough and crusty eyes. Most of them wouldn't survive the drive home, and they might be the lucky ones.

Is this it? I wondered. *Is this all there is to life?*

CHAPTER TWENTY-EIGHT

The Fruit of Knowledge

"I don't believe in colleges and universities. I believe in
libraries, because most students don't have any money.
When I graduated from high school, it was during the
Depression and we had no money. I couldn't go to college,
so I went to the library three days a week for ten years."

—RAY BRADBURY

2004

Thad and I quit the puppy-delivery gig the moment we returned to
Iowa.

Weeks later, I moved to Denver, Colorado.

It wasn't at the top of my list of places to live, but I'd met a girl in
a bar who was on her way to the Mile High City, wanted me to come
with her, and offered to pay for everything for the first few months.
I'd struggled to save enough money to get out of Iowa, so this was an
enticing offer. We parted ways shortly after arriving in Colorado—she
turned out to be as fearful of downtown Denver as I was enamored
of it.

This was long before Denver's economic boom from legal weed,
and I was able get myself a tiny room in a run-down house (no kitchen,
bathroom down the hall) for a hundred dollars a month. I centered my
life on my writing and my books, with everything and everyone else in a
distant second place. Not that anyone was clamoring to be my copilot
in this life of poverty and cheap wine in a hundred-square-foot box.

I adopted the look and manner of a sloppy poet, emulating the
bohemian fashion of Arthur Rimbaud, Patti Smith, Jean-Michel Bas-
quiat, and Pete Doherty. I longed to develop a powerful wit and intellect, while looking like a Dickensian street urchin. I lived by the Oscar
Wilde conviction that "Man is least himself when he talks in his own

person. Give him a mask, and he will tell you the truth." I didn't want to look like a conservative evangelical from the Midwest; I wanted to be Bob Dylan in 1966.

Living downtown afforded me the luxury of not having a car, since I could bike or walk everywhere I wanted to go. Not only did this drastically reduce my cost of living, it also gave me the opportunity to listen to hundreds of audiobooks, rented from the library just down the street. The intellectual filters I'd placed on myself throughout school were gone, and now I was free to indulge every whim of my curiosity.

Walking home from the library each night, I would test my memory of everything I'd just learned, assembling all the threads of information into a vast tapestry that lived just behind my eyes.

My life soon revolved around the Great Courses series, those large packages of books and recordings of lectures given by professors at Yale, Harvard, and Sarah Lawrence. This amounted to having the whole class, in your hands, ready to come home with you, free of charge, from the library.

Though I was far too intimidated to apply to college, I soaked up courses on everything from behavioral economics to the Peloponnesian War. I checked out most of them with a "Why not?" shrug of my shoulders, but the lectures of Bart D. Ehrman, a New Testament scholar and bestselling author from the University of North Carolina, were as revolutionary for my mind as any psychedelic.

When I plucked *The History of the Bible: The Making of the New Testament Canon* off the library shelf, I was taken back to my teenage years in school, when I had been endlessly curious about religious history, yet terrified of wounding my belief in God.

"Many of my students assume that the New Testament appeared one day shortly after Jesus's death," Bart Ehrman says in the first lecture. "But in fact, not only were the books written decades after Jesus's death, they weren't considered scripture until a long time after that, and they weren't collected into a canon until a long time after that. It went on for centuries."

I must admit, I was one of those people who viewed the Bible as a singular entity, presented to humanity by God, all at once. Sure, there was a lot about it that seemed contradictory or inconsistent to me—

not to mention morally questionable, such as its approval of owning slaves or beating your wife and children—but I had chalked all that up to my own lack of understanding.

Now, at the age of twenty-two, I was confronting a whole new galaxy of information about the Bible. Apparently, the identities of the original authors of most books of the Bible are a mystery, their original texts lost to history (Biblical historians only have copies of copies of copies of the manuscripts), often because first-century Christians thought Armageddon was coming any day now, so why bother preserving them?

Not only were there dozens of other gospels floating around with conflicting accounts of Jesus's life, but the ones we do have—Matthew, Mark, Luke, and John, which are merely titles, not names of the authors—aren't terribly credible pieces of journalism.

"What happens if you play the game of telephone, but it's not with people from the same socioeconomic background who speak the same language?" says Ehrman in his lecture, referring to the accounts of Jesus's life. "You play it for thirty-five to sixty-five years, among people who live in different countries, who speak in different languages, who have different contexts and different concerns. What happens to the stories? They inevitably change, sometimes accidentally, sometimes because people want to make a point."

Throughout the 1990s, many evangelicals (including me) wore cheap bracelets with the acronym WWJD ("What Would Jesus Do?") stitched into the side. These were more for religious exhibitionism than theological debate, but after listening to Ehrman's lectures, it seemed to me that the only reasonable answer to this question was: Who knows?

Around the same time that I was listening to Ehrman's lectures, I watched *Monty Python's Life of Brian*, which portrays the days of early Christianity as a vast marketplace of religions, deities, and prophets, with followers of Christ constantly misinterpreting his words, and eager zealots viewing random acts of their messiah—like losing one sandal while running—as a doctrine they must build their lives around.

Apparently, this was historically accurate.

"The various beliefs of Christianity in the second and third centuries make the modern diversity of denominations and theologies pale by comparison," Ehrman says in his lecture. "Some said God created this world, others said an evil deity created it. Some said Jesus was human, some said he was divine, others said he was human *and* divine. Some said Jesus's death brought salvation to the world, others said it had nothing to do with saving the world, while others said he never actually died. And they all had books to prove that's what happened."

By the third century, there was an urgency to divide Christianity into orthodoxy and heresy, with one holy book to rule them all.

There are estimated to be as many as three hundred thousand manuscripts of the New Testament—and they're all a bit different. This is because ancient writings were all copied by hand, and each copier made little changes based on their political or theological underpinnings, or just differences in the translation of languages. The assembly of the books of the Bible wasn't finalized until the fifth century, and even then, debates raged on about the validity of rejected scriptures like the Gospel According to Judas or Mary—as well as the invalidity of canonized scripture, like the book of Revelation—until the Catholic Church ratified a final collection in the *sixteenth century*.

It was difficult for me to wrap my head around the idea that God was guiding this messy process every step of the way, not to mention why He didn't just send a comprehensive text down all at once (as He was said to have done to Muhammad and Joseph Smith).

As I rode my bike down the Cherry Creek bike path in Denver, I found myself trembling with rage. I'd devoted so much of my youth to feverishly investigating God's teachings (as interpreted through the Bible, via my church leaders), always finding myself just beyond understanding, and therefore just beyond belief—and therefore just beyond salvation from Hell—to the point where I was cutting myself in the basement while awaiting the Apocalypse. Only to learn years later that the reason I couldn't make heads or tails of the book of Revelation was that it was written—most scholars agree today—not as a prophecy of the coming Antichrist, but as an allegory for the Roman Empire in the first century.

We had been obsessed with finding the number 666 in the Mossimo Clothing logo or an Iron Maiden song as evidence of Satan's rise in America, never realizing it was just a reference to the Roman Emperor Nero, spelled out numerically in Hebrew. If I hadn't been raised as a fundamentalist, none of this historical information would've been so devastating to my faith. In one lecture, Ehrman explains that the Bible was viewed symbolically, not literally, by a great many Christians throughout history (until Martin Luther made a big deal during the Reformation about its being infallible). Over the years, I would come to meet Christians who defined their faith by Christ's teachings, not their unwavering belief in his resurrection or divinity. They'd had no trouble viewing the Bible as a fallible creation of man, which nonetheless still had some spiritual wisdom. Thomas Jefferson pioneered this idea when he edited out all of the miracles and supernatural activity from the gospels—while keeping Jesus's teachings about tolerance, forgiveness, and caring for your neighbor—and created his own Bible, titled *The Life and Morals of Jesus of Nazareth*.

But this option was never afforded to me.

I was raised on the apologetics of C. S. Lewis, who said Jesus was either divine, evil, or mad. Never did any of us consider that perhaps the source of Jesus's teachings, actions, and claims about himself were historically unreliable.

When faced with this information, I found myself at a crossroads.

I could dismiss it all as propaganda, a creation of the atheistic, liberal, government-run education conspiracy machine, secretly manipulated by a campaign of demons to sway children toward evolution, mind control, and eternal torture in Hell.

Or I could accept that I'd been fed a load of bullshit, and had a great deal of work to do to provide myself with a proper education.

Kent Hovind once said, "Seventy-five percent of kids from Christian homes who go to secular schools lose their faith after one year." And I suddenly understood why.

When I'd heard this statistic as a teen, I'd attributed it to the spiritual warfare occurring on college campuses. Now I was beginning to understand that the evangelical worldview simply could not thrive outside of its own intellectual ecosystem, and therefore it was necessary to keep all contaminants of the secular world beyond the reach of

young people. Even the apologetics of C. S. Lewis and Francis Schaef-
fer couldn't withstand the intellectual inquiry of scholars like Ehrman,
because, at its core, apologetics begins with the assumption that the
Bible is factually reliable (if not infallible), and all of its arguments
work backward from that conviction. Just as creationism finds the
birthday of the Earth through (very sketchy) genealogical records, and
then goes in search of geological and hydrological evidence to support
that premise retroactively.

Does this mean you no longer believe in God? Caldonia asked me.

I still wasn't ready to answer that question, but I could at least reject
the notion that academia had any kind of agenda to destroy conservative Christianity, and consider that the literal demonization of these
institutions by evangelicals was at the very least essential to maintaining our simplistic worldview when it came to history, theology, and
the childish binary of good versus evil.

You may now think college is cool, Caldonia said, *but that doesn't mean
a penniless bumpkin that flunked out of high school is going to be welcome
there.*

I knew she had a point.

I didn't even know how to apply to college, let alone how to choose
one, or what my options even were. The fear that college would be just
like high school—bullies, alienation, failure—kept me from exploring
the idea, as did a crippling fear of debt.

After a lifetime of watching my parents sink into debt and self-
loathing, and given my experiences at the debt-collection call center,
I had a deep-seated aversion to owing money to any institution. Still,
there lingered a pang of regret when it came to missing out on college. Visiting my sister at Evangel had given me a sentimental view
of the higher-ed experience—the dorms, the parties, attending early-
morning classes in your pajamas—and I couldn't help but feel I was
missing out on an essential milestone of young adulthood. I'd never
attended a school dance, or a sports game, or a high-school graduation of my own. Never had the eyes of my community trained on me
in a state of maudlin pride. All I'd gotten was a silent, unceremonious
disappearance into the western sunset.

In time, I would grow confident that I could handle whatever academic workload college could throw at me, but by then I'd realized I had access to all the information I needed at the library (at least when it came to feeding the beast of my curiosity). I could tell that the essays and short stories I was writing each night were getting sharper and clearer, with more humor and insight. My voice as a writer was taking shape, like a sword I was learning to wield with more grace and power.

Yeah, but you're still a loser who's never accomplished anything in his life, Caldonia was always there to remind me. *What could you possibly have to write about?*

CHAPTER TWENTY-NINE

It's Work

2006

I was walking home from a graveyard shift as a bellboy one night when a taxi driver offered to pay me for sex.

I'd never been inside a five-star luxury hotel before I was hired at one in downtown Denver, and I didn't really understand the purpose of a bellboy. Naturally, bellboy service wasn't part of a guest's stay at the roadside motel my mom worked at in Clear Lake.

Most of the time, I was just carrying a small bag for one person, walking alongside them from the lobby to the elevator to their room, and then there was this awkward silence when they decided whether or not to give me some vague amount of cash. Tipping in general always felt weird to me, because it seemed designed to deflect labor costs away from the employer and onto the consumer. Also, the forced smiles and mindless salesmanship necessary to seduce a few bucks out of each patron's pocket simply reminded me too much of my days as an evangelical.

Since no public transportation ran at night, I often found myself walking home down the brutally sketchy Colfax Avenue at three or four in the morning. I'd try to pretend I had no money to steal, which often wasn't an act. I would twitch, zig-zag as I walked, mumble obscenities under my breath.

I was walking home that night, still in my uniform—looking like a roadie for Sgt. Pepper—when a taxi slowly rolled up beside me. It was dark inside the cab, and I could barely make out the driver's face from behind his lit cigarette. I'd never even ridden in a taxi before, so when the man offered me a ride, free of charge, I accepted. My feet hurt, and I had a Zadie Smith book at home I was eager to get back to.

He was a large, sweaty man, his red face swollen with the signs of alcoholism.

"What's a cute kid like you doing walking home at this hour?" he asked.

"Just got off work," I explained. "And I'm too broke to own a car."

"I know how you could make some money," the cab driver said, his voice suddenly going high-pitched like a child's, though he was simultaneously out of breath.

"Oh yeah?" I asked. "How?"

After a few minutes of chitchat, this sweaty man offered me a hundred dollars if I'd allow him to do things to my body.

I'd met a handful of sex workers since moving to Denver, and found that theirs wasn't always the desperate, exploitative practice that Christian conservatives made it out to be. Without question, there are tragic and brutal avenues of the sex industry all over the world, but—similar to the War on Drugs—the laws that fundamentally ban rather than regulate this practice are what allow the violence and exploitation of sex workers to continue.

In recent years, various Christian-right organizations have taken up sex trafficking as their humanitarian cause. Like their efforts to feed the homeless, care for victims of natural disasters, or offer substance-abuse treatment to addicts, many of these anti–sex-trafficking organizations do good, necessary work.

But, more often than not, conversion is the ultimate goal.

These charitable efforts often come with a good deal of proselytizing. And within this rhetoric is the unimpeachable conviction that sex outside of straight, monogamous marriage is *always* a bad idea—particularly if money is involved—even though prostitution is literally the oldest business in human history.

In the Gospel of Matthew, when Jesus is confronted by the chief priests of the Temple—after throwing out the money changers for defiling the holy sanctuary—he angrily dismisses them: "Truly I tell you, the tax collectors and the prostitutes are entering the kingdom of God ahead of you."

The idea that sex work can be conducted without exploitation, or physical or mental danger, within a framework of respect, empowerment, and social acceptance, is inconceivable to most evangelicals. But that hasn't stopped many of them from wrapping themselves in shame and jumping crotch-first into the transaction.

Particularly when it comes to male evangelists hiding in the closet.

I didn't know it then, but at the very same time I agreed to the cab driver's offer, one of the nation's most prominent evangelical leaders was purchasing meth and sex from a gay prostitute only a few miles away.

I'd attended Pastor Ted Haggard's New Life megachurch in Colorado Springs a few months earlier, not out of any pursuit of spirituality, but to see what those worship services, those sermons, those offering plates looked like through these new eyes of mine. And New Life Church was certainly worth the two-hour bus ride from Denver.

Known at the time as "the Evangelical Vatican," Colorado Springs was home to the headquarters of Focus on the Family and an air-force academy with a notorious evangelical presence, and frequent host to the Koch brothers and their mega-rich masters of the universe gatherings. It was also the birthplace of State Amendment 2, a 1992 ballot initiative that overturned all gay rights in Colorado and prohibited the passage of new ones. Known as "the Colorado Model," this provision would be duplicated by Christian-right political operatives in other states throughout the next two decades.

As president of the National Association of Evangelicals, Pastor Ted Haggard was the face of Colorado Springs throughout the 2000s, with his megachurch as the social and spiritual hub of the scene. Haggard advised President Bush once a week on the trends and temperatures of evangelical voters, and was a regular guest on political talk shows, representing the conservative Christian viewpoint on nearly any issue. He was a quick wit, with a somewhat Muppet-like (yet nonetheless handsome) face, a bright smile, and electric confidence.

Gay marriage was the pool-table issue of the 2004 presidential election, and though Ted Haggard wasn't as aggressively homophobic as many of his peers, there was no avoiding the Christian right's relentless obsession with gay sex at this time. Haggard often referred to homosexuality as a sin and against God's plan, as plainly stated in the Bible.

All the while, he was regularly ingesting meth and paying for gay sex.

When Denver prostitute Mike Jones outed Haggard for having purchased the meth from him before they had sex for money, it forever obliterated the pastor's career. Haggard lost his job at the National Association of Evangelicals as well as New Life Church. He'd end up living out of campers and cheap hotels in Arizona, unable to get a job, reduced to hanging fliers on doorknobs for minimum wage.

A few years after this, the co-founder of The Family Research Council and "conversion therapy" pioneer George Rekers was discovered traveling throughout Europe with a sex worker from Rentboy.com. Rekers had devoted his career to preventing gay couples from adopting children and keeping gay men out of the Boy Scouts, and had written several books about raising children to be straight—and yet was (allegedly) hiring young men to give him nude massages with happy endings in Spain, according to Jo-Vanni Roman, the Rentboy.com escort Rekers traveled with. Rekers maintained he'd only hired Roman as a "travel assistant," and no impropriety ever took place.

The taxi driver's offer was enticing, in part because the things he wanted to do to me weren't uncomfortable, and even if they were, I'd been selling my body for years by that point. The broken bones, bruises, pulled muscles, hearing loss, chemical burns, cuts, scrapes, and inflamed joints I'd endured at my previous jobs were all far worse than what the taxi driver was asking of me.

But what about the emotional distress of prostitution? you may ask.

After years of suffering disrespect in the service industry, dangling from windmills or scaling icy roofs in anxious vertigo, wiping pubic hairs off toilets and shower drains, submitting to random drug tests, searches of my bag, and condescending bosses who viewed me as an inherently replaceable cog in cheap machine . . . I thought the twenty-minute rental of my body for a hundred dollars was a fine offer. (Again,

I know there are many victims of sex trafficking around the globe enduring tremendous pain while making others rich. I'm just relaying my experience.)

After it was over, I noticed the man was slumped over, heaving desperate sobs into his hands. "What's the matter?" I asked. He flinched when my hand touched his shoulder and hurriedly threw a wad of twenties at me, telling me to get out of the car.

Of all the madness of the last thirty minutes, this felt the most familiar, making me think of something a sex worker who lived in my building told me the week before. "Sometimes sex work is just work. It's a job: sometimes it's fun, sometimes it's not. It's work, like anything else."

I opened the car door and had one foot on the ground when I stopped.

The cab driver turned and looked at me, with the sun rising in the window behind him.

"I'm married," he mumbled, tears dripping down his wrists. "I'm gay but married . . . to a woman . . . I have three kids with. Why . . . can't . . . I . . . stop this?!"

My heart collapsed. Suddenly he wasn't a disgusting, wicked symbol of life in the big sinful city, but a scared little boy who didn't know what to do with himself. Something I could certainly relate to.

I got back into the car and wrapped my arms around the man, feeling the weight of his despair as he hugged me back, his pulsing sobs jolting both of us. I felt his fear, his self-loathing, his confusion. It was enormous and overwhelming, like grabbing a live electrical wire.

Looking over his shoulder at the Denver horizon spiced with morning light, I wondered how many people out there were living lives of quiet desperation. I thought of my dad as a frightened child, then as an angry husband and father. I thought of Thad being too afraid to dance, afraid to have passion and ambition, disappearing into the warmth of opiates instead. I thought of my mom, so talented and useful to the world, yet defined by her failure as a housekeeper. I thought of all the working-class faces from church, all seemingly desperate for a moment of authenticity, just a few minutes in which they could stand naked before the world and admit, "Yup, this is who I am."

Feeling the weight of that taxi driver's sorrow while holding him in the back seat of his car, I realized what sex work was really all about: confidently, expertly taking on the buried sexual neuroses of adult humans who'd spent decades channeling all their fears of failure, humiliation, and death into their sexuality, and carefully, empathetically removing the whole burden without showing the slightest flicker of distaste, without exacerbating their cycles of shame and repression and compulsion.

Which, honestly, seemed like *way* too much work for me.

I thought I'd rather just write about it instead.

So I took this cab driver's money, headed home to pack a bag, then walked to the train station and bought a ticket for San Francisco.

CHAPTER THIRTY

Boy on Fire

In 1949, Billy Graham was having a crisis of faith.

His ministry had yet to explode and transform America's relationship with Christianity (and the very identity of Christianity itself). His revivals were poorly attended. His sermon-writing partner, Charles Templeton, had lost his faith in the Bible's fundamental truth following an academic investigation into its history and theology, which he had undertaken after witnessing horrifying newsreel footage of the Holocaust and finding himself unable to square the idea of a loving, all-powerful God with such carnage.

Kneeling in the California wilderness, Graham opened his Bible upon a large tree stump and declared, "O God! There are many things in this book I do not understand. There are many problems with it for which I have no solution. There are many seeming contradictions. There are some areas in it that do not seem to correlate with modern science. I can't answer some of the philosophical and psychological questions Chuck and others are raising."

Graham recalls in his autobiography *Just As I Am* that as he prayed he felt the Holy Spirit move in him as never before, and then his tears splashed upon his Bible. Suddenly all those lingering questions felt irrelevant, and Graham proclaimed, "Father, I am going to accept this as Thy Word—by *faith*! I'm going to allow faith to go beyond my intellectual questions and doubts, and I will believe this to be Your inspired Word."

Nearly sixty years later, I was looking out the window of an Amtrak train speeding through California as we passed the same tree stump where Graham had committed—in my estimation—his intellectual suicide. During my time in California, I would have precisely the opposite revelations, yet they would be equally comforting.

After I bought the train ticket on impulse, I would arrive with only $120 left in my pocket.

I didn't know anyone in San Francisco. I was obsessed with the counterculture of the 1960s, so I naturally had a great deal of interest in the birthplace of psychedelic music, the epicenter of the Summer of Love and the student protest movement. But honestly, I just wanted to feel free. I wanted a literal and metaphorical gesture of life's anarchic whimsy; I wanted to reject any sense of a "master plan" from Daddy God in the sky—any attachment to destiny, purpose, responsibility—and just *go*.

I knew the Apocalypse wasn't coming.

I'd known it for a long time; I just hadn't been ready to say it.

As I sat on a beach beneath the Golden Gate Bridge, with goose bumps crawling up my arms, I said aloud to myself, "I don't think God exists."

Dogs chased one another across the beach, splashing into the water of the Bay.

By saying this, I was knowingly damning myself to a Hell I no longer believed in. I thought of all the children's ministers, summer camp counselors, and youth-group preachers who'd insisted that my salvation from eternal torture could be purchased only through belief, but here I was, actively tearing my belief to pieces.

"I don't believe," I said aloud, "as the Bible commands me to, that Jesus died for my sins, or that God raised him from the dead. I think the Bible is a politically infected, historically inaccurate, poorly translated mess. I do not believe in *any of this* and will no longer fear an eternity of torture in Hell, because I can find no evidence that such a place exists. I will live by reason, science, and observation, not on faith or fear."

I was overcome by a dozen conflicting sensations.

The terrified child was screaming for me to stop, expecting a beast with seven heads to rise out of the Bay to drag me swiftly beneath the water and into the fires of Gehenna.

There's no time to change your mind.

Trouble!

Then a soft wave of liberation rippled through me.

I was free, pure, and authentic, for possibly the first time in my life.

I bought a joint in the park, went dancing, and fell asleep in an alley.

Within a week of arriving in San Francisco, I'd found myself with a job at one of the largest youth hostels in the world.

Thad agreed to pose as a reference for me over the phone, pretending to be my former boss in a fictional Clear Lake restaurant that, we decided, had burned down last year (this way, no potential employer could double-check any outside information about our ruse). We had done this for several jobs I'd landed in Denver as well, and it had worked every time.

The hostel gig paid only minimum wage, but San Francisco had the highest minimum wage in the nation, and the job came with my own rent-free apartment on the top floor. I managed a small breakfast café in the hostel's kitchen, selling coffee, bagels, cereal, juice, and fruit. I ate a lot of free food, and thanks to the free rent, most of my paycheck became disposable income. I traveled a lot that year, touring the museums of D.C., attending the South by Southwest festival in Austin, and hooking up with a mandolin player in Portland. Running the café gave me a sense of independence and personal responsibility I'd never felt in a job before. I took pride in my work, seeing the café as an extension of myself. I had no bitterness toward my boss, and often went beyond my prescribed duties, working extra hours, feeling that sense of achievement in my work that conservatives had been telling me about for so long.

Where was this feeling when I was working at Walmart, Red Lobster, or the Gap? In the San Francisco hostel, I would've felt embarrassed if the café and kitchen weren't sufficiently clean, or open on time, or if the inventory or bookkeeping wasn't correct. This was *my* operation, and I took it seriously.

I had never been able to inspire myself enough to give a shit at any of the disposable jobs, never felt any personal connection with my work. I'd had a similar experience in school—both public and Christian—never engaging my own, personal desire for learning or academic achievement, just responding to the threats made by my Christian authority figures. In both cases, I had been constantly bathed in fear—paranoid about liberal indoctrination at the public school, and unable to square fundamentalism with my own internal logic at Forest City Christian School, all of it threatening my eternal soul—and consequently I couldn't make it through a single homework assignment without crippling anxiety.

But when I was creating my own homework assignments, in my own quiet space, graded on my own terms, for my own ends, I was a fucking machine of passion and productivity. I had to care, genuinely, in order to learn or be good at anything.

I was writing for eight or nine hours at a time, averaging three thousand words a day, sometimes as many as seven thousand, cranking out what would eventually become a series of six novels—homoerotic psychological thrillers starring a mentally ill, teenage preacher—under the title *Carnality*. At the time, it never occurred to me actually to show anyone my writing, or send it to an editor in hope of a publication. I just wanted to put all these ideas, images, and characters in my head onto the page.

Like many people at the time, I became obsessed with Malcolm Gladwell's ten-thousand-hours rule from his book *Outliers*. According to Gladwell, one of the consistent aspects of highly accomplished people is their having spent ten thousand hours on their craft—a feat that could only be reasonably accomplished by someone who has unlimited free time without the constraints of a full-time job or raising children. Suddenly my lonely life of poverty and low expectations started to feel like an advantage.

Now the seven or eight decades of an average human lifespan didn't feel enough to achieve what my spirit was asking of me.

My entire life, I'd been preparing for eternity, told that this life was just a test, and that we'd have an endless stretch of existence after death either to bask in our rewards or to suffer our punishments. But now, viewing death as the end of my story, I felt a fire under me to write as much as possible, if I had any hope of kissing the sky of eternity with that one golden sentence before life slipped through my fingers. In this way, I wasn't unlike my dad as a teen, desperate to start a family before the Apocalypse—only, instead of babies, I was desperate to make books.

San Francisco had been my Walden, my *Seven Years in Tibet,* my Mississippi Crossroads, where I made a deal with the devil to learn to play the blues.

But it was also very lonely.

Everyone I met was a traveler, offering no shortage of adventure but only ephemeral connections. I certainly blossomed in both my queer and my hetero sexuality at the time, but I missed the friends I'd made during my years in Denver, and was finding the bustle of an international city a bit too menacing for me.

So, after a year, I left San Francisco as quickly as I'd arrived and headed back to Denver, finally ready to show the world my writing and try my hand at journalism.

Interlude: Hounded by Fox

2023

I'm sitting in a diner in downtown Clear Lake, watching Fox News on a nearby TV, and thinking about storytelling.

On the TV, Kevin Sorbo is promoting his latest editorial for the Fox News website, "Let's Make Hollywood Manly Again." The former *Hercules* TV star has become the most recognizable face in Christian movies ever since starring in the 2014 megahit *God's Not Dead,* and the most recent *Left Behind* reboot last January.

"There's an attack on men being men," I hear him say from the TV. "They're trying to break apart the family unit, which they've been doing for a long, long time." He rejects the existence of "male white privilege," and says terms like "toxic masculinity" in the media and on university campuses are used to "rob men of their masculinity."

He points to the glittery wardrobes of Timothée Chalamet and Billy Porter as evidence of his concerns: "Your grandfather wouldn't have been caught dead dressed like Chalamet."

I've probably watched more Fox News than anyone I've ever known, including my conservative Christian relatives. And not out of a "know your enemy"-type espionage, but simply because I am curious. If I subscribe to any kind of ideology, it's the transcendent power of curiosity in all areas of life, particularly journalism. I've often described what I do for a living as "getting paid to be curious," because satiating my own inquisitiveness is always the driving force behind my work (and then an editor helps make it palatable to an audience beyond my own head).

This is what makes it so fascinating to hear from people who are different from me. My mother had the same mindset as a teenager; it's what fueled her to join the debate team, and live with a family in Argentina for three months. She always told me you could never truly understand an issue unless you could articulate both sides of the argument, for and against, without bias.

As hordes of Midwestern families stream down the sidewalk outside this restaurant—headed for the Fourth of July carnival by the lake—I'm thinking about how amazing Fox News is at storytelling, and how terrible it is at curiosity.

Seeing its new catchphrase flash across the screen—"Most Watched, Most Trusted"—reminds me of the decision to jettison the old one, "Fair and Balanced," in 2017, because of its associations with the network's disgraced founder, Roger Ailes. A series of costly sexual harassment lawsuits may have destroyed Ailes's reputation, but his *Music Man* legacy of manufacturing fear of liberal journalists while creating the most aggressively conservative media machine is still very much alive.

Just as the GOP strategist Paul Weyrich exploited abortion to galvanize the Christian right in the late seventies, Roger Ailes brilliantly wielded a "P is for pool!" strategy in his creation of the religious, patriotic, family-friendly Fox News—which, as of 2022, is literally the "Most Watched" cable TV channel in America.

For decades after the Scopes Trial and the Civil Rights Movement, evangelicals ignored journalists and listened exclusively to preachers, who created their own media ecosystem via radio and TV programs.

These preachers were phenomenal storytellers, partly because they were never subject to the restraints of journalism, which, at its best, seeks to understand an issue objectively, from all angles—a process that severely complicates (if not cripples) most storytelling. Easily digestible narratives require a narrowing of facts into an accessible, subjective structure, a clear binary with heroes and villains, rights and wrongs.

So popular and unrestrained were these evangelical radio preachers in their conspiracy theories, conservative politics, and end-times theology that the Federal Council of Churches (the same progressive Christian organization that inspired the creation of *Christianity Today* magazine as a conservative counterpoint) called for networks to ban any religious broadcasting deemed not "responsible," that asked for financial donations, and was not affiliated with any larger denomination.

In 1943, they were successful at getting NBC, CBS, and the Mutual Broadcasting System to agree to the proposed regulations, which wasn't difficult as most station owners preferred mainstream Protestant programming to the wild conspiracy theories and divisive social commentary of the Pentecostal radio preachers. In the decades leading up to this, the Federal Radio Commission would often only grant licenses to these programs on low-frequency channels in unpopulated areas.

The following year, a group of 150 evangelicals formed the National Religious Broadcasters, seeking to push back against what they saw as persecution of fundamentalists, conservatives, and those warning of the coming Armageddon. Even stripped of their access to the big radio networks, these preachers still held tremendous sway over their congregations—and their pocketbooks—giving them the grassroots and financial support needed to reclaim their place on the airwaves.

The NRB relocated its headquarters to Washington, D.C., where it began a long campaign of pressuring regulators to return them to the airwaves. In 1960, a new policy from the Federal Communications Commission ruled that radio networks could sell airtime to evangelical organizations—mainstream religious programming was often given free airtime, per FCC regulations mandating segments of airtime operating in "public interest"—and there were a lot of well-funded ministries that could finance a good deal of programming.

This conflict added fuel to the narrative that a cabal of intellectuals, government regulators, journalists, media elites, and progressive

Christians were collectively working to silence evangelical voices that had grown too popular. The NRB was viewed as a sanctuary from this persecution, an isolated media ecosystem blending sensationalist news reports with dramatic, tent-revival sermonizing.

They were free of "experts," intellectuals, journalists, or theologians, but they were still broadcasting on airwaves owned by the federal government, and—similar to public schools banning prayer or integrating racially—any move against evangelicals by FCC regulators would be portrayed by radio preachers as persecution.

In 1964, the evangelist and host of the right-wing radio show *Christian Crusade,* Billy James Hargis, attacked journalist Fred Cook for his book *Barry Goldwater: Extremist of the Right.* Goldwater was not only the godfather of the libertarian movement, he was that year's Republican candidate for the presidency.

Sweaty and angry, Hargis, who had once been a speechwriter for Joseph McCarthy, was a wildly popular preacher who railed against the long-haired Beatles, women's liberation, the Anti-Defamation League, and sex education in schools on 500 radio and 250 TV stations coast to coast. He said that electing Goldwater was essential "to the survival of a free America" and called Cook a "professional mudslinger" who was falsifying his reporting and affiliating with communists.

Cook demanded that Red Lion Broadcasting, the owner of the radio station, give him an on-air rebuttal, citing the Federal Communications Commission's "Fairness Doctrine," which mandated news programs giving equal time to opposing sides of an issue. The rule had yet to apply its teeth to evangelists on the radio, but Cook's lawsuit forced their hand when it was upheld in court—only to have Hargis and Red Lion Broadcasting sue the FCC for violating their First Amendment rights.

When the case made it to the Supreme Court, they found that government regulation of the radio airwaves was necessary, and wholly different from restrictions against individuals' speech. "Without government control," stated Justice Byron White, "the medium would be of little use because of the cacophony of competing voices, none of which could be clearly and predictably heard."

The Supreme Court's ruling in favor of a mudslinging journalist over a popular evangelist enraged many fundamentalists. Just as evangelicals were fleeing public schools for "segregationist academies" that taught creationism and patriotic history, a desire was growing for a Christian media ecosystem with no ties to the federal government—and the obliteration of any pesky regulations against such a thing.

Roger Ailes saw this writing on the wall years before anyone. Long before he created the Fox News empire, Ailes was helping to rebrand Richard Nixon's image for television in 1968. He was the Karl Rove of his time, intuitively understanding how to package conservative politicians for a religious, working-class audience who were tuning in to the TV or radio after a long day at work.

Ailes later worked on the "Morning in America" campaign to re-elect Ronald Reagan in 1984, where he was known as "Dr. Feelgood," telling Reagan to avoid policy and instead rely on charm and wit, nurturing America's desire for political comfort food. "You didn't get elected on details," he told the Gipper. "You got elected on themes."

In his second term, Reagan appointed a former campaign staffer to head the Federal Communications Commission, who argued that the Fairness Doctrine violated the First Amendment by limiting free speech, thereby launching a fight that would see the ruling repealed by George H. W. Bush's administration (another presidential win that Ailes was largely credited for) a couple years later.

Almost immediately, the world was introduced to Rush Limbaugh—the corpulent clone of Billy James Hargis—whose right-wing radio show could now simultaneously rail against "the liberal media" while also spreading half-baked conspiracy theories, racist justifications for the War on Drugs, and blatant homophobia. Before the repeal of the Fairness Doctrine, Limbaugh's program would've had to devote time to an equally leftist viewpoint on every issue discussed (which, to balance out the man who coined the term "feminazi," would have had to be some kind of trans-Marxist revolutionary).

Limbaugh said that meeting Ailes in 1992 was like "finding a soulmate."

Ailes created a late-night TV program around Limbaugh, one that blended news and comedy, personality and outrage, focused on issues important to (white) Christian Republican voters. This would be the prototype for Fox News, which Ailes launched in 1996 with the conservative media mogul Rupert Murdoch, intending to create a "Fair and Balanced" counterpoint to the untrustworthy, liberal media.

Fox News tapped into America's fear of unseen threats (terrorist plots, drug-dealing immigrants, Planned Parenthood, socialized medicine) as well as the repressed sexuality of American conservatives (Ailes was known for casting leggy bombshells in short skirts to read the news), better than any megachurch could have aspired.

Throughout history, the media—and preachers—have faced the choice of potentially boring their audience with nutritious wisdom that would expand the public consciousness, or gaining power and wealth by promoting more narrow, fearful, and inflammatory rhetoric. A vengeful God will always grab an audience more quickly than a peaceful one; and reporting on the sex lives of celebrities or a kidnapped beauty queen will always get more attention than consequential shifts in economic policy.

Curiosity has no agenda, narrative, or ideology. It is never completely satisfied; always hungry for new perspectives, new information that makes everything infinitely more complex, yet endlessly fascinating.

Roger Ailes's Fox News is possibly the most effective storyteller of the modern era. Complex world affairs and public policy have been boiled down to shiny soundbites in the hands of Sean Hannity, Glenn Beck, and Bill O'Reilly (along with their teams of producers and directors). The world is a simple place on Fox News. It's the TV news equivalent of a rom-com or a *Fast and Furious* movie.

Kent Hovind was brilliant in his use of narrative to explain the science of creationism, while creating links between the theory of evolution, communism, and end-times prophecy.

Hal Lindsey was great at storytelling, too. Reading *The Late Great Planet Earth* in my twenties, I found myself captivated by his narrative's blend of Revelation and world affairs, often having to stop and remind myself: The world didn't end in 1988.

Progressives have never been terribly great at storytelling. Relying on experts to craft policy means dealing with a lot of nuance and hedging language, too many options, too much data. Science is complex.

Civics is complex. And complexity makes for shitty slogans, war cries, or headlines.

As I sit in this diner in Clear Lake, waiting for Thad to join me, I watch Kevin Sorbo contribute his two cents to the 24/7 anti-woke campaign on Fox News.

Sorbo's career had nearly evaporated when he agreed to star in *God's Not Dead*. He played an atheist, a Richard Dawkins–like college professor, who forces all of his students to sign a contract declaring "God Is Dead" or else he'll fail them. One Christian student stands up to him, leading to a David and Goliath debate between them.

The two-million-dollar film would go on to net sixty-four million dollars, giving a massive boost to the Christian film industry (which began in Iowa with *A Thief in the Night*), and would lead to a series of *God's Not Dead* sequels, all centered on stories of the persecution of Christians in modern America. Now Sorbo is using this narrative of persecution to claim that the existence of effeminate boys is due to a conscious effort among liberals to destroy masculinity once and for all.

History has taught us that you can never go wrong ginning up fear among conservatives of a gender identity crisis. Throughout the 2000s, the megachurch pastor Mark Driscoll led a hypermasculinity revolution against what he saw as the "feminization" of Christianity, saying, "I cannot worship the hippie, diaper, halo Christ because I cannot worship a guy I can beat up," and he blamed Ted Haggard's affair on his wife's "letting herself go." He was aggressive, crude, misogynistic, and popular with the kind of insecure men who idolized *Fight Club*'s Tyler Durden.

There's no room for emotional intelligence in this worldview, only instinct fueled by patriotism, religious fervor, and the cinematic myth of the American cowboy.

No one who saw the rise of Mark Driscoll could have been the least bit surprised when Donald Trump became the new evangelical strongman (or when pictures of his head Photoshopped onto Rambo's ripped body abounded on the social-media pages of incels and QAnons). Both Driscoll and Trump are great storytellers, and the world is a scarier place because of it.

Bathrooms, pro sports, and teaching jobs have now become battlegrounds of gender politics, thanks to the brilliantly spun narratives of a few evangelical meatheads. Sitting in this diner, I notice my short-shorts creeping up again, revealing scars on my thighs.

I feel eyes on me, a narrative forming about the city boy in the small town. One of those sissies that Hercules on the TV over there has been warning them about. He tells them all they need to know about me. Any conflicting information—like the fact that I lived in this town for twenty-two years, and have generations of ancestors in the local cemetery—would only complicate their narrative. Which isn't likely to make them any more inquisitive, only potentially dangerous.

I sure wish Thad would hurry up and get here.

Monetizing Trauma

2010–16

In his outrageous memoir, *Catch Me If You Can,* the prolific con man Frank Abagnale chronicles the life he has spent successfully pretending to be a university professor, a commercial airline pilot, an emergency-room doctor, and a practicing attorney, despite being a high-school dropout teenager living on millions in phony paychecks. Throughout the book, Abagnale first learns a sufficient amount about each of these professions—their esoteric lingo, routines, and hierarchies—and then forges some documents and applies for the job.

I thought of Abagnale often throughout the first few years of my journalism career.

I viewed myself as a kind of con man, disguising what I saw as humiliating and discrediting details about myself—uneducated, poor, a former evangelical Young Republican—whenever entering the Denver Press Club, or some cocktail mixer hosted by one of the publications I was writing for.

It was Denver's *Village Voice* alt weekly paper, *Westword,* that gave me my first paid journalism gig after I pitched them a story about Scum of the Earth, a semi-progressive punk-rock church founded by members of the Christian-rock band Five Iron Frenzy (who were more or less the Rolling Stones of my generation). *Westword*'s editor in chief, Patricia Calhoun, and copy editor, Jane Le, mentored me for the next two years, teaching me about journalism ethics, dangling modifiers, and (in Patty's case) how to drink five beers in under an hour and still manage to pitch a variety of stories to a team of editors in a noisy bar.

I wrote dozens of articles for the local LGBTQ paper, *Out Front Colorado* (one of the oldest in existence), profiling my queer heroes like Peaches, Tegan and Sara, and Wanda Sykes.

For my first few years I covered mostly the arts, finding myself in an overcrowded corner of journalism where editors' budgets were constantly slashed. So I sought out underreported avenues of Denver journalism—marijuana legalization, DIY stand-up comedy—and, Abagnale-style, positioned myself as an expert on those topics (despite knowing very little about them). This led to bigger platforms, like Colorado Public Radio, *The Denver Post,* and eventually to national publications like *Esquire, Politico,* and *Vice,* the last of which published around seventy of my stories between 2014 and 2024.

Though I felt like a fish out of water when I compared my background to the education, culture, and stable, middle-class upbringings of my journalism colleagues, I was very much at home in the poverty that came with being a freelancer.

I was never formally employed at any of these publications, despite doing the same amount of work as an employee for long stretches of time. (At one publication, I had my own desk and weekly writing assignments, and attended six hours of editorial meetings each week, while earning around half the minimum wage when my hours were calculated against pay.)

Freelancing is the ultimate conclusion of rugged individualism and free-market economics. It bypasses all of the labor laws that helped build America's middle class, because freelance work isn't subject to the same regulations that govern other forms of employment. Like farmers, freelancers don't get holidays, vacations, health-care benefits, or overtime. We have to pay for our own equipment, and are taxed by the IRS at the highest rate of any workers (yes, you can deduct some expenses, but that will shoot you in the foot when it comes time to prove your income for a bank loan).

In addition to writing the stories, you must also be conducting a 24/7 marketing campaign to promote your work—and life—on social media, an incessant charm offensive of photos, videos, and witty quips, where your work is evaluated based on your charisma instead of the quality of your reporting. Just as with multilevel marketing schemes, as a freelancer, you get to "be your own boss," selling your wares to unsuspecting friends and family on Facebook. Just as in evangelicalism, our lives have to become an advertisement for our success, because this is how more opportunity arises.

I would eventually learn how to negotiate contracts, articulate my worth, and (most important) say no to shitty pay for time-consuming stories, but during my first few years as a journalist I lived on around ten thousand dollars annually (sometimes less), despite working around the clock. I could do this only because of Denver's crust-punk community, who taught me all the tricks to live on very little money in the city (dumpster diving, collective living, not owning a car, learning to DIY everything). And my stripped-down lifestyle of no kids, spouse, or hobbies left me plenty of space to give the work everything I had.

I was fueled by passion, financial anxiety, and Adderall.

Impostor syndrome kept me on my toes at all times.

It's only a matter of time before you humiliate yourself, Caldonia often reminded me in those years. *Soon enough, they'll learn who you really are, and then it's back to Walmart for you.*

For years, I successfully kept my background as an evangelical a secret. I was so immersed in high fashion, so effeminate, and, worst of all, such an "intellectual," that none of my journalism colleagues ever suspected I came from a small farming town in Iowa and had spoken in tongues every day until the age of eighteen.

But all of that changed one night when I was visiting Iowa in the summer of 2014.

A murderer in my hometown had just been declared not guilty by reason of insanity, and the reason for this was so inconceivable to me, I pitched an idea to my editor at *Vice.* Eventually, I wrote a story that revealed to the world my childhood trauma.

The previous year, Tom Barlas, Jr., had stabbed his father to death in their Mason City home. His mother arrived shortly after, finding her son standing in his underwear in the garage, dripping with blood, explaining to her, "Mom, I killed Satan." He then fled to the local Greek Orthodox Church, where police found him hours later, repeating the words "God and Jesus Christ" over and over again.

I had written only a handful of crime stories by this point and was surprised to find that Barlas's insanity defense was legitimized by the fact that he thought his father was infected by the devil. I was intrigued by this strange exception in our criminal-justice system, carved out for mentally ill defendants, and that it seemed to apply only to people with the same spiritual beliefs I was raised on: namely, that angels and demons always surround us, occasionally infecting our bodies; and that sometimes God literally asks us to kill people (as He does *many* times throughout the Bible).

At the time, I hadn't established any sources in criminal justice, so I rang up my old colleague at *Westword* Alan Prendergast, who not only had reported on crime for decades (producing many excellent books), but also taught journalism at Colorado College.

"There are all sorts of people who could be observed to be psychotic or deranged, but they don't necessarily meet the legal definition of insanity," Prendergast explained to me. "Someone who kills their kids and says God told them to do it, they have a chance with an insanity plea . . . In weird family tragedies, where there's a history of bizarre behavior or claims of demonic possession or someone thinking their kid is Satan, it's more difficult for the prosecution to establish [sanity and guilt]."

Evangelicals do have a history of attempting to inject supernatural beliefs into criminal courtrooms. The ghost hunters Ed and Lorraine Warren were present in Connecticut the day after Arne Cheyenne Johnson murdered his landlord with a pocket knife, insisting that Johnson was possessed by a demon at the time, and was therefore innocent. His defense team attempted to plead that he was not guilty because he had been infected with supernatural evil at the time, but the judge dismissed it instantly.

And yet the jury found Johnson guilty only of manslaughter.

Blending memoir and journalism, I conjured a story juxtaposing the common supernatural beliefs of evangelical Americans (who, at the time, were nearly a quarter of the population) against the practices of the criminal-justice system. My editor at *Vice* loved it, and began asking me for more stories about evangelical politics and culture, particularly ones with a dark, confessional angle about my childhood. Since I had a mighty arsenal of pitches along these lines, I soon found another unique little corner of the industry for myself, giving me a leg up on my more educated and privileged colleagues.

Up until that moment, I'd mostly been writing thoughtful essays from the safety of my bedroom, occasionally leaving to conduct an interview or attend a political rally, but always able to retreat to my peaceful ecosystem at home, modeled after my time at the alternative school in Iowa. I had yet to immerse myself in the jungle of breaking-news journalism, which demanded razor-sharp thinking and instant response to new information.

So, when I found myself fielding a call from an editor at *The Guardian*—the centuries-old left-leaning British paper—asking me to report on a mass shooting at a Colorado Springs Planned Parenthood, I was equally flattered and terrified.

I never let on that I had zero experience covering a breaking news story, and had only written a handful of crime stories in my life.

Since I still didn't own a car, I ordered a $220 Lyft ride to Colorado Springs (which I didn't know until later would be reimbursed by *The Guardian*). I was dropped in the King Soopers parking lot across the street from the Planned Parenthood, which was cordoned off with police tape and swarming with TV reporters in the process of giving live broadcasts for the six o'clock news. I had no idea what to do with myself.

It was dark; a blizzard was stinging my face and neck with blowing snow.

Just before I arrived, the shooter, fifty-seven-year-old Robert Dear, had killed two Planned Parenthood employees and one policeman and injured nine more, then conducted a five-hour standoff with police while other Planned Parenthood employees hid in safe rooms, before he was convinced to surrender.

Over the next few days, I cranked out story after story about the shooting, interviewing religious leaders, women's rights activists, and those arguing for and against gun control. I attended vigils, political rallies, and press conferences. My piece on the political history of the area, "Colorado Springs: A Playground for Pro-Life, Pro-Gun Evangelical Christians," was a hit with the British paper, creating a demand for stories from *The Guardian's* Australian and U.S. divisions about violent religious fanatics in America.

While reporting on evangelicals, I often thought of the Scopes Monkey Trial, and the swarms of journalists who were there not to further readers' understanding of the intersection of education, government, and religion, but merely to point and laugh at the freak show of backwoods Christians.

I also thought of the GOP strategist Paul Weyrich in the late seventies, who stirred up fear and anger among a demographic of voters who cared nothing for the abortion issue until nearly a decade after *Roe v. Wade.*

I thought of the Chick Tracts I'd read as a kid, like *Baby Talk* and *Who Murdered Clarice,* which emphatically portrayed abortion as murder, and anyone involved—from the doctor administering the abortion to pro-choice Supreme Court justices who sanctioned it— as complicit. The practice was akin to child sacrifice, we were told, evoking images of violent horror against toddlers.

I then thought of Robert Dear—who was later found too incompetent and delusional to stand trial—living alone in his rural trailer home, likely raised on the same Chick Tracts and militaristic language that I was, believing himself a vigilante, a hero rescuing innocent babies from systematic murder.

I was naturally horrified by him—and the pro-life movement that radicalized him, which has led to eleven murders, forty-two bombings, 196 arsons, and 491 assaults against abortion providers since 1977—but I could also understand his worldview in a way few of the reporters in the area could. That doesn't mean I had the right, as a man, to lecture anyone about reproductive rights, or how they should feel about this kind of terrorism against doctors who were providing an essential medical service that all women were entitled to. But I was lecturing myself, as a journalist, wondering whether I was really trying to enlighten the world on how religious politics in America influenced laws around guns and abortion, or to stir up outrage and fear against religious fanatics living deep in the Rocky Mountains.

I was afraid that, by highlighting the most outrageous (yet titillating) aspects of evangelical culture, embracing narrative over curiosity, I was contributing to the stereotype of the liberal journalist attacking conservative Christians, thereby justifying their sense of martyrdom by the mainstream media.

Following the Planned Parenthood attack, *The Guardian* would call me whenever a mass shooting occurred within a thousand miles of Denver, which was fairly often. I experienced a disgusting thrill at news of carnage breaking out in America—whether it was at a grocery store in Boulder or a lawnmower factory in small-town Kansas—because it meant I was about to make some money (in my defense, I was very broke and happy to get the work).

At the same time, I kept reminding myself to be grateful.

I was free of disposable jobs, garnering international recognition despite my ninth-grade education. I may not have been making very much money as a freelance journalist, but it was giving me access to an almost endless catalogue of professors, authors, doctors, politicians, and activists, who would have a thirty-to-sixty-minute conversation with me about whatever was tickling my whimsical curiosity. More than that, I was using journalism to further my understanding of where I came from, to get an outside perspective on my people, why they think and behave the way they do, what traps had been laid for them by the Music Men of politics and religion, and how I fit into all of it.

At the time, I never considered the flip side to being a journalist with a personal, traumatic connection to the topic they're covering: that, throughout each workday, I'd be wading through the swamps of my childhood terror, exploring emotions, memories, and new perspectives, all on a public stage, all for a day's wages.

Think of the Children

2017

In Marion L. Starkey's chronicling of the Salem Witch Trials in *The Devil in Massachusetts,* she repeatedly theorizes that the extreme terrors of seventeenth-century Puritan culture—where nearly every action was a damnable sin, avoidance of Hell was unlikely, and the relentless sufferings of pioneer life were caused by either an angry God or a hateful Satan—drove the young girls to such madness that they actually hallucinated the specters they claimed to see in the courtroom.

She posits that, though the girls may have been delusional, they genuinely believed that those they accused were guilty. Published in 1949, this is one of the earliest descriptions of religious trauma syndrome of which I'm aware (and certainly conflicts with Arthur Miller's portrayal of the girls as bratty tricksters stirring up trouble in *The Crucible*).

Religious trauma syndrome has been widely discussed in psychological-medicine and academic journals over the last two decades, but has yet to appear in the *Diagnostic and Statistical Manual (DSM-5),* the Bible of mental-health disorders.

Often categorized as a subset of complex PTSD (trauma that continues over a long period of time, instead of as an isolated incident), its primary symptoms include emotional and cognitive impairments in childhood, based on the interpretation of ordinary thoughts and feelings through a supernatural lens, leaving children constantly hypervigilant about the spiritual minefield they live in each day. This can lead to a whole battery of problems in adulthood, including "depression, anxiety, guilt, and addictive or compulsive behaviors," writes the psychologist Alyson Stone. "The intellectual realm can become restricted, promoting legalistic, black-and-white thinking and difficulty with . . . problem solving."

I certainly fit the bill for religious trauma syndrome, in its description of both childhood terror and of the aftershocks into adulthood. And I was not alone.

Following the 2016 election of Donald Trump—in which 81 percent of evangelicals supported the candidate—a movement of "exvangelicals" began forming little digital communities, through podcasts, social media, and Zoom events. I found a great deal of solace among these former believers, all of us discovering we had the same childhood stories about fearing we'd been left behind in the rapture, learning to hate our bodies in sexual-purity classes, and suffering sleepless nights as we obsessed about spiritual warfare.

Ryan Connell was one of a handful of exvangelicals from Denver that I met online, then in person in 2017, when I learned he lived just a few blocks away from me. Together we'd host rapture-movie nights with other former zealots, often getting stoned before watching films like *A Thief in the Night* or the *Left Behind* series (both the Kirk Cameron *and* Nicolas Cage editions), all of us laughing at what once terrified us.

Validating one another's trauma went a long way toward soothing my emotional turbulence; but my career as a journalist covering all the insidious avenues of the Christian right was on the ascent, and while my instinct told me I wasn't emotionally stable enough to deal with this kind of work, my poverty and ambition forced me to push through.

I'd actually seen Ryan Connell several years earlier, before the word "exvangelical" existed, in the documentary *Hell House*. He'd played a priest of the Church of Satan in a theatrical production from Trinity Church in Dallas, Texas, back when he was still a Christian. Hell Houses were an evangelical tradition created by (who else?) Jerry Falwell in the 1970s. They were haunted houses with a message, using gore and immersive art to reveal the supernatural warfare behind social issues like drugs, abortion, and gun violence. By the 1990s and 2000s, they'd entered the mainstream consciousness, and in 2017 the topic came up in conversation with my editors at *Vice.*

Connell's church in Dallas was notorious enough to warrant a documentary largely because of the outrage they spawned with their 1999 Hell House, re-creating the Columbine School massacre only six months after the tragedy took place.

Smelling a story, I asked Connell to revisit the Trinity Church Hell House in Dallas with me, thinking it would be a fun "exvangelical" adventure as well as provide a decent paycheck. I would quickly learn there was a big difference between giggling at rapture films while stoned on my couch and jumping into the kinetic headfuck of a Hell House.

Just like the Hell Houses I participated in as a teenager at Agapé, Trinity's was a chaotic assault on the senses, a gauntlet of pop-culture references and culture-war touchstones. In one scene, Black Lives Matter protesters clashed with Trump supporters, leading to gunshots and bloodshed, followed by demons celebrating the violent chaos they'd successfully orchestrated.

In addition to racial strife, women's issues were also at the forefront of the play: a girl meeting a Tinder date winds up kidnapped and forced into a sex-trafficking ring; another is so distressed by her father's sexual abuse that she kills her mother before slitting her own wrists; a different mother encourages her daughter to get an abortion, which we are treated to a viewing of, in intimate detail.

As they all do, Trinity's Hell House climaxes with a tour of Hell, where a multitude of screams, banging metal, flashing lights, and demons in goth makeup successfully terrified both Connell and me for several minutes.

Hell Houses are perhaps the only realm of the arts where evangelical conservatives surpass the secular counterparts that influenced them. Their stories, performances, and production are always wildly effective at scaring the shit out of their audiences, because everyone involved is operating under the urgency of saving souls from eternal torture in Hell.

After the Hell scene, Trinity guests were brought into a brightly lit room, where church counselors explained how they could avoid burning alive forever by reciting a prayer and inviting Christ into their hearts. It was the same routine at my Hell House in the nineties, which led to protests and being called out for brainwashing on the evening news.

That seemed hyperbolic to me as a young believer, but I had no trouble using the term when writing about Hell Houses for *Vice* in 2017. After all, the most common tactics of brainwashing are overloading the targets' senses, reducing their critical and independent thinking skills, and questioning their moral goodness, to get them to change their beliefs or values. Practitioners will create urgent, terrifying problems in their subjects' minds, and then offer themselves (and/or some idea or practice) as the only solution.

I'd gone into the story intending to illuminate readers on this evangelical novelty they may not have heard of, peppering in a few anecdotes from my childhood and a bit of lighthearted cynicism (this was for *Vice,* after all). But the immersive qualities of the Hell House were often just too much for me, drawing me back to my childhood when I was cutting myself in the basement to keep away the demons, or to the vision I had at church camp of my eternal torture in the underworld.

This only continued when I flew back to Denver to write the story; I trembled as I listened to the audio recording I'd made of our tour through Hell. No amount of hipster detachment could keep me from being sincerely terrified while writing this story, leading me to drink even more alcohol than I already had been.

Though I never fell as far down the addiction rabbit hole as many of my friends in Iowa, during these years in Denver I was living an unsustainable life of chaos and intoxication that only got worse the more time I spent writing about evangelicals. I was consuming a case of Milwaukee's Best every night (eventually switching to IPAs once I could afford them), along with a few Adderall pills and a pack of cigarettes to stay focused, and a constant stream of marijuana to deal with the anxiety, along with the occasional opiate, benzodiazepine, or line of cocaine here and there. I was living each day like Ellen Burstyn in *Requiem for a Dream*—sweaty, paranoid, and delusional.

I couldn't maintain a relationship for more than a year or two, all of them beginning in a whirlwind of romance and cohabitation and ending with tearful fights and bitter isolation. My relationships with colleagues, editors, collaborators, and friends were equally fraught with conflict, though I never consciously *decided* to start shit with anyone, and certainly didn't enjoy it. In addition to RTS, I likely suffered from chaos addiction, wherein a tumultuous childhood can lead to a compulsive (yet unconscious) craving for drama as an adult.

This was reflected not only in my relationships, but in my writing. Though it was never a conscious decision, so much of my work attacked sacred institutions: I wrote sassy essays about tipping, voting, Christmas, or Denver's cherished Cruiser Bike Ride (resulting in the only death threat I've ever received as a journalist). I also covered murder, child abuse, cults, police brutality, homelessness, and climate change, validating my misanthropic worldview and justifying my nihilism surrounding the human experience.

The darker my stories became, the hungrier my beast of addiction grew.

The deeper I fell into substance abuse, the less focused and productive I became, sparking a panic of financial ruin, which only ramped up the need for more drugs.

I couldn't write in public, couldn't sit in restaurants with my back exposed (feeling unsafe everywhere I went, yet unsure why), and was obsessed with the idea that everyone around me thought I was a pretentious hipster who needed to go away.

Once again, I wanted to get out of Denver, this time to run away from all the conflict I'd wrought. So I moved myself and my floppy-eared mutt of a dog, Iggy, into a cheap, run-down cabin in the Rocky Mountains.

Without realizing it, I was following in the footsteps of my predecessors, unable to cope with the problems they'd created, thinking they could run away from it all.

My grandfather, who literally kicked his family out of his life.

My dad, who couldn't muster the trust, vulnerability, and patience to connect with his mentally ailing wife, so instead got high, screwed around, divorced, married again (and again, and again), while spending most of my childhood alone in his bedroom.

My mom, who surely loved me but found refuge from motherhood in extreme dissociation, then channeled that energy into building a very successful career. That's an endeavor I fully applaud her for, yet I still harbor a bitter suspicion that my existence as a child was a conundrum often too overwhelming for her to look at, let alone navigate. (She, too, spent a good deal of my childhood hiding in her bedroom, when she was home.)

What I desperately needed at this time was professional help, but instead I told myself to keep typing, keep building my career, keep climbing the ladder of success, never asking where it led, or if I even wanted it anymore.

CHAPTER THIRTY-THREE

Exercising Demons

2018

The cabin I'd moved Iggy and me into was poorly insulated and heated only by a wood-burning stove. But I had a reliable WiFi connection to keep the freelance journalism machine turning, and my forty-pound dog to cuddle with on cold nights.

In addition to journalism, I continued tinkering with the *Carnality* novels. Writing dark fiction late into the night—surrounded by a deafening silence, randomly pierced by the screams of marmots being torn apart by packs of coyotes—brought me to ever-darker recesses of my childhood memories, conjuring new layers of pain and vivid imagery I could use in these semi-autobiographical stories.

Despite growing up surrounded by rural farmlands, I'd had very little experience with "real" nature, since most of the ecology of Iowa had been plowed, drained, and turned into cold factories of flora and fauna. But I was in the real shit now, surrounded by mountain lions, black bears, and isolated weirdos with stockpiles of guns.

For the first few weeks, I was too scared to explore the trails that surrounded me, only playing with Iggy in the fenced-in yard behind us. But one evening, my anxiety was so overwhelming—my body trembling as though I were having a seizure, my thoughts racing and heart pounding—that I had to get out of the house, had to move my body lest it explode.

So I popped a ten-milligram marijuana edible, laced up my shoes, put on my headphones, and headed out with my dog, into the wild. The sun was setting behind the distant mountains, and a brisk chill electrified the air. Iggy sprinted up the dirt road, and I ambled along behind him.

I'd never enjoyed exercise a day in my life—as a kid, I was often mocked in gym class for being too slow, too weak, too easily frightened of dodgeballs—but right now, feeling slightly stoned, with my favorite tunes in my ears, my beloved dog by my side, I found my feet bouncing off the ground with a bit more lightness than usual; my brain was processing it more like dancing than jogging.

I started to feel like I weighed fifty pounds.

All the little hairs on my body stood on end.

The edible was certainly kicking in, delivering a smooth body high and steady enthusiasm, notably different from the manic spikes and dips of smoking cannabis.

A euphoric chill rippled up my spine, and I quickened my pace.

I was keeping up with Iggy (who ran like a chugging greyhound on those long, skinny legs of his) when the sun went to bed and a thunderstorm rolled in. Iggy hated thunder, but he loved running more, so he stuck by my side as we jogged along the road, eventually turning onto a dark trail surrounded by aspen trees in autumnal bloom.

It was beautiful and menacing at the same time; conflicting emotions of elation and dread swirled within me. There was something soothing about the hypnotic rhythm of my running footsteps, combined with the safety of my favorite music; and the ancient indifference of this mountain was humbling me, forcing me to find and maintain a strong sense of self, a confidence that I could confront the things that terrified me, that I could handle the darkness and the overactive imagination it inspired.

I suddenly found I could put all that anxiety—all that existential terror of abandonment and shame and unworthiness and damnation—straight into my surprisingly nimble legs, and burn it all up.

Iggy and I picked up the pace and ran at full tilt down the mountain trail.

I looked to my left and saw a pair of glowing red eyes approaching me from the dark woods. I looked to my right and saw the same thing, just as my playlist randomly switched to the 1981 David Byrne and Brian Eno song "The Jezebel Spirit."

The art-rockers first made this hypnotic, Afrobeat track with an audio clip of Kathryn Kuhlman performing an exorcism, but her estate denied their permission to release it. Instead, they used an anonymous recording of an exorcism in which a preacher asks the woman, "Do you hear voices? You do? So you are possessed. You have a Jezebel spirit within you." As with most art surrounding the macabre nature of fundamentalist Christianity, I both adored and was horribly terrorized by this song. So it was perfect for such an occasion.

As I ran down the muddy trail, heavy bullets of rain assaulting my face, I saw more red eyes approaching from the dark woods, coming at me from all angles. I paused under a tree and let my eyes focus, seeing a dozen jittery Caldonias, a flock of gleefully sociopathic witch demons closing in on me. Their familiar cackles overpowered my headphones, coming not from my ears but from inside my head, delivering the greatest hits of shame and self-loathing I'd heard throughout my life. They chanted in unison:

Pervert!

Sinner!

Faggot!

Lazy, undisciplined stoner!

You and your whole family are pathetic losers with no friends or money!

Soon we will take you to Hell for your weakness!

Eternal torture, eternal torture!

I sprinted away, but they kept pace. I felt helpless, my skin crawling at the sound of their voices.

Part of me wanted to slow down, to stop running and go home; I told myself that I'd never been a runner and never would be, that I was embarrassing myself and should just go back to the cabin and get drunk, like the unlovable deadbeat that I was. I thought of the day I flunked out of school and crashed my car, and how I'd tried to run along the gravel road in Iowa, craving the ability to sprint out my emotions but never being able to last more than a minute or two.

I had been divorced from my body then, an anxious head balanced on a numbed anatomy. But here in the mountains, my brain and my body had fused with each other, creating feedback loops of pleasure and empowerment, wonder and enthusiasm.

As a boy, whenever Caldonia appeared in my dreams, I'd try desperately to get away, but it was like running through a swimming pool, every movement heavy and exhausting. The more frightened I became, the slower I would run. Tonight, however, I was endowed with a power I'd never known I had, able not only to run fast for a long time, but also to see myself as a person capable of such a thing.

I'd written novels, hundreds of articles, built a whole writing career with no guidance or education. I had escaped Iowa, traveled the world, had experiences most folks back home couldn't conceive of. I was not a lazy worm watching TV all night. I wasn't a hopeless welfare baby with nothing to offer society.

I could write.

I could work.

I could run.

Suddenly the Caldonias disappeared into the darkness, their bouncing red eyes falling behind me as their hateful words faded into the distance. I laughed and cried hysterically as I sprinted through the rain, knowing that they had never really been there, but that the shame and self-loathing of evangelical culture they represented certainly was.

In that moment, I felt empowered to stand up to God. To tell him and his Caldonia minions I did not deserve their torture.

I turned to look at the God I no longer believed in, who had given me a life of such confusion and fear, and I saw Him for what He really was: a sadistic monster that, whether real or imagined, had kept me locked in an endless loop of misery.

When we returned to the cabin, Iggy zipped past me, shook the rain from his fur, and curled up by the fire. I took off my jacket and caught my reflection in the mirror. Staring back at me was a wet, apple-cheeked face, sporting an enormous, Cheshire Cat grin, the unmistakable look of pure joy. I felt clean. Emptied. Suddenly running (particularly under the influence of cannabis) felt as natural an impulse as sleep, food, or sex—and I couldn't wait to do it again.

A week later, I quit smoking cigarettes, just so I could run more.

I also cut *way* back on the booze and pills to better maintain my heart rate for extra-long runs. I started eating healthier food and sleeping longer and deeper. Over the next two years, I not only ran like a madman—working my way from 10Ks to marathons to a 50K ultramarathon up the side of a mountain—I wrote a book about the science behind cannabis as an aid to fitness, and the open secret of its popularity among a majority of professional athletes.

Runner's High: How a Movement of Cannabis-Fueled Athletes Is Changing the Science of Sports would become my first book with a major publisher. It was a significant boon to my career, but the emotional catharsis I experienced on that trail was only the beginning of a very long journey of wrestling with unpleasant shit. Accepting that I couldn't spend every minute of the rest of my life running on mountain trails to a soundtrack of Norwegian black metal, I knew I needed to get some help.

I needed therapy, a community, and to love myself for who I was.

I didn't want to follow in the footsteps of my dad and grandfather, retreating from the world, from their families, every time their rage, humiliation, and self-loathing overwhelmed their faculties, preventing them from seeing a way through.

The acclaimed family therapist Terrence Real once said: "Family pathology rolls from generation to generation, like a fire in the woods taking down everything in its path, until one person, in one generation, has the courage to turn and face the flames. That person brings peace to his ancestors and spares the children that follow."

I would never have children, but I was up for the task of healing myself.

CHAPTER THIRTY-FOUR

Satan Versus Psychology

2019–21

The Christian right has always had an adversarial relationship with psychology. To seek out therapy was an admission of weakness. To discuss your childhood trauma was to shirk personal responsibility for your behavior.

Evangelical zealots view mental-health treatment alongside feminism, yoga, Dungeons & Dragons, and evolution on their religious-hysteria bingo card. Psychology represented secular humanism and godless intellectualism, and sought to replace the Bible with Freud. The whole concept of mental-health care threatens the fundamentalist teachings of spiritual warfare. If, as evangelicals claim, all humans are given free will, and sufficient mental faculties to navigate the good and evil forces of the spiritual realm, then all morality exists within a clearly defined and understandable framework that tests us all equally, right?

If you see humanity through the modern lens of neuropsychology and socioeconomics, there are an endless number of factors that individuals have no control over—the family and environment we're born into, the genes we inherit, the childhood experiences that shape us— and we're severely limited even in our scope of understanding these matters and how they affect our emotions.

But in church we were told not to worry, because "God's got it," and to have any questions beyond that was to out ourselves as having weak faith. Most of us weren't even aware of our feelings when they arrived, the sensations they inflicted in our bodies, until they'd grown into problematic behavior that, left untreated, could lead to divorce, abuse, prison, or death.

I certainly had little emotional awareness or intelligence when I showed up for my first therapy session and was simply asked how I was feeling.

"Fine," I replied, unsure what else to say.

"I mean, tell me an emotion, and where you feel it in your body."

"I don't know what you mean," I said, "I don't feel anything in my body. I feel fine. Normal."

In time, the therapist explained to me that there was likely a busy world of emotional activity buzzing inside of me—hence my panic attacks, anger issues, insecurities, intrusive thoughts, drug abuse, and endless string of failed relationships—but I had no awareness of the emotions when they first arose, which is crucial for regulating them. She theorized that, long ago, I'd divorced my mind from my body (a split that is common among sufferers of complex PTSD) as a way to avoid bad feelings, and that a connection would need to be restored.

To begin with, she recommended I try body-scan meditation therapy to restrengthen that connection. The practice involves a series of breathing exercises, followed by focused concentration on specific areas of the body, starting with the toes and slowly moving upward to the head. The whole thing can take anywhere from five minutes to an hour or two. It's a mindfulness practice that sharpens the mind-body connection, leading not only to a greater understanding of your emotions, but also to better control of them.

When I started trying this at home, it didn't take long for me to freak out. My feet twitched, legs trembled, every muscle fiber shaking as though millions of bugs were traveling under my skin. Still, I continued, moaning with displeasure when scanning my pelvis, hips, then gut, which had terrorized me for so long. As I reached my torso, chest, and arms, I began to growl—honestly, *growl*, like a rabid animal—and my whole body quaked with spastic movements and inhuman noises.

If someone had walked in just then, they might have thought I was undergoing an exorcism.

Scenes from my childhood flashed behind my eyes.

Chased home by bullies calling me a faggot. Hiding from the Antichrist in the basement while cutting my legs and punching myself in the crotch. Wailing at church camp over the shameful lust I believed no one else but me suffered. Visions of bloody, screaming torture in Hell as I lay on my bed each night, and a few others I'm not prepared to write about just yet.

When it was over, I felt not unlike I did after running in the mountains, exhausted yet euphoric, as if I'd shed something large and toxic that I'd been carrying for years.

I thought of my years at Pentecostal churches, and how the kinetic activities of dancing, quivering, shouting gibberish, then collapsing to the ground in exhaustion made me feel so clean and weightless. At the time, I'd attributed this to the presence of the Holy Spirit. But, as with my experiences with secular music, I realized I could access that same catharsis outside of church.

The mindfulness therapy techniques I was learning about constantly emphasized how essential it was to feel my feelings—if I embraced them, they would pass. Whereas I had been taught that negative emotions were likely caused by Satan, something to fear, to reject, and to pray away. And if they returned, it was likely due to your sin.

After my first year of therapy, I read *The Body Keeps the Score,* a book on the science of overcoming trauma, and learned that disturbing emotions are often stored in the body and manifest in physical as well as emotional ways. Running, meditation, and therapy were giving me an opportunity to purge these dark sensations from my body, creating a space of strength and healing.

Just as I did with church events as a teenager, or writing in my twenties, I threw myself into healing my emotions with everything I had, centering my life on my weekly therapy sessions, while attending religious-trauma support groups, and reading everything I could get my hands on about complex PTSD, chaos addiction, and childhood psychology. It took me years to fully uncover what was going on within me, and navigating these dark emotions will be a lifelong journey of mindfulness and self-compassion, knowing my triggers and trying to keep myself calm.

Though the impulse to hurl myself into the deep end of covering the Christian right—and the need for more money—would always be there, and I would continue to overestimate my ability to handle it.

CHAPTER THIRTY-FIVE

God's Plan for Your Investment Portfolio

2022

As I watched Tim Tebow compare saving souls to signing with the Patriots, I thought of my parents' relationship with money. I was standing in a crowd of thousands at Life Surge, a nine-hour Christian finance conference in Denver; Tebow, *Duck Dynasty*'s Willie Robertson, and the Auntie Anne's Pretzels lady were some of the keynote speakers at this event, which combined practical investment and business seminars with culture-war campaign rallies.

If any of the finance talk became too boring for anyone, a worship service of inspiring music, a light show, and beach balls descending from the arena ceiling would rouse our spirits every few hours, before we returned to our lectures about Christian entrepreneurship and which stocks God thinks you should buy.

I was there to write a story for *The Guardian,* but couldn't help thinking about the intersection of emotions and money in my family. When I was a kid at Agapé and our Pentecostal services would get really wild, Pastor Jim would tell the congregation to "go home and *laugh* at your bills, *believing* God's got it!" We would sing and dance, weep with joy, then confidently hand over 10 percent of our income (in addition to "seed faith offerings"), rejecting any hint of doubt, lest we damn ourselves to poverty.

Our financial futures depended on our emotional connection to God. So we sang with bright smiles; we danced to make it rain (so to speak). We viewed money in strictly emotional terms, always as either a source of fear, anxiety, and shame, or as one of explosive celebration and crucial self-esteem.

Any sensible financial advisers will tell you that economic advancement is born of slow, steady investment and practical, long-term saving and budgeting. They will warn you not to succumb to anxiety during a stock-market fluctuation or become seduced by get-rich-quick seminars or promises of wildly high returns on investments in new trends like bitcoin, NFTs, or multilevel marketing businesses.

But this kind of financial literacy isn't prioritized in our culture, or public education. It's passed down generationally. And to many working-class people, like so many of my friends in Iowa who have no idea what their credit scores are, the maneuvers necessary to advance in our financial system are often intimidating and esoteric.

I didn't have a credit card until the age of thirty-five, or a bank loan until I was thirty-seven, and was even older before I learned about retirement accounts, or that money you keep in a bank account will simply, organically appreciate in value. (I was well acquainted with the opposite end of that spectrum, however, charged, over the years, thousands of dollars in fees *for not having enough money*.)

According to the Pew Research Center, nearly half of evangelical Protestants never attended college, and more than half earn less than fifty thousand dollars annually; a third earn less than thirty thousand.

Living within these tight margins means that every purchase, every surprise, every decision is weighed down by an exhausting level of stress and anxiety, impairing your cognitive functions, driving people like my mother to a numbed catatonia in bed.

Meanwhile, back at church, it's give, give, give!

You want a nice car, a lakeside home, and new suits like the pastor? Well, invest your seed faith today and you'll be with us on the boat in no time!

There were a few references to the familiar evangelical materialism of sports cars and expensive vacations at the 2022 Life Surge conference, but the more consistent theme of the day was the "Great Commission."

Tim Tebow's story about the sacrifices he made in order to sign with the Patriots was kind of superfluous, because he ultimately lost the Patriots gig anyway. But, as with so many evangelical speakers I've heard throughout my life, this very boring anecdote functioned as a self-reflective provocation to the audience, asking them, essentially: What would you do to win the culture wars for Jesus?

"I was willing to make that sacrifice for football," Tebow said, "but would I be willing to do that for the Great Commission?"

The "Great Commission" comes from the Gospel of Matthew, where Jesus "commissioned" his disciples to "Go therefore and make disciples of all nations, baptizing them in the name of the Father and of the Son and of the Holy Spirit." It's where the word "evangelical" comes from, the mandate to go out and win lost souls. Some Methodists, like my grandma Marilyn, or Baptists, like Jimmy Carter, saw this as a charge to go out and help those in need, particularly the poor, sick, imprisoned, marginalized, and dying, but most conservative evangelicals viewed the Great Commission as a command to proselytize, to convert, and to grow the congregation.

At Life Surge, the Great Commission was being weaponized to fight the culture wars, not just to proselytize to nonbelievers, but to truly "own the libs" once and for all. "Why on earth are *we* not buying Twitter?" asked the Minor League baseball player, HGTV star, and cohost of Life Surge, David Benham. "Why can't *we* get our money together and buy Disney, who have been so open-minded lately their brains are falling out? How many of you are sick and tired of seeing the devil take all the influence in this culture?"

It was a clever angle, since most of the people in this audience were, myself included, likely raised in an evangelical culture that fetishized Christian persecution. And after eight hours of seminars on building your business and investing in the stock market (via subscription to investment apps from Life Surge presenters), we finally got to the point: You must become rich so you can fund the fight to dominate American culture for Jesus, silencing the godless liberals once and for all.

Nearly every seminar at this conference, no matter how fiscally focused, was filled with jokes and ominous warnings about the "woke snowflakes" in Hollywood, Silicon Valley, and the mainstream media, who were working hard to rid the world of Christianity. Many speakers shared their stories of being "canceled" for their faith, and stirred fears that the government would come for your guns, monitor your cryptocurrency, and assemble an army of IRS agents aiming to bankrupt America's churches.

But in becoming wealthy, you would be able to launch your own movie studio, social-media company, news organization, or influencer brand, all centered on the message of Christ, so that you might more effectively fight the coming army of transgender socialists aiming to indoctrinate your children into becoming shoplifting atheists fighting for the right to marry their cats. Okay, I'm paraphrasing, but not much.

There was much to be afraid of in 2022, according to Life Surge, and God's war against Satan would be waged not only in flesh and blood, or even in the spirit realm, but in the stock market and on social media as well.

The anti-woke frenzy in conservative media circles—from podcasts, to conferences, to streaming services, to, as Jon Stewart pointed out, "over seven hundred book titles about being 'canceled' "—appeals to working-class evangelicals. They view the left as bullies, and people like Trump, Charlie Kirk, and Jordan Peterson as their protectors. But fear among the poor and uneducated of being mocked by the stylish urban intellectuals has been weaponized at Life Surge into creating not just a powerful voting class, but an economic army ready to storm the gates of Silicon Valley.

Prosperity gospel simply tapped into the materialism and vanity of poor churchgoers—promising them cars, boats, vacations, and mansions—but this was something far more insidious. As a twist on the same old ploy of getting poor people to view money in emotional terms, these people, instead of being aspirational, were being encouraged to tap into their own bitterness toward an elusive "other," contributing what little money they had toward silencing their supposed political enemies.

It seemed unlikely to me that anyone would get rich by following any of these investment strategies—or even find security in their finances—but the Life Surge business model isn't dependent on the return on investment from their ticketholders.

It cost anywhere between $50 and $500 simply to get into the building (admission included a box lunch from Chick-fil-A!), but that turned out to be just the beginning. In addition to the app subscriptions for stock-market investment, there was an endless series of follow-up classes to sign up for after this event, providing countless opportunities to fleece the financially illiterate in the crowd for every dime they were worth.

Walking out of the Life Surge conference, I had the same feeling I did when watching the January 6 insurrection on TV: *I know these people.* For good or ill, they're my people. Watching them cheer on the calls to "reclaim America for Christ"—both at Life Surge and on January 6—I knew what was going on behind their eyes and in their hearts.

After all, I was once one of them.

As I hopped on the light rail back home, I felt a hunger to articulate all of this on an intergenerational scale, pulling back the curtain on the Music Men who'd emotionally, psychologically, and economically manipulated my people—and myself. I began to see the intersection of mental health, poverty, and religion as a mighty whirlwind, upending the lives of working-class Christians, draining them of all their wealth, energy, and spirit, while conditioning them to be grateful and never complain, lest they be left behind.

Later that night, I booked myself a flight back home to Iowa, thinking there might even be a book in all this. As usual, my enthusiasm far outweighed my caution, and this time it would nearly destroy me.

The Swamps of Sadness

2023

As my dad and I sit in the parking lot of the old Sleepy Hollow Water-bed store, I marvel at how comfortable he is with himself.

I've been back in Iowa for two weeks now, interviewing friends, family, historians, farmers, and economists about a variety of topics concerning how the Christian right has used fear and shame to manipulate the working-class people of Iowa. Understandably, not everyone I've spoken with agrees with this premise.

Many of them are guarded, suspicious of this big-city journalist writing a memoir that (many assume) will make them look like snake-handling simpletons who can't be trusted not to stare into the sun. I no longer feel like a sixth-generation local, but something closer to H. L. Mencken at the Scopes Trial, who characterized the good people of Dayton, Tennessee, as "a universal joke."

Yet my dad has been remarkably humble, honest, and courageous throughout this whole process, even saying, "This project of yours has the potential to really help people." The endless rage that consumed him throughout my childhood has been gone for some time, which he largely attributes to "no longer caring what people think of me, like I did when you were a kid."

For so many years, Dad centered his entire self-worth around the numbers in his bank account, a toxic form of self-esteem encouraged by the prosperity gospel of our church. He's had so many waves of boom and bust—working sales jobs that he hated but that provided security, then risking it all on passion projects that left him broke—his self-esteem has always been on shaky grounds.

Shortly after his third divorce, Dad moved into a small house on the south side of Mason City and, because of his numerous medical ailments, was able to collect Social Security disability payments. Before this, he'd been homeless on more than one occasion, at times searching for loose change to buy himself something to eat. The government assistance didn't provide him with a glamorous lifestyle—travel and dining out were still luxuries beyond his reach—but cared for his basic needs sufficiently so that Dad could take the time to address his mental health.

He spent several years in almost complete solitude in that house. "It gave me the space I needed to reflect on my life," he recalls today. "I thought about my childhood, my marriages, my businesses—successes and failures. It helped me find some compassion for myself, accepting me for who I am, growing comfortable being my authentic self and not what I thought everyone needed me to be."

In those years, he also abandoned the dark theology we were both reared on, particularly the concept of Hell. "I thought about you kids, how I would do anything to save you from pain, and couldn't imagine how a loving God would allow His children to be tortured for all eternity." Unlike myself, though, Dad never became an atheist; he is still praying, still believing, still smiling brightly whenever the name "Jesus" crosses his lips.

Long ago, I stopped sharing my views on God's existence with him—or other family and friends in Iowa—in part because I have no interest in debating anyone out of their faith. I didn't lose my belief voluntarily; it slipped through my fingers like sand, and I don't wish that experience on anyone else. It's likely my dad doesn't have much time left on this Earth, and the peace he finds in believing Heaven awaits him is nothing I want to mess with.

Besides, I really envy the calm vulnerability he presents to the world.

Within hours after landing in Iowa, I could feel the feminine mannerisms I typically carry myself with beginning to fall away, my voice getting lower and posture more masculine; I was returning to the inauthentic boy they all know and remember.

Looking at the old Sleepy Hollow store, Dad recalls the darkest period of his adult life, a time when fear and shame drove him to destructive behavior. "I felt like everyone in the church abandoned me in those days," he says, his voice heavy with emotion. "After the divorce, and bankruptcy, I no longer fit their image of success and wasn't wanted anymore."

It's been years since Dad has been on a meth binge, but many of his friends haven't found the strength to pull themselves out of hard-drug abuse. Earlier today, he took me around to visit a few of them, folks I knew from childhood or my days dealing weed in Mason City. I remember them as full of laughter and energy, but now they looked like hospice patients—pale, confused, and desperately malnourished. Those who'd spent decades on meth were twitchy and covered in sores from picking at their skin; they spoke rapidly, but I could only understand a handful of their words. And even though those who were strung out on opioids talked slowly, they were equally unintelligible, often passing out midsentence.

Both camps carried themselves with slumped shoulders and downcast eyes, as if apologizing for their own existence.

Cerro Gordo County, where Mason City and Clear Lake reside, has some of the highest rates of methamphetamine use in the state—and along with that, a lot of violence. It's not uncommon for dead bodies to be found in the area (one was discovered not far from my dad's house a year earlier), and a whole book could be written on the drug-fueled murders in my hometown.* In 2022, some tweaker randomly shot a woman in the abdomen with a bow and arrow on a downtown

---

* The most notorious being the disappearance of Jodi Huisentruit, a twenty-seven-year-old blonde news anchor at KIMT, who is believed to have been abducted one early morning in June 1995. The cold case remains open to this day, but Huisentruit was declared dead in 2001, when I worked as a KIMT camera operator. There are many theories surrounding her disappearance, including retaliation for her investigation into meth trafficking in the area.

sidewalk—only days after two separate high-speed police chases that ended in gunfire.

For leaders of the Christian right like J. D. Vance, the antidote to this chaos is for churches to play a larger role in the lives of American families. But many of the addicts I met today grew up in the same evangelical culture that I did and, like me, were told it was unlikely they would reach adulthood, because the Apocalypse would arrive at any minute. So why finish school? Why build a career? Why save for retirement?

Often, these failures to advance in life lead to drug addiction.

Around the same time that Donald Trump became a working-class hero and J. D. Vance released *Hillbilly Elegy*, two economists took a deep dive into the massive spikes in suicide, drug addiction, chronic pain, and mental illness among uneducated white men in America. *Deaths of Despair and the Future of Capitalism* paints a bleak portrait of poorly educated men who can't seem to muster the get-up-and-go of their forefathers, and unpacks the economic shifts in labor and agri-culture driving the unemployment, low wages, and dying towns that fuel this existential hopelessness.

"Deterioration in job quality, and detachment from the labor force, bring miseries over and above the loss of earnings," write Anne Case and Angus Deaton in this 2020 book. "Many of the jobs that have come with lower wages do not bring the sense of pride that can come with being a part of a successful enterprise ..."

For most of us, this fork in the road presents itself just after high school.

"Those without a college degree are seeing increases in level of pain, ill health, mental distress, and ability to work and socialize," Case and Deaton report. "A four-year degree has become the key marker of social status."

Self-worth and opportunity were never part of the discussion dur-ing the War on Drugs of the eighties and nineties. We were taught to shame drug users, calling them losers and burnouts, trailer trash with meth-mouth. This had been going on in my hometown since the KKK marched down these streets in 1925, promising "Death to all bootleggers!"

Up until recently, few considered that the isolation and shame perpetrated by the War on Drugs—and the political operatives of the Christian right who made this happen—were actually exacerbating the drug problem.

In Johann Hari's 2015 book, *Chasing the Scream: The First and Last Days of the War on Drugs,* he challenges the notion that addiction is formed by a drug's rewiring of the brain, and instead points to a lack of community as the problem.

To illustrate this, he cites the "Rat Park" experiments, wherein lab rats are presented with the familiar scenario of access to morphine-laced water, but in an environment two hundred times the size of most cages, with balls and wheels to play with and a number of other rats to socialize and have sex with. Though these rats tried the morphine water, they never became addicted to it, consuming nineteen times less morphine than their caged counterparts.

"The opposite of addiction isn't sobriety. It's connection," writes Hari. "Punishment—shaming a person, caging them, making them unemployable—traps them in addiction. Taking that money and spending it instead on helping them to get jobs and homes and decent lives makes it possible for many of them to stop."

Isolation has become a common theme throughout my interviews in Iowa.

"All the farmers around here used to know each other," says one third-generation farmer I spoke with. "You used to help each other out when someone's kid was sick or you fell on hard times. Now you don't even know who's working the land next to you, or who owns it."

More than half of Iowa farms today are owned by people who don't actively farm; 20 percent of them don't even live in Iowa.

Driving with Dad around Mason City, I think of the joy he's found in accepting himself for who he is, and how difficult it was for him to achieve this inside the world of high-stakes evangelicalism. Back then, he longed for the support and connection of a community; but connection requires vulnerability, and vulnerability requires knowing who you are, accepting it, and not fearing what others think of it. However, for many of us working-class Iowans who no longer have farms to inherit or decent-paying manufacturing jobs to apply for (the place where many laborers once found their community), it's difficult to find an identity to embrace and be proud of.

My dad was able to achieve this without attaining social status in part because he bravely faced the wounds of his past, identifying the negative self-talk that had kept him angry, needy, and addicted for so long. But this process was also midwifed by the gift of time. Once his kids were raised, his dreams of wealth were abandoned, and the government provided for his basic needs, he had the space to work on himself.

Time is a luxury not often afforded to working-class Americans.

It takes time to get sober, to go to college, to carefully plot a life course.

Those raised with a certain level of privilege have the support of their families and communities during these times of transition and healing. But people who are working multiple jobs for wages that don't cover their living expenses, while trying to raise a family, don't have the time to deal with what's in front of them; they're living each day in a state of emergency, like my parents did.

There's a cold irony in the fact that our Norwegian ancestors came to the Midwest in the nineteenth and early twentieth centuries looking for a better life, considering all they missed out on. A generation after the Homestead Act lured so many of them to the Midwest, Norway developed "the Grand Compromise" between labor, government, and industry, leading to robust social programs like free health care, education, maternity leave, and the regulation of wages and working conditions. Meanwhile, in Iowa, child-labor laws have been repealed, and a new flat tax bolsters the wealthy while defunding education and health-care programs that support the most vulnerable.

It's the perfect breeding ground for self-loathing, isolation, and addiction.

From Billy Graham's sermon declaring, "Social problems of the world are a result of sin," to Ronald Reagan's chestnut, "Government is not the solution to our problem; government is the problem," working-class Americans have been conditioned to reject the notion that a system like Norway's could be an antidote to the deaths of despair in the Rust Belt. Decades of Christian-right propaganda have conditioned them to believe government assistance is for the lazy, the weak-willed, and those lacking moral fortitude.

But, like industrialists who will happily accept government subsidies while demonizing food-assistance programs, many low-income Americans on welfare view themselves as one of the rare, truly justified recipients of assistance, dismissing others like them as "profane loafers," nodding along to Fox News pundits who declare that "nobody wants to work anymore."

Like the railroad tycoon Jay Gould, who got "one half of the working class to kill the other half," the Christian right has managed to convince working-class Americans to hate not only themselves but one another. And this includes my dad, whose newfound inner peace has its Achilles' heel in the issue of welfare.

As we drive around "The Loop" in downtown Mason City—a three-mile circuit that generations of North Iowans "cruised" on Saturday nights, à la *American Graffiti*—the song "Rich Men North of Richmond" comes on the radio. Oliver Anthony's folk song about working-class malaise has connected with millions of Americans, becoming one of the biggest hits of 2023. Its commentary on low wages and dwindling opportunities mirrors the songs of leftists like Pete Seeger and Woody Guthrie—that is, until Anthony turns his attention to government assistance, singing "If you're five foot three and you're three hundred pounds, / Taxes ought not to pay for your bags of Fudge Rounds."

"Such a toxic lyric to an otherwise great song," I say to my dad. "Bullying people for accepting food assistance is so disgusting."

"Well, some people do need to hear it," my dad says. "Socialism is taking over this country, and it needs to stop."

We've come full-circle to our earlier conversation on the beach two weeks ago, but this time I don't hesitate to voice my opinion. I ask him how he can lack compassion for welfare recipients, when he was shamed for being on welfare as a kid; additionally, programs like Medicaid and Medicare have kept him from owing a fortune in healthcare costs, and the years he spent working on himself came courtesy of Social Security disability checks.

"Yes, but I worked hard for many years and paid into Social Security," he says, "so I'm *owed* that money."

"And you think other people on government assistance haven't worked hard?"

"Some have, but many people are abusing the system. It's been proven that some women will have multiple children just so they can get more government support."

"Dad, that's not a thing anymore, if it ever was!" I say. "A lot of resources have gone into rooting out welfare fraud, and the rare cases that exist represent a tiny fraction of those who sincerely need it.[*] Government assistance programs have been defunded to such a degree, especially here in Iowa, that having a baby just to get a welfare check would be the most idiotic investment strategy imaginable."

"You just watch, Biden's socialism is going to usher in the Mark of the Beast."

Even though he said the same thing only weeks earlier on the beach, my jaw still drops.

I want to ask him how he can continue to believe in the Tribulation—and all its horrors described in Revelation—but doesn't believe God will allow humanity to be tortured in Hell.

Instead, I bite my lip and look out the window.

We drive silently for a while after that.

Cruising around town, I recognize the site of the Klan rally in 1925, when laborers were made to fear immigrants, booze, and jazz music, and were promised that the purchase of a robe and hood—along with a bit of domestic terrorism—would keep them safe.

We pass the old KIMT studio building, its 1937 construction bankrolled by working-class Christians who, awed by phony miracles, were made to fear being left behind in the modern world and were promised that building a megachurch would keep them safe from humiliation, only to be stiffed with debt and bankruptcy by a fast-talking preacher

---

[*] One 2018 study from the Congressional Research Service found an average of fourteen cases of legitimate welfare fraud, out of every ten thousand food-assistance recipients.

who stuffed his pockets with cash and drove into the sunset. Next, we drive by the site of the old Good News Center, where my dad's childhood fear of abandonment—and a generation's fear of the world's collapsing—were soothed by the promise of a welcoming community and the assurance of knowing the "one true" interpretation of Biblical prophecies.

While Dad's mini-sermon about the Mark of the Beast jolted me at first, the feeling doesn't linger as it did weeks earlier, on the beach. Since then, I've gotten a thorough look behind the curtain of the Christian right's manipulation of working-class America and am left with a heady malaise that I'm not entirely sure what to do with.

We've been doing this interview for more than three hours now (along with four hours yesterday), and I can tell my dad is exhausted, both intellectually and emotionally. So, instead of confronting him with data-driven arguments against right-wing politics, I point out to him all the touchstones of my childhood, focusing on the warmest memories I have of him as a father.

"Remember when that was a video shop, and you let me rent my first R-rated movie?" I say, pointing to a tiny Dutch-style cottage. "You lived in a studio apartment in that red house, over there. All four of us, including Phin and Faith, slept together in that giant waterbed, left over from Sleepy Hollow, watching *Pet Sematary* on a six-inch TV screen. Later that night, I couldn't sleep, and you took me to Cash Wise at one a.m., telling me I could have whatever I wanted, and I got an entire apple pie."

Dad, though, has few memories of those years that aren't tainted by self-loathing.

While I loved lying in the grass at the park as a kid, he hated himself for not being able to afford a proper vacation. While I was thrilled by twenty-five-cent arcade games at the laundromat, he felt shame at being unable to afford to buy us a Nintendo.

I do recall his depression in those years—as well as my mother's. He didn't bear that weight alone. Keeping Dad's spirits up was a preoccupation of mine as far back as I can remember. And it continues to this day. Our father-and-son dynamic has always been problematic, but I'm glad we've grown into close friends, providing each other with the patience, acceptance, and compassion that only a community can provide.

Even if it's only made up of two people.

CHAPTER THIRTY-SEVEN

Reach Out and Touch Faith

I'm beginning to wonder what it is I'm looking for in these interviews.

If my aim is to prove my people have been manipulated by the Christian right, I must address their misconceptions about politics, class, and mental health. But what purpose would it serve for me to bully them over (what I perceive to be) their ignorance about these issues?

Also, I'm not sure if I'm really up for it myself.

I've tried my best to maintain a journalistic distance from all this despair, but it's been quite taxing, especially when I still have so many unhealed wounds from childhood, still open to infection. (Therapy is profoundly helpful, but the pain never fully disappears; therapy just turns down the volume.)

Interviewing Phin and Faith is particularly awkward, because I inherited the same dynamic with them that my mother had with her elder siblings. Namely, I hunger for their approval and attention to such a degree that a genuine connection is impossible. Every memory I have of them is some scrambled version of that evening in the corn-field, chasing after my big brother and sister, as desperate to find them as they were to get away from me.

But now circumstance requires me to be a probing journalist, not a clingy sycophant.

"I think the whole woke political agenda is a bunch of BS," Faith says as I nod along, thoughtfully. "Teachers telling children that they should use whatever bathroom they want to, or that they can be a unicorn instead of a horse or a donkey, or whatever. I mean, did *we* think about who we were attracted to in elementary school? No. We're causing more confusion in kids than we need to. Shoving all this moral, political crap down their throats is just wrong."

I want to interject and say that I *definitely* thought about who I was attracted to in elementary school, and could've used someone telling me I wasn't a demon-possessed pervert for these sensations in my body. I want to say that we had *plenty* of moral, political crap shoved down our throats as kids. I want to say that her mythologizing the 1990s as a more sensible era of childrearing is merely a perpetuation of the conservative impulse to view sociological issues through the lens of childhood sentimentality, just as our father did with the *Ozzie and Harriet* world of the 1950s, just as Jerry Falwell did with the Baptist revival of the early 1930s, or the Klan and Bob Jones, Sr., did with the "old-time religion" of the 1870s.

But instead, I just continue to nod.

I've been feeling guilty about putting the journalistic screws to my family, knowing that they didn't sign up for this. They're not politicians running for office, or musicians promoting an album. I've just shown up on everyone's doorstep, put a microphone in their faces, and demanded they account for things that happened forty years ago.

Also, the confidence I typically feel while conducting interviews has completely vanished. I'm unable to place my zeal for debate—inherited from my mother—at the forefront of my conscious mind. Instead, I feel the way I do when Caldonia visits me in dreams: terrified, desperate to act but unable to move or speak.

You should've known better than to think you're a real writer, she says in my mind, as if on cue. *Or that you're worth your family taking you seriously.*

When my interview with Faith fizzles to a close, I am very disappointed in myself.

I conceded to all of her arguments, offering up no rebuttals.

It took all of my energy just to maintain the façade of the Josiah she knows, terrified she'd get a glimpse of the real me. When I finally meet up with Thad in Clear Lake the next day, I feel raw and vulnerable, hungry for soothing, for authentic connection with my old friend, desperate to drop the hypervigilant maintenance of a specious personality.

Some kind of orientation, a sense of home.

I've had moments of that with my dad, but we've mostly spent this trip talking about our childhood traumas (in my case, much of it inflicted by him), and the experience has left me rattled. But Thad has always been my refuge of authenticity when visiting Iowa. After spending too much time with my family, I'd often meet up with him at a local bar, and an audible sigh of relief would pass through me when I first saw his face.

I'm currently sitting on a park bench in the middle of the Fourth of July carnival in Clear Lake—Guns N' Roses' "Welcome to the Jungle" blasting out of the nearby Gravitron, the smell of funnel cakes and diesel generators in the air—waiting for Thad, who is almost an hour late. Searching for the comfort of his face in this crowd reminds me of a cold night in the parking lot of a cheap motel in Michigan, twenty years earlier.

It was in the middle of our puppy-mill odyssey, both of us vomiting and running high fevers. Though we were supposed to keep driving 24/7, we had checked in to the roadside motel out of desperation, spending what little money we were making on the gig.

At some point in the night, I awoke to find myself in the parking lot, in my underwear, in January. I had sleepwalked out of the hotel room and was now staring back at an endless row of doors, having no idea which was ours.

Helpless, I randomly knocked on the first door I walked up to.

Shockingly, Thad answered.

I let out a shriek of relief, grabbed him tight and wept into his neck. It was more than escaping humiliation or hypothermia; it was a rush of oxytocin at being reunited with the face I'd most associated with the word "home."

My memories with Thad are the greatest hits of my youth. Driving down gravel roads in the middle of the night, smoking weed and Pall Malls, choking down Mad Dog 20/20 while blasting Radiohead, Tool, or The Smashing Pumpkins at full volume, feeling spooky yet sublime, with nowhere to go, nowhere to be, just lost in the headlights, chasing along the cornfields.

I'm looking forward to spending time with an ally, someone who knows me, knows my worldview, my writing, and is on board with the premise of my book without my even having to articulate it.

"Hey, loser," he says, startling me from behind.

Thad has lost a lot of his boyish handsomeness; his red hair has receded, and deep lines around his mouth and forehead (along with a few ill-gotten scars) give his face a kind of world-weary, Clint Eastwood effect. He's gained some weight, but that's mostly from his year of sobriety from meth and opioids (while still enjoying a few other, softer substances). For the most part, he still has that muscled, capable, farm-boy body he had when we were teenagers, partly because he's spent the last few years working the fields around North Iowa.

He's late meeting me after spending the day spraying pig shit—collected from a local industrial hog lot—onto fields of corn and soybeans. This is one of a handful of industrial farm practices poisoning the water, spreading E. coli to the crops, and contributing to Iowa's second-highest cancer rate in the nation. Thad worries about the impact this work could be having on his health and that of his community, but it's one of the few jobs available to him.

Until recently, every dime he made in those fields went straight into his arm. When I saw him two summers ago, he looked as pale and gaunt as Christian Bale in *The Machinist*.

"You wanna rent some bicycles and ride around the lake?" he asks.

"Fuck yeah," I say.

Like me, Thad has found intense exercise to be a less problematic alternative to hard drugs. This was the case with many former addicts I interviewed for *Runner's High,* people who used to binge-drink, inject hard drugs, and get arrested in bar fights, but then discovered that ultramarathon running was just as insane a life—and, at times, just as hard on your body—yet didn't result in as much emotional instability or mornings in jail with a hangover.

"I did the math recently," Thad tells me as we escape the din of the carnival and hop on our rented bikes, "and I've amassed over ten thousand hours of withdrawal time. Ten thousand hours of moaning and grinding my forehead into the carpet, sick all day and night, no sleeping or eating, constant vomiting, diarrhea, and wishing I was dead."

Though it's terribly selfish, in this moment I can't help but think: *Why didn't that happen to me? Would that have been my fate if I'd stayed here?*

I had really wanted Thad to come with me when I moved to Denver. I wanted us to start a band, or a radio show, like we'd always talked about as kids. I wanted to take him out dancing at my favorite clubs, introduce him to other musicians, watch him blossom into the artist he was meant to be. I feel guilty whenever talking to him about my writing career, like I'm rubbing his nose in it. He's still the shy boy who wanted me to teach him to dance, wanted to make the world laugh or be in awe of his songwriting, but was too deeply smothered in shame to perform his songs anywhere beyond a handful of shows in Mason City bars.

Thad is a master oral storyteller, able to bring an audience to tears of laughter, assuming it's an audience of friends he's comfortable with and he's chemically stimulated. But when I try now to get him to recount a few of the classic gonzo tales of his past, he only looks at the floor and mumbles, full of regret and self-loathing.

"I've done a lot of things I have a hard time forgiving myself for," he says, his voice carrying a tremendous weight of sadness. This is something new: we'd always viewed our hedonistic exploits, no matter how debauched, illegal, or questionable, as charming tributes to our liberation from evangelical Christianity. As far as I'm aware, we never hurt anyone, so I don't know of anything we need to feel guilty about.

I've often viewed Thad as my Neal Cassady, the real-life inspiration behind *On the Road*'s Dean Moriarty, and Randle P. McMurphy in *One Flew Over the Cuckoo's Nest*, characters full of zest and humor, sucking the marrow out of life. I'm good at writing stories, but Thad *is* a story, a walking, breathing poem.

I ask him what he's done to warrant all this sorrow, but he doesn't want to say on the record.

Thad has made a handful of attempts to move out of his parents' home, relocating to nearby cities like Minneapolis or Des Moines, laboring to get a band together and join a creative scene of ambitious people. But he's always returned after a year or two, following some epic bout of self-destruction. For the last few years, he's been living in a small room in his dad's machine shed, several miles north of Mason City; the surrounding farmland and livestock were long ago sold off to a faceless corporation.

Whenever I turn my recorder off, he's his old self again, the misanthropic prankster, the hyper boy interrupting himself with one story after another about Christian school, sexual misadventures, and our drug-fueled fantasy life before everything went sour. When I turn it back on, he returns to the monologue of self-loathing, full of regrets and perceived failures, as if he didn't believe he was worthy of feeling good about himself.

At one point, we pull our bikes off the road and grab some drinks at a lakeside diner.

Even though our interview hasn't gone the way I'd hoped, I'm still comforted by being with my old friend. The self-conscious anxiety I had around my sister—or when I was sitting in a diner watching Fox News, with Kevin Sorbo ranting about how effeminate men are a threat to society—is slowly fading away, like coming into a warm house after hours in the cold.

I can feel my mannerisms softening again, my voice returning to its normal (higher) register, my wrists going limp and my speech dramatic.

Then Thad looks at me sideways, with a bit of suspicion and possibly a hint of embarrassment. It's a look I recall him giving me when I first started at Forest City Christian School, when my bullies suddenly turned their eyes on him.

"Could you have found any shorter shorts, Josiah?" he says with a laugh, pointing at my retro basketball shorts. I chuckle along with him, though I do pull the shorts' legs down a touch, suddenly aware of my exposed scars.

For the first time, I notice his grubby farm-boy clothes, steel-toed boots, buzz cut, and good-ole-boy slouch in his chair as he drinks a light beer—contrasted with my vintage booty-shorts, fishnet tank top, and Timothée Chalamet curls, sipping on a Cape Cod. For a brief moment, I feel the conflicting impulses both to protect him and to be protected *from him.*

The sun has set, and a thunderstorm is brewing on the other side of the lake. Lightning flashes, briefly illuminating the air.

"Fuck you!" I say, playfully kicking him under the table. "I don't know what happened in the mid-nineties to make men so scared of their own thighs, but for most of the twentieth century this was what men's shorts looked like, you philistine."

"Doesn't bother me, so long as you're not into the whole pronoun thing."

At first I'm confused, wondering if he's suddenly making an argument about grammar. "I'm sorry, what pronoun thing?" I ask.

You know what he's talking about, Caldonia says, *and you're gaslighting him. You're just a big-city journalist trying to make your only friend look stupid.*

"Are you referring to transgender people?" I ask.

"Yeah," he says, sitting up in his seat. "I don't hate them, I'm just not down with that, especially when it's used to confuse children."

I want to ask what he means by "that"—trans people in general? Or just preferred pronouns? I'm a bit taken aback; I've never heard Thad talk about any culture-war issues before, yet he seemed to bring it up out of nowhere, shoehorning the subject into our conversation when we'd otherwise be talking about gobbling ecstasy at raves in 2002 or fighting over the last box of Tuna Helper when we were broke.

I'd made the classic mistake of the modern era: assuming that because you share affection with someone, you also share the same worldview. Before I can ask a follow-up question, he volunteers more opinions about gender expression, critical race theory, and why he refused the COVID vaccine, sounding like the right-wing pundits we used to laugh at. Gently, I ask him about his "media diet," wondering where all of this is coming from.

"I don't watch the news anymore," he says. "Common sense is where I get my news."

I roll my eyes at this. It's the same response I get from every conservative I speak with (despite their eventual admission that they watch conservative programs on One America News, Newsmax, or Fox, or read right-wing blogs like *The Epoch Times* or the *Washington Examiner*). I suspect they feel condescended to when I ask about their media diet, as though I'm dismissing their views as propaganda, accusing them of being brainwashed and ignorant.

In some cases, I suppose I am.

What else is left to conclude when someone's opinions on matters they'd previously shown no interest in are in lockstep with that week's Sean Hannity monologue? Most of the time, though, I try to keep a poker face in these moments, not wanting to rouse defensiveness or a sense of martyrdom in the people I'm interviewing. In this moment, however, while I'm sitting here with my oldest friend in the whole world, my guard is down, and I give Thad my unfiltered reaction, unleashing a geyser of repressed frustration I've amassed over my last two weeks in Iowa.

"Oh," I say, "I suppose it must be a coincidence that you happen to unload a screed of anti-trans rhetoric, provoked only by the length of my shorts, at the same time the Iowa State Legislature is considering a bill to ban gender-affirming care for minors? You just happen to parrot all the conservative talking points on this issue—what?—through the ether?"

"Must be," he says, repeating that he never engages with any news source. His voice is beginning to tremble, as my own blood pressure climbs. "Just because I don't agree with trans people doesn't mean I don't love them, as a Christian. I'm just tired of being called a bigot for not being down with all this."

"Wait, when did you start identifying as a Christian again?"

Before I realize it, I find myself uncrossing my legs and broadening my shoulders.

"I've always been this way," he says. "It's you that moved away and changed. Isn't it interesting how people who move to big cities always become gay and trans?"

"That's a ridiculously hyperbolic statement," I say, hearing my voice get loud and angry, my muscles twitching. "It's true that a lot of queer people move out of places like North Iowa, but that's because they *don't feel safe* here!"

I stop for a moment, setting aside the news that he's now a Christian (who, I also learn, plays guitar in the worship band of his parents' church). Though he was never an angry atheist like me, I do recall that Thad identified as agnostic for most of our adult years. But in this moment, I set aside my need for a comrade in rebellion and think about the other thing he said: "I'm tired of being called a bigot."

I know that Thad retreated from social media a while back (a few months after this conversation, I'll hear from many people who unfriended him on Facebook because of his political statements about trans people), and is not in touch with any of our old friends from our twenties—the ones who are still alive.

I think of my dad, ostracized from the church he helped build.

I think of the books *Deaths of Despair* and *Chasing the Scream,* and how being accepted by a community is the antidote to self-destruction.

Thad's isolation on his parents' farm has made him bitter and arrogant, yet terribly thin-skinned. I later learn that he does indeed have a media diet—it just consists of podcasts and YouTube videos from conservatives like Jordan Peterson and Ben Shapiro—and that he's been regularly consuming psychedelic mushrooms and kratom. I can picture him in that crawl space of his dad's machine shed, tripping day and night, falling down rabbit holes of conspiracy theories about COVID and "the trans agenda."

Suddenly I could picture Thad in 1925, warned by the KKK about the threat Black men posed to white women. Or as a young hippie in the Jesus Movement, flattered into thinking he was part of the "chosen generation" that would see the end of the world. They felt rejected by society and went conservative as a rebellion against the progressive establishment of the Christian left, just as many disaffected young white men today buy into the narrative that going MAGA is a punk-rock move.

In the early days of Nazi recruitment, Hitler never bothered soliciting the decadent intellectuals in Berlin, who were preoccupied with a renaissance of Expressionist filmmakers, cross-dressers performing at the cabarets, or those at the Institute for Sexology arguing for acceptance of queers in society. Hitler's goons went to the countryside where poor, young farmers and laborers felt left behind, both cultur-ally, in this sexual revolution of the 1920s, and economically, given the high inflation raising grocery prices.

After several years of covering mass shootings, I found that the culprit was almost always a straight white male, isolated, bitter, and usually celibate, consuming hours of conservative blogs and YouTube conspiracy-theory videos day after day.

As a working-class high school dropout, raised in evangelical schools and churches in rural Iowa, and a onetime member of the Young Republicans, I really should've suffered the same fate. But for some reason, I didn't. Perhaps, as desperate as I was to find a home with any group that would accept me, the right-wingers always knew I wasn't one of them. At one time I thought of Thad as my home, because we were the tender misfits who listened to Bright Eyes and got nervous when our crushes walked into the room. But now he's quoting Elon Musk and I don't know how to respond.

Sure, I could debate him, pointing out that trans people have always existed in nature and throughout human history (the Talmud recog-nizes multiple genders, as do many Native American tribes), and that gender tropes such as pink for girls and blue for boys are relatively new marketing gimmicks of suburban capitalism.

And I could show him the Xeroxed news clippings I have about the Mason City cross-dresser Miss Tillie Yensen, who in 1938 was championed by her community, attending parties and civic functions, photographed for the newspaper alongside business leaders and poli-ticians. I want to point out that his favorite movie, *The Matrix*, was written and directed by two transgender sisters aiming to create an allegory for the trans experience.

I want to rant about the variety of animals in nature that change their gender, convincing him that the conventional hetero binary we've been prescribed by our conservative Christian culture is as ridiculous and primitive as the belief that the sun revolves around the Earth. But I can see that this will only be taken as an attack, a condescension from the liberal city boy to the supposedly ignorant farm boy, yet another accusation of bigotry, contributing to the cycle of shame and rebellion animating our political times. (And part of me is afraid he's gone down some "flat Earth" rabbit hole on YouTube and may believe the sun really *does* revolve around the Earth.)

Ultimately, though, what hurts me the most is not that Thad holds these views disparaging queers and journalists, but that he seems perplexed by why I'd find them objectionable. And then I realize that I've never been terribly vocal, or even articulate, about my own sexuality, particularly when in Iowa.

I can't even say I've ever really landed on a satisfying label for these things, myself.

When I first arrived in Denver, and later San Francisco, I struggled to find my place in gay bars and clubs. When I was absorbing anti-gay propaganda at the Christian schools and youth groups, I was secretly drawn to the glitter freaks on parade floats we saw in videos warning us about "THE GAY AGENDA!"

I watched news reports about the homoerotic photography of Robert Mapplethorpe—the fisting, sadomasochism, and latex bodysuits that led the evangelical Senator Jesse Helms to try to destroy the National Endowment for the Arts[*]—and assumed that was what awaited me beyond the gates of Iowa.

But when I finally encountered men at gay clubs, most of them looked like the Abercrombie & Fitch bullies who had beaten me up in high school. There were plenty of effeminate men that I was attracted to, but most of them only wanted to hook up with muscle-bound jocks, not other twinks like me.

Obviously, there were exceptions to this, and I've enjoyed the company of enough gay men and trans women to know I check some kind of queer box. But at the same time, it's mostly been straight women with a David Bowie fetish who've been drawn to me, and I've remained insecure enough to engage only with those who make the first move.

Surely, though, Thad has always known I'm a bit . . . different.

I suppose I could identify as "gender-nonconforming" and "pansexual," but these somewhat esoteric terms feel aggressive in the context

---

[*] Helms was unsuccessful at this, but his efforts eventually came to fruition under the first presidency of Donald Trump, who severely defunded the program.

of my conversation with Thad. Perhaps they shouldn't, and I should feel proud of who I am and what I want. There is still a little boy within me who is seriously pissed off at every conservative in Iowa for making me feel like I had to be an inauthentic version of myself in order to be accepted.

And I'm starting to recognize a similar feeling in Thad, this time directed toward me. What he needs most is a community that makes him feel good about himself. But it's difficult to feel good about who you are when your childhood best friend comes back to town, puts a microphone in your face, and more or less asks: *So, how is it that you managed to waste your entire life shooting up heroin?*

I suppose he's found acceptance in the Christian right, as tragic as that seems to me.

Like all of us, deep down, Thad doesn't want to be left behind.

"What's the most embarrassing thing you're going to say about me in your book?" he asks, after a long moment of silence.

"I don't know how to even answer that," I say. "You're certainly welcome to take a look at it before anything is published, if you want."*

(During many attempts, Thad will consistently reject this offer.)

We are able to be civil long enough for me to agree not to divulge a number of details about Thad in this book, which is seriously disappointing, because many of these are stories I was eager to, with his help, bring to life in vivid detail, our teenage ambitions coming full-circle.

But then, on the bike ride back to the carnival, I begin to wonder: Am I the Music Man in this situation? Am I exploiting the pain of my people just to advance my career?

Am I so eager to view their story as tragic, and mine as heroic, that I'll manufacture a sociopolitical narrative to reflect that retroactively?

Perhaps.

But when I see Thad carrying himself with the same defeated, self-conscious posture as so many working-class Iowans, unable to muster an ounce of the creative passion we were bursting with as kids, it

---

* Some of this exchange happened after our interview, via text, though I have included it here for storytelling purposes.

becomes apparent to me why I never sank into the Swamps of Sadness that seem to have consumed him.

I certainly felt pulled into that muck before I escaped Iowa at the age of twenty-two. Since then, however, I've diligently worked to preserve the dreams Thad and I had cultivated so many years ago. More than just creating, it was the *caring,* the excitement for ideas, aesthetics, and a sense of awe, that I didn't want to lose. Choosing tenderness over aggression, curiosity over convention, was what kept me from sliding down the dark tunnel of a syringe. It was less geography than a mindset that I escaped.

But where does that leave me with Thad?

I was so desperate to see him today because I was searching for a home, a place of grounding, somewhere I could be authentic and understood, particularly for my effeminate manner and (admittedly) pretentious speech. I don't need him to agree with me, just to *see me.* But perhaps that's not possible in the politically charged times we live in.

Perhaps, like in the Christian novel *This Present Darkness,* Thad, Faith, and others here believe that I have been corrupted by the forces of evil, as evidenced by my "woke" politics, "gay agenda," and efforts to subvert God's master plan for humanity, helping to usher in a revolution of Satan-worshipping vegans coming for your guns, oversized trucks, and MAGA flags. Maybe they see me as one of those characters from the Hell Houses, the passion plays, and the *Left Behind* films, who had the chance to be saved but succumbed to the deception of Satan's tricks, lured by science, curiosity, and logic.

We have an awkward and silent bike ride back to my car.

Afterward, Thad texts me that my "soul is broken."

As of this writing, we have not spoken since.

CHAPTER THIRTY-EIGHT

Mama, I'm Coming Home

I once interviewed the celebrity dog trainer Cesar Millan, "the Dog Whisperer," and afterward felt like shit about myself.

After discussing canine psychology and why buying a puppy is usually a bad idea, I took the chance to ask a question about my dog, Iggy. He was getting into fights whenever I took him to the dog park, yet when my roommates drove him there without me, he was perfectly happy and playful with the other dogs.

Millan's response, though practical, flooded me with shame.

"The fact that your dog does not have this reaction when you aren't with him indicates that something in your state of mind is setting him off," he told me. "Because of his behavior in the past, you're probably worried that the same thing is going to happen again, and your worry travels to your dog, saying, *Something here is dangerous. Prepare to defend.*"

He was right. I was often an anxious wreck when taking Iggy to the park, turning into a hyperventilating helicopter mom. My mental-health issues were preventing him from enjoying his life.

I'm thinking of this while walking into my mother's home for my final interview. It's the same house she and my dad bought in 1979, the same house I spent so many sleepless nights in, guzzling coffee in front of the TV, convinced I was surrounded by demons.

When I give her a big hug—the six-pack I brought awkwardly bouncing against her back—I look around at the house, feeling overwhelmed with memories. Like Dad with his anger, Mom has worked hard to shed her reputation as a hoarder from years past. She's come a long way, and I am very proud of her, but I still see so many remnants of years past in every corner. Some of the memories are wonderful: Mom cleaning to Amy Grant records; wrestling with Dad on the brown shag carpet. Some not so much: the porch window I put my arm through; the word "Fag!" shouted at our house, punctuated by smashing eggs. For a moment, I get lost, staring at the door to the basement, just off the kitchen.

"Do you have any concerns about how you're portrayed in this book?" I ask my mom, as the two of us sit down at the kitchen table.

"A little. I have visions of *Mommie Dearest*," she says, as quick-witted as ever.

"No wire hangers!" I say, and we both laugh a bit.

Suddenly I am flooded with gratitude that the state of Colorado offered me a no-cost vasectomy so many years ago. It was bad enough having a dog take on my anxiety; I can't imagine how I'd handle passing all my neurosis on to a human child—especially if said child returned to my doorstep decades later, asking me to be interviewed for a book about how miserable they were as a kid.

Both Phin and Faith expressed their disapproval of my writing about our family history, mainly, I suspect, out of concern for our mother, whose emotional stability we've all worked very hard to protect throughout our lives.

But even though she's had her breakdowns, it would be tragic for me to paint my mother as fragile or helpless. The strength it took for her to pull herself out of a spiral of panic and self-loathing, to work two jobs while attending night school and raising three children, has been very inspiring to me. Our father once held it over her that he had twice the income she did without an education, but she is now the comfortably middle-class one, able to treat her grandchildren to all kinds of material wonders.

With this in mind, my journalistic autopilot kicks in, and I begin asking questions, starting with her childhood in the north end of Mason City, her academic life, her time as an exchange student in Argentina, the Jesus Movement, her marriage to Dad, and the experience of running the waterbed store. She's brave, funny, wise, and at times contrite, tackling stories that were once too overwhelming to even verbalize.

She tells me about the high inflation rate when she and Dad launched the waterbed store, so they had to get a business loan at 21-percent interest.

"Was that why you switched from volunteering for Carter's campaign in '76 to voting for Reagan in '80?" I ask, cracking my first beer of the night.

"Well, our economy was in a tailspin in 1980," she says, leaning back in her chair. "And Reagan seemed more rational, more supportive of small businesses, getting inflation under control."

I resist the urge to go on a long rant about voodoo economics and how the promises of wealth trickling down clearly didn't pan out, considering that a third of America is currently earning less than fifteen dollars an hour and we've got the highest income inequality since the Gilded Age. Because, though I disagree, I really enjoy hearing her perspective.

Living in downtown Denver, I'm surrounded by a diverse spectrum of liberals (from moderates to anarchists to libertarian Marxists), and so I rarely get the chance to chat face-to-face with a conservative who might offer thoughtful rebuttals to my progressive worldview. Far from a MAGA zealot, my mom is more of a classic Republican—a John Kasich, George Will conservative—with views far more nuanced and practical than the myopic rants of Sean Hannity or Jesse Watters.

When I mention all of the labor jobs that had their wages slashed during the big mergers of the Reagan era, she mentions how many of the businesses would've gone under if not for those mergers. When I refer to agriculture subsidies as corporate welfare, she goes into long detail about efforts to wean the ethanol industry off of subsidies and fully into the free market.

Neither of us convinces the other of much, but it's the best way I've discovered to bond with my mother. In these moments, I can see the zealous teenage captain of the debate team she once was, and how this thirst for knowledge and understanding was passed along to me. Like a judo fighter, she steps out of the way of my attacks, letting the silence hang after I'm done ranting, allowing me to trip over my excessive passion and realize I have not made a cogent argument, but five fragments of arguments.

When I try to get her to comment, on the record, about Donald Trump's revolution in her beloved Republican Party, she skirts the issue, using her time in Argentina as an allegory.

"People often ask me if January 6 was a coup, and I say that I saw a coup, up close, in 1976, I know what a coup looks like," she says, seeming to imply that January 6 was, indeed, an attempted coup, though I can't be sure, as she would rather not make any definitive political statements on the record. "I recall asking my Argentinian mother about when the next election would be held, and she said, 'Oh, we had to get rid of that, for our own safety.' I remember tanks rolling down the street every night, or in parades—can you imagine?"

"Well, Trump wanted to parade tanks through our capital, so it's not too difficult to imagine."

Again, she doesn't say anything, just gives me a nod of recognition.

I feel like a son trying to get his dad to play a game of catch with him. I know how intelligent Mom is, how knowledgeable she is about world affairs and economics, but I'm frustrated at her maneuvering, her unwillingness to take a direct stand on contemporary issues while being interviewed for my book.

It's not that she's avoiding the questions, she's just profoundly careful, though she's still saying a great deal. When I ask her about immigration, she again pivots to Argentina, telling the story of how her first teacher introduced my sixteen-year-old mother to the class: "I am so sick of Americans: they're dumb, lazy, and entitled."

"I was so humiliated at being othered," she recalls, "and think about that feeling a lot. Everyone is someone else's 'other,' and othering people is a powerful, but manipulative, thing to do."

I decide to ask a more direct political question through a personal lens. "How did you feel being on welfare during the Reagan and Bush, Sr., years?"

"I felt a lot of shame," she recalls. "I told the woman at the food-assistance office, 'I only need a couple weeks' worth, just while my husband is in drug treatment.' She gave me an incredulous look and started with six months' worth of food stamps."

Years ago, I overheard my mom locked in a heated conversation with a group of local businessmen, and when one of them described welfare in America as infinitely abundant, accessible, and endless for America's poor, she was quick to correct the man: "Look, as someone who once depended on welfare to feed my family and keep our house warm, I can attest that what you're saying is not true."

It's a dizzying responsibility, interviewing my mom about those dark years, but it's also very illuminating for me to get her perspective on experiences I only saw from the vantage of a three-foot child.

"I had years of only dealing with what was in front of me," she says, her voice much quieter than when discussing politics. "Years of 'I just gotta get through today.' There are stretches of time that I really don't remember . . . I know I could have fed you better, I could've cleaned you better, I could've cleaned the house better. I was just hanging by my fingernails for years."

I see a heavy emotion twitching beneath her typical veneer of composure. In an attempt at compassion, I acknowledge how impossible a task she was presented with as a young mother.

"When I think about myself at the age of twenty, living in Des Moines," I say, "I couldn't hold down a job at the Gap, couldn't pay my rent despite having several roommates. But you were dealing with two failing businesses, raising two kids while pregnant with a third, and married to a cheating, verbally abusive husband with anger issues. I'm forty, and I *still* don't think I could handle all of that."

"I remember when you called me from Des Moines, asking me to help you pay your rent," she says. "Telling you no was one of the hardest things I've ever done, and I cried hard afterward, not sure if I was doing the right thing. But, looking back at myself, I think having a period of being absolutely desperate served me well. And I wanted all my children to go through a phase of desperation, because I think it was so good for me."

I know what she's saying, and on the surface I don't disagree.

I think having no safety net, no Plan B, virtually no financial security throughout my life, forced me to work harder than my colleagues in journalism who had parents supporting them throughout the bumpy phases of their careers. Fear of homelessness certainly kept my fingers typing. But, sitting here in my childhood home, a little tipsy, yet bolstered by this project, I can feel the bitterness returning, manifesting in a bit of partisan belligerence.

"I think too often that mindset of 'What doesn't kill you makes you stronger' is used by conservatives to justify cutting aid to the poor," I say, as I crack another beer. (I don't drink regularly anymore, and typically only nurse one or two beers in the course of a night, but tonight I find myself guzzling them down like Bukowski.) "Years ago, that argument was used to attack Social Security and Medicare; then it was food assistance, unions, or attempts to raise the minimum wage. Now it's rent control, student-loan forgiveness, or unemployment checks. All my life, I've heard conservative evangelicals like J. D. Vance rail about how these programs become a crutch that make people lazy and entitled, and how 'nobody wants to work anymore.' But so many Americans have fallen far below the stage of healthy desperation, and have landed in pure despair, which takes more than gumption to climb your way out of. It's an epidemic, a crisis. We're headed back to the fucking Gilded Age!"

I cut myself off from rambling any longer, and let my argument hang in the air.

"I see your point, up to a point," my mom says. "I think social programs are great when they give you a step up, but not indefinitely."

I'm starting to wonder if my mom really does enjoy clashing swords with me as much as I do. Perhaps too much has happened since her days on the debate team, too much pain and chaos, for her to have that playful charge for political discourse she once did, particularly when the issues come so close to home.

Listening to the recording of this interview later on, I will be embarrassed to hear a bit of slur in my voice from the alcohol, and a childish yearning for validation from my mother—as though I'm a ten-year-old with a skinned knee, rather than a forty-year-old playing journalist. As my empty beer bottles start to fill the kitchen table, a part of me feels like this was my one chance to really unpack all that's never been said. (Only someone like me would think that an interview for a book is the appropriate time to clean the closet of your childhood trauma.)

Until the TV show *Hoarders* introduced the disorder to the mainstream, none of us had a word for Mom's aversion to cleaning, or even throwing things away. Neither I nor my siblings have ever used that word in relation to our mom, because it feels aggressive—yet entirely accurate. Instead, I tiptoe around it, asking about "the state of the house, when I was a kid," and ask if she has any insight into "this issue," the one we all lived with for so long yet none of us ever spoke of.

Whether it was ADHD or OCD (both of which I've been diagnosed with, but Mom has never been tested for) or whatever, a traffic jam of conflicting thoughts in her brilliant mind prevented her from being able to maintain a house. And her anxiety disorder and depression (which she has been diagnosed with) can often make the most casual duties seem insurmountable. Often it was the same faculties that made her so brilliant in some tasks—academics, economics, politics—that would work against her when it came to other tasks, like cleaning and organizing a home.

"It's something I've struggled with for decades," she says of her hoarding behavior. "I felt very overwhelmed, very ashamed [when you were a boy]. I knew how it affected you, and I was mad at myself for that, and then I would panic and shut down, go to my safe place in bed."

I want to stop myself, knowing how humiliated she feels by this topic, how much it grates against the need to maintain an image of success in the world of evangelicalism. But I press on.

"So . . . you knew how much misery I was in as a kid?"

"Not exactly," she replies, shifting in her seat. "There was a moment about a year or so ago when I read something that said, 'Children can't tell you they're anxious, all they know how to say is "my stomach hurts,"' and that just broke me, thinking of how often you told me your stomach hurt. We had you checked out by doctors, but couldn't figure out what was wrong, why you were flunking school, why you were having so much trouble in life."

"I felt very scared and alone, and you became so distant toward me."

"Well, I was in a really awful place at that time," my mom says, defensively. "If I'd talked about any of it, I'd just fall down and cry, and that wouldn't have helped anyone."

"Well, how was I to know that?" I say, angry yet tearing up. "I think it might've helped me understand where you were at, that it wasn't *my fault* you were like that. It might've helped give me some emotional intelligence to see my mother as a vulnerable human being, just like me."

I can feel my pulse quickening as memories flood my brain. This is no longer a professional interview—just a child stomping his foot in a tantrum, but with fancier words.

I can tell my mom is growing tired, reaching her limit for heavy conversation. But the floodgates of my heart have been unleashed, and my compassion for her emotional needs is clouded by five beers and the surreal vibes of sitting in my childhood kitchen, with the whole house feeling like a living, breathing member of my family that we never talked about.

I think of what my therapist asked me, more than once: "Why do you work so hard to protect the people who failed to protect you when you were a child?"

So I lean forward and let 'er rip, listing all of the dark theology that crippled my mind and boiled my heart as a child: pervasive confusion around sin, the rapture, and salvation from Hell, the incessant conviction that I was doing it wrong and would be tortured throughout eternity for my lack of understanding. (But I hold back details about cutting myself in the basement as I awaited the Antichrist; that feels unnecessarily gruesome.)

I had relayed these same stories to my sister earlier in the week, and Faith, genuinely perplexed by it all, simply replied, "You were really overthinking all of this. It's not that complicated. Didn't you ever have an emotionally transformative experience when you were baptized in the Holy Spirit?"

"Sure," I said, "but I've also had the same sensation thousands of times at raves, concerts, plays, movie theaters, or running mountain trails under the influence of cannabis. That feeling at church camp, in retrospect, was just the fever of the music, the sentiment of Heaven, Hell, the love of Jesus, surrounded by kids weeping, shaking, speaking in tongues. Yeah, that'll certainly make you feel something when you're ten years old."

My older brother, Phin, though he's a staunch conservative who lives for talk-radio conspiracies, was never much seduced by evangelical theology or rituals; he mostly hung with the other rebels at the back of the church-camp sanctuary, while the rest of us were wailing and gnashing our teeth at the altar.

We've never been close, and my interview for this book was one of only a handful of sincere conversations we've ever had. He was genuinely taken aback to learn how constantly menaced I was by the supernatural pitfalls I believed surrounded me as a kid.

"Didn't your real-life experiences show you that life isn't that dramatic?" he asked, sounding truly curious.

"Life always felt pretty dramatic to me."

"But when I'd read about all these miracles happening in the Bible," Phin said, "I'd always ask: Why aren't they happening today?"

"I was told they *were* happening today; you just don't see them because you don't have enough faith."

"I was told that, too, and I called bullshit on that. Maybe part of it was that I was older and saw the world differently than you. Another part was probably that I just didn't have the anxiety that you did, and didn't take everything so seriously. I've never really worried much about the future."

I laughed with no hint of sarcasm, because I was genuinely amazed by this statement.

Phin's always been a fairly laid-back guy, but his casual admission that he'd never worried much about the future filled me with shock and envy. I doubted I'd gone a whole hour of my life without worrying about the future.

"Don't you remember Dad telling us about the coming rapture and Tribulation, and that we may have to hide from the Antichrist in the wilderness?" I asked him.

"Oh yeah," he said, throwing his head back with a smile, suddenly remembering. "We were gonna have to plant our own gardens and live on vegetables, and never get the Mark of the Beast. I remember that, for sure."

Seemingly lost in memories, Phin began to laugh; this irked me for a moment, but then I laughed, too, reflecting on how ridiculous it all was, how arbitrary. This was probably the first time we'd shared a laugh together in thirty years, and it meant the world to me, briefly filling me with the nourishing light of validation.

But that was yesterday.

Tonight, as I sit across from my mom in the house where I endured endless panic attacks, self-mutilation, and crippling loneliness throughout my formative years, neither of us is laughing. Mom is subtly wiping away tears, and I'm drunk and surly, thinking about all the anguish I endured over a mistranslation of the book of Revelation.

But it's unfair of me to dump all of this on my mom's lap now. Though she believed in the same rapture theology that I was taught, she was far, far down on the list of people who caused me to obsess over it. When I look back, I realize that she rarely mentioned Hell or the Tribulation to me during my childhood.

Talking about it today, she's confused as to why I would be so troubled by the mysteries of sin and the threat of eternal torture. "Didn't you assume that, even if you didn't understand everything about the Bible, you were a good person? That God loves you, that you're safe with your parents, and everything will be okay?" she asks.

"Honestly, I never felt any of that, even for a moment, in my entire life," I say.

I let that comment hang in the air, knowing it was true yet instantly regretting it.

"I don't have any memories of you paying me a single compliment, as a child or an adult," I say, aggressively. "Why is that?"

"And here I thought I was one of your biggest cheerleaders," she replies, her chin beginning to tremble. "I'm very sorry I didn't say the words you needed to hear, but I've always been very proud of you and have tried to show that the best I can."

"It's not just you," I say, leaning forward. "I can't remember anyone here ever paying me a compliment."

"Part of that's cultural. Our people, stoic Scandinavians, don't often gush over you until after you've left the room."

"No, that's not it!" I growl: "I've never really felt of value to anyone here, because I never started a family, never earned a lot of money and bought a house. Instead, I got a vasectomy and a literary agent. Maybe, if I'd stayed at the Winnebago factory and sprouted a brood of towheaded children, I'd be of value to my family, to my working-class brethren, and J. D. Vance would think I'm worthy to vote in America. Our capitalistic system rewards families with tax breaks and job opportunities. People view you as reliable, as *good*, as *winning at life*, if you're married with kids, especially in a house you own. But all my novels and sassy essays aren't worth *shit*. I ain't worth *shit*, to anyone, especially in Iowa. I am all *alone*, left behind."

I can hear a voice inside telling me to slow down, to notice how I'm the only one talking, and that I just slurred "capitalistic system" like a 1950s wino.

But I cannot stop myself.

I drain my sixth beer and ask, "Honestly, why didn't you just get an abortion when you found out you were pregnant with me?"

"No, never," she says, looking me in the eye.

"I just think life would've been better, for you and everyone else, if you'd gotten one."

"Oh, I don't think so," she says, meekly.

I'm searching for a compliment, a justification for my existence from the human that made me. But after a moment of silence, I let out a long sigh, realizing how I sound. I'm forty fucking years old, for Christ's sake. Why am I drunkenly yelling at my mother for not aborting me as a fetus, like we're in a scene from *Prozac Nation*?

What drives this relentless need in me for reassurance?

Why do I have so few memories of ever feeling truly safe, even when sleeping?

Was it Dad's screaming throughout Mom's pregnancy with me that pickled my little fetus in cortisol? Was it just my OCD—the intrusive thoughts and obsessive overanalyzing of every ethical conundrum—that explains Caldonia and my maddening search for salvation from Hell at the age of four? What is it that leaves me feeling so unworthy of love and acceptance, or even peace in my own mind?

"I guess what I'm looking to have validated by you," I say, sitting straight, attempting to sober up, "is the idea that I was in one place when I lived here, when I was a teenager flunking out of school, or working disposable jobs in my early twenties, and that I'm now somewhere else, somewhere new and better, and the acknowledgment that

I worked really hard to get here, that I'm not lazy and useless after all. I do have something to offer this world."

"I think you're in a vastly different place now," she says, wiping tears from her cheeks. "And I am very proud of you."

I smile, not feeling any better, but wanting her to feel better, just as I did when I was a kid.

I realize I'm just as vain as any prosperity-gospel evangelical, just as insecure, just as anxious to project an image of success—even if it's on my own terms—to my family, my hometown, my people.

Like the poor, working-class Americans who feel forgotten by the economy, feel bullied by popular culture (yet equally obsessed with its approval), I find myself drunkenly berating my mom over the politics of economic and social issues, when I really just want her to say I've done a good job at life.

Isn't that what we all want? Someone to convince us we're doing a good job?

Someone to validate all of our hard work and difficult decisions.

I don't think I'll ever truly be capable of feeling validated by anyone, at least when it comes to my labor or morality. For years, I've exhausted my therapist with the insistence that I'm bad for humanity, that I must be a sociopath or a narcissist and I'm terrified that I'm going to hurt someone. And, every time, she sighs, holds the bridge of her nose, and says, "Narcissists don't show up to therapy twice a week terrified that they're an awful person, worried they'll hurt someone."

After eighteen years of daily propaganda insisting that I am inherently corrupt, I am a sinner, I have an evil nature, interpreting the common sensations of puberty as demonic possession, viewing my body as an enemy to be conquered (with violence, if necessary), feeling ashamed of letting my schoolmates go to Hell because I was too embarrassed to witness to them, my brain has been conditioned to view Josiah Hesse as a weak, cowardly, untrustworthy waste of human flesh.

Never wanted in the first place.

Fantasizing of a 1982 abortion, but told to *Smile*, because *your mother chose life.*

After a long moment of silence, Mom asks to be excused to go to the bathroom.

I stand up to get myself a glass of water and stumble over my feet, suddenly realizing how drunk I am, and grateful my mom didn't see it. As I hear her walking up the creaky wooden stairs (still covered in the same brown shag carpet from my childhood) I walk over to the door leading to the basement staircase, allow my trembling hand to grab the brass doorknob, and pull it open. When I smell the air drifting from under the door, and feel the creak of the knob turning, it's suddenly 1997, and I can hear a tornado siren roaring in my mind.

Gooseflesh ripples across my arms.

Suddenly I am five, eight, ten years old, convinced everyone but me has been taken in the rapture, trying to muster the courage to redeem myself in that basement, knowing I deserve to be abandoned, I chose this with my sin, there's no time to change my mind, the Son has come, and I've been left behind.

I can hear the rumble of thunder in my mind, even though the air is still.

My therapist once asked me why, if I suffered from so much anxiety, nightmares, and paranoia as a child, I spent so much time watching horror movies and reading *Goosebumps* and Stephen King novels as a kid. "It's because they validated my worldview," I told her. "I had a horror movie playing in my own head twenty-four hours a day, so it was comforting to have my inner world reflected back at me in books and movies."

A musty, wet smell tickles my nose when the basement door opens, instantly drawing me back to the summer thunderstorms that would flood this basement. It's dark down there, but the kitchen light barely leaks down the steps and onto the stone floor. I can almost hear DC Talk's cover of "I Wish We'd All Been Ready" emanating from an old boom box with cracked speakers. I'm just about to flip the light switch on the staircase wall when I see two red eyes floating at the bottom of that dark stairwell.

It's like they're a thousand miles away, but still visible enough for me to see the flames dancing in the pupils. The voice doesn't come from the basement; it's deep inside my skull, each syllable tickling the hairs of my inner ears.

You belong down here, Caldonia whispers to me. *Degenerate, pervert. Lazy sinner. You've blasphemed the Holy Spirit, you've denied belief in God, and we're waiting for you down here. You can run as long as you want; death will find you, eternity will find you.*

My gut lurches, and I barely get to the kitchen trash can in time to vomit.

When Mom comes back downstairs, I'm already packing my stuff up. I thank her profusely for agreeing to participate in all this, but I'm gonna hop on my bike and head back to Dad's house (a phrase that makes me feel even more like a child).

I stumble down the front steps, and as I prepare to mount my bike (on the very same sidewalk where I learned to ride one), my eyes drift toward the dusty basement window of my mom's house. There I see those two red eyes looking back at me, flames dancing in their pupils, and I hear that awful, screechy laugh in my head.

I hop on my bike, slip on a pedal, and nearly collapse to the ground; then I right myself and am about to speed away when I stop and stare back at that dark face in the window.

What do you want? I ask Caldonia in my mind, feeling scared but determined.

To keep you safe, she replies.

CHAPTER THIRTY-NINE

Beach Buddhist Bingo

Until I really dug into it, I never realized that Buddhism is actually quite goth.

I don't identify as a Buddhist, and don't subscribe to the theology surrounding karma or reincarnation, but I was taken by the religion's embrace of pain and suffering when, during a particularly nasty breakup last year, a friend loaned me the book *When Things Fall Apart,* by the Buddhist nun Pema Chödrön. She has a warm, wise presence that's gently seductive, though her words can sometimes read like the lyrics to a Joy Division song.

"Instead of asking ourselves, 'How can I find security and happiness?,' " Chödrön writes, "we could ask ourselves, 'Can I touch the center of my pain? Can I sit with suffering, both yours and mine, without trying to make it go away? Can I stay present to the ache of loss or disgrace—disappointment in all its many forms—and let it open me?' "

Another Chödrön book, *The Places That Scare You,* is all about the inevitability of suffering, and how you must make suffering your closest friend if you're ever going to transcend the fear of it.

All of this comes to mind as I ride my bike around Clear Lake under a full moon, lazily drifting from one side of the street to the other. The Fourth of July carnival has just left town, and yet the spirit of roller coasters, flashing neon, and sizzling deep-fried Twinkies still hangs in the air, even though it's deathly silent.

I'm feeling better the farther I get from my mom's house, but I'm still pretty wired, and need to be alone. So I decide not to go just yet to my dad's place in Mason City (where I typically crash while I'm in town). Instead, I pop a cannabis edible into my mouth and ride out to City Beach.

I lean my bike against a tree, take off my shoes, and walk across the sand. In the quiet solitude, I can almost hear my nerves screaming with anxiety, like neglected babies. Taking a cue from Pema Chödrön, I lean into the discomfort, feeling an unpleasant warmth in my face and chest. I take a few slow breaths and start to feel better.

It's no fun, but it sure beats cutting my thighs in the basement.

Twenty-four hours ago, this beach—and the whole circumference of the lake—was swarming with families here to watch the fireworks show, evidenced by the glow sticks, empty sunscreen bottles, and a "Trump 2024" beach towel littered across the sand.

I'm sobering up a little, and begin reflecting on the last two weeks.

For most of the people I interviewed, it was their first time articulating stories and feelings about the past. Whether it was my parents and their divorce, or other exvangelicals sharing their dark church-camp horror stories, many had never brought their pain to the surface, and I found myself straddling the roles of journalist and therapist—which come with very different agendas.

I was naïve to think I could stir up these old ghosts without consequence.

As stoic Iowans, we bury our emotions quickly and deeply, and it's an ugly and unfamiliar feeling when someone insists on dragging them into the sunshine.

That's why it was such a shock to hear about my mother's breakdown. All I saw at the time was her detachment, the vacancy in her eyes, the coldness of her skin. I had no idea how much she was suffering, or why, or that it wasn't my fault, mine to fix.

That's because she never felt permitted to show it.

There are some wild discrepancies between Mom's and Dad's recollection of their marriage (particularly the end of it), but one detail they both share is a sense of feeling abandoned by the other, that their partner shut down and shut them out when they needed them most, when they were desperately trying to find a solution. Mom would stop talking for long stretches of time, and Dad refused to participate seriously in therapy or marriage counseling.

Each of them felt left behind by the other.

Neither of them had the ability to identify and articulate their feelings, let alone embrace and learn from them. They couldn't simply tell each other that they felt scared, confused, overwhelmed, and lost, and desperately needed someone to just listen for a bit, to validate their pain, to accept them with compassion and understanding. Instead, they both shut down and disappeared into their own minds, their TVs, and their bedrooms with locked doors.

Perhaps Mom was right, and there is something about our Scandinavian heritage that leaves us silent about our emotions (even the positive ones that would inspire a compliment), but surely some responsibility can be pointed toward the *Music Man* grifts of fear and shame perpetrated by the Christian right—all of prosperity gospel's magical thinking, telling us not to worry, because "God's got it!" and we should "laugh at" our bills; the demand that we *believe,* even when it doesn't make sense, protect that belief against our own logic, our own reality, and hide any emotional evidence to the contrary.

Become rich so others will see how God has blessed you.

Become rich so you can help fight the woke agenda.

Become rich so your family will respect you.

And if you're not there yet, just fake it till you make it. Don't be a victim. Don't look behind the curtain. Don't blame the rich, just work harder; the wealth will trickle down soon. After all, this is America, and if you don't become rich here, it's your own fault. So keep up appearances, live on credit, and let everyone see that you've got that joy-joy-joy-joy down in your heart.

Remain on fire for God, or else.

Revelation 3:16: "So then, because you are lukewarm, and neither cold nor hot, I will vomit you from My mouth."

Be afraid, but don't look like you're afraid.

Be afraid of baby-eating witches, of nuclear-armed communists, of demons in the supernatural realm, of eternal torture, of poverty, of falling behind, of being *left behind,* of letting everyone down; be afraid of your bodies, your natural sexual desires, of immigrants coming for your paycheck, of trans women hiding in your bathroom, of unions, of socialists, of being a "profane loafer," of being "on the welfare," of "libertine men and scarlet women" dancing to "shameless music" around pool tables on the north end of Mason City.

Trouble!

America needs the old-time religion!

All of this is still with me today, even though I haven't believed in the Christian God (or any other) in twenty years. It fundamentally shaped the architecture of my brain as a child, which is a very difficult thing to undo. I still have nightmares, still hear Caldonia's cruel voice in my head, and sometimes see her when I awake with sleep paralysis.

When the voice of Caldonia in the basement window of my mother's house told me she wanted to keep me safe, it was obviously a bit puzzling. This wretched figment of my imagination has caused me a colossal amount of terror throughout my life, so it's difficult for me to think of her as laboring on behalf of my safety.

But now, sitting on this beach, away from my childhood home, it starts to make sense.

One of the hallmarks of PTSD is an incessant revisiting of the traumatic episode in your mind and nervous system, hearing the breaking glass of a car crash every time you drive through an intersection, or experiencing the disorienting jolt of a punch to the face when someone approaches you too quickly. It's not a conscious desire to relive the pain, but a subconscious "safety check," demanding you stay hypervigilant so as to avoid ever being harmed again.

The voice—and, at times, apparition—of Caldonia was a manifestation of all the rhetoric the Christian right fed me as a child, and her incessant taunting about sin and how I was a wretched person was a survival mechanism I'd developed at an early age, attempting to warn me about the threat of eternal torture that awaited me if I didn't follow the rules.

And even though I no longer believe in any of it, my nervous system is still hard-wired around that religious trauma, even manifesting in secular ways, like the paranoid fear that I'm a narcissist or a sociopath.

I long for the day when I can handle life sober, when I can feel at peace with all sides of myself, when I can experience sexual energy without a tsunami of fear and self-loathing. When I can make major life decisions based on a carefully considered plan instead of emotional impulse. When I can be authentic and vulnerable, when I can trust.

For the first time, I feel that may be a possibility.

Conducting these interviews has provided me with an immense perspective on matters I'd previously only known through a child's eyes, and with that comes the first stirrings of catharsis. My therapist once said to me (after a discussion about growing up in a house filled with garbage), "Hoarding is about not wanting to let go of the past."

I don't want to hold on to the garbage of the past.

Standing on the lake's shore, I can still feel the warmth of the afternoon sun in the sand between my toes, even though it's well past midnight. The deathly quiet of the town is randomly punctuated by the sound of tiny waves lapping on the beach. I haven't seen a car around for a while and decide it would be a good idea for me to get naked.

I certainly streaked around this town plenty of times with Thad when we were kids (equal parts terrified, aroused, and confused, even though it was two a.m. and we never encountered another soul). Now that all the twenty-four-hour businesses have closed and its population has dwindled by two thousand people, Clear Lake is even more deserted at this hour than it was decades ago.

Brain drain.

I throw my clothes on the dry sand and stroll into the lake, naked as the day I was born.

Previously, I don't think I would have had the courage to go swimming in Clear Lake alone at night. Not only have I seen all the *Jaws* movies a thousand times, but the horror-novel series I wrote, *Carnality,* is largely based on my hometown, and some seriously spooky shit goes down at the bottom of this lake in those books.

Beyond the fiction, I have too many legitimately bad memories here. I can too easily recall being pushed into that dark-green water, feeling it grow darker and colder the farther I sank. But, taxing as it was, the interview with my mom—and the peek into the basement— have left me feeling empowered to lean into that which scares me.

Also, my edible is kicking in, and the water feels amazing.

The sand is soft, the water still warm from today's hot afternoon.

The sound of tiny waves lapping on the shore grows quieter as I wade into the dark lake. A cool breeze tickles my hair and chest, and I take a deep breath. Once I'm far enough out, I dive beneath the surface, then splash back out of the water with a gasp of joy. Though I'm certainly not a great swimmer, I have developed some skills since I was a kid. My arms and legs are strong now, and I tread water easily.

The full moon is reflecting off the lazy ripples of the lake's surface. Fireflies encircle me above the water, their rich yellow lights flashing on and off, lazily. I swim past the buoys, deep into the middle of the lake, to the same spot where I was pushed off a canoe for refusing to kiss another boy's penis.

Looking back at City Beach, the grand "Seawall" to the south of it (another one of FDR's New Deal projects), and the vast firmament of stars encasing us, I feel calm and safe enough to call this place my home, and perhaps even part of my identity.

Whether they welcome me or not, these are my people.

That doesn't mean I'm ready to re-enlist in the Christian faith like Thad, or buy a house in the suburbs like my siblings. The Dalai Lama once said, "There are many different religions and cultures in the world and each has developed to suit its own people. Because of that, I always recommend that it's best to keep the religion you were born into."

I could never imagine an evangelical preacher making that argument.

How does Mr. Lama ever expect to make any money with *that* angle?

Though this may change someday, at the moment my only associations with Christianity are fear, shame, and poverty—nothing I'd ever want to make a part of my identity. After the last few weeks of reflecting on my childhood, I can see that I didn't choose atheism out of a logical deduction of the facts (à la Richard Dawkins), but from a desperate yearning for God to *not be real,* because the Christian God of my youth scared the fuck out of me.

Ever since that first day in San Francisco, I've attempted to soothe my childhood religious trauma, essentially to parent myself, with the reassurance that none of it was real: Hell wasn't real, the spirit realm wasn't real, the vengeful God wasn't real, Caldonia wasn't real.

There were no monsters under my bed.

God is not real, and therefore cannot spew me from His mouth and into the mind-shattering tortures of Hell. I will never have to be on fire for God, in any way. The fear never leaves completely, however, and that's why I still can't sleep at night.

Thinking of the Dalai Lama's recommendation that I embrace the religion in which I was taught—and Pema Chödrön's instruction to lean into that which scares me—I lie back into the waters of Clear Lake, arms stretched out like a crucifix, and begin to sing:

Life was filled with guns and war,
And everyone got trampled on the floor.
I wish we'd all been ready.

I float effortlessly atop the water, now that I know not to panic and tense my muscles the way I did as a child. Looking up at the stars above me, I continue to sing in a barely audible whisper:

Children died, the days grew cold,
A piece of bread could buy a bag of gold.
I wish we'd all been ready.

I don't think anything defines my image of Christianity more clearly than this song. For better or worse, it's the anthem of 1990s evangelicalism (and the Jesus Movement of the 1970s).

I know a lot of exvangelicals who retained their Christian faith while adopting a more progressive worldview. There's a rich legacy of left-leaning Christians throughout history, and plenty of scripture—particularly the teachings of Jesus—that reinforce their perspective. But there are just as many to justify a brutal right-wing philosophy as well.

Having so many authors over such a long period of time, their writings mutating with each translation, and now with over three thousand versions in print, the Bible is remarkably versatile. It contains so many contradictions of morality, theology, and history that you can use it to justify literally any behavior: genocide, slavery, rape, murder. Take your pick.

As the Dern Foley character in Tom Robbins's *Villa Incognito* said, "There's not much behavior that can't be justified by one verse or another in [the Bible]. Ambiguities and contradictions, that's what biblical guidance is made of."

As an adult, I've resisted having any ideology, beliefs, or consistent worldview. After spending the first half of my life believing so fundamentally in an ultra-specific definition of reality (Heaven, Hell, God, Satan, eternity), only to have it slip through my fingers in the sands of logic, I've been reluctant to orient myself around any kind of essential truth, instead blanketing my mind in the opiate-like comfort of nihilism.

And for this reason, I've resisted ever being in a position of leadership.

Like Charles Barkley, I am not a role model.

I do not want to be a thought leader. I do not want to spearhead a revolution.

If sharing my story brings anyone some comfort, validation, or even empowerment, I think that's wonderful. But I don't want to become like Jim Bakker, hawking his survivalist buckets of Apocalypse chow on infomercials; or the prosperity televangelist Robert Tilton, promising that if you purchase one of his "prayer cloths," it will heal whatever ails you. I'm much more comfortable dealing in provocations than in resolutions, questions than answers.

But just because I no longer wish to evangelize doesn't mean I can't find beauty in the faith I was born into, and possibly even a loosely defined identity.

Within all the colonialism, genocide, slavery, criminalizing of other faiths, and the entire Spanish Inquisition, I have to admit that Christianity has also given the world some of its greatest treasures: Renaissance art, church architecture, Black gospel music (and, by extension, rock and roll), the novels of J. R. R. Tolkien and C. S. Lewis, the social gospel of defining your faith by caring for the poor, the abolition of slavery, the Civil Rights Act, Christian environmentalism, the music of U2 (don't judge), Belle and Sebastian, The Staple Singers, Little Richard, and Johnny Cash.

There is plenty in the Bible that I would happily adopt as part of my identity: pacifism, romance, gratitude, tolerance, forgiveness, collectivism, charity, meditation, fasting, and the obligation of always being a courteous host (which, fun fact, was the intended lesson of the Sodom and Gomorrah tale). There is even brilliant humor to be found in Christianity, such as Saint Augustine's classic line "Oh Lord, give me chastity, but do not give it yet."

But I am forced to acknowledge that none of these things can be found in the brand of Christianity I was raised in (white, evangelical, nationalist, Republican). There's no room for humor in authoritarianism. Have you ever seen Donald Trump emit a hearty belly laugh? This is why conservatives have never had a successful comedy program, and why the only musicians who turn Republican are creatively washed up (Meat Loaf, Kid Rock, Alice Cooper).

I wish my people could appeal to their better angels and embrace the peace, tolerance, and (oh, let's just say it) *socialism* present throughout the Bible, instead of the cold, authoritarian tenets of the Christian right, which wrangles desperate people into voting for a political party that has no interest in bettering their lives.

But, as Buddhism teaches, I must accept life as it is, not as I want it to be.

Though I cannot, at this time, embrace Christianity as part of my identity, I can place humble curiosity about it at the center of my being. And hope that one day I can view spirituality beyond the lens of fear and shame, and perhaps connect with something divine.

For the moment, I am not okay, and that is okay.

I can accept and love my family, even if I don't agree with them.

I can forgive all of them, even though I'm still in pain.

I can share my story, even if I don't have any answers to the questions it poses.

But do I still wish my mom had had an abortion?

I ask myself this question after swimming back to the shore and getting dressed. My clothes get wet and stuck to my body, but it's a warm summer night in Iowa, and I dry quickly as I ride my bike to the paved trail connecting Clear Lake and Mason City.

Cruising alongside the endless cornfields—moonlight shining on their perfectly symmetrical rows, creating the optical illusion of movement—feeling the humid air in my lungs, hearing the crickets singing in the fields, I feel connected to the history of this land, these people. My people. I can feel their stories in my bones. Their triumphs and failures, their love and their hate, their better angels and spiteful demons. I think I'm finally strong enough to hold all of this within me, and accept it all with compassion, patience, and gratitude. I think I'm finally ready to say I'm glad to be alive.

Acknowledgments

It's such a cliché to say "no book is written alone" in the acknowledgments section of your book, but sometimes clichés exist for a reason (which is, itself, another cliché). Though this tired chestnut is truer in the case of this book than in any other project I've undertaken, as it required more emotional and intellectual energy than I could ever muster on my own.

Without Jane Le's editorial guidance, morale boosts, and late nights chatting about classic rock and Tennessee Williams, I would've cracked up halfway through this thing.

And, of course, I'll always be grateful to my editor, Denise Oswald, for believing in this project when it was still in its infancy, and for exercising profound patience and determination through the several drafts it took to bring the story into focus.

Without my wonderfully tenacious agent, Laura Nolan, I wouldn't have the career (and well-negotiated contracts) that I currently enjoy. In addition to the endless nights drinking old-fashioneds and listening to me rant about the Klan 2.0 and the Scopes Trial, Stephanie Wolf was also gracious enough to lend me her charming cabin in Frisco, Colorado, for weeks at a time. Without that crackling fire, those gorgeous mountain views, and the excellent running trails, I don't know how I would've gotten through the last few drafts of this book.

And, similarly, I'm very grateful for the relentless encouragement from my old friend Dan Landes, who also lent me his Santa Fe ranch house (with the bitchin' sound system) for a few weeks when I first began writing this book.

My favorite exvangelical, Ryan Connell, made himself available at all hours for any random question I had about the theology of Christian rock or the symptoms of religious trauma syndrome. He was also a wonderful researcher and gave very helpful notes on several drafts of this book, as did Anders Bartleson, Amanda E. K., Jacob Thomas, Anna Montoya, Djuna Martinez, Jeremy Grace, Henry Hesse (a.k.a. my Dad), Jane Le, and Pantheon's wonderful assistant editors Shanna Milkey and Natalia Berry.

My early interviews with Mason City's premier historian, Terry Harrison, sparked an electrical storm of curiosity in me, inspiring the writing of this book's initial proposal. My subsequent interviews with Terry (which primarily centered around drinking Schlitz at the local Moose Lodge) helped fill in a lot of cracks in the historical chapters of this book, and the hours he devoted to combing through the Mason City Public Library archives with me was a dream for any journalist digging into the esoteric past. And on that note, I also want to give a shout-out to the many employees of the MC library, as well as the Clear Lake Public Library, for all their assistance tracking down random clippings on Clark Gable or Kathryn Kuhlman whenever another bolt of inquiry struck me.

Scott Carney, as always, offered a lot of professional and creative guidance throughout this project, and was always a sympathetic ear when I needed to gripe about the decline of journalism.

I was humbled by how available the members of my family made themselves for interviews and follow-up questions over the last few years. It wasn't easy, and you didn't have to do it, but I'm very glad you did.

Oscar Jiménez-Solomon and Bethany Moreton gave me a tremendous amount of facts and insights about income inequality's cultural and psychological impact on America. Don Hofstrand, George Cummins, and Kevin Mason offered a great deal of essential information about Iowa's agricultural history, as did Robert FitzPatrick about the predatory tactics multilevel marketing organizations use against working-class evangelicals.

Big thanks to my favorite socialist, Stephen Polk, for all the nights we closed down City, O' City with our heated debates about economics and academia, which inspired several sections of this book.

The *Globe Gazette*'s excellent reporting on the events of North Iowa—both in the present and over the last century—was endlessly helpful in the research done for this book. David Di Sabatino, Brad Onishi, and Marsha Stevens-Pino were all crucial to my reporting on the Jesus Movement. Bart Ehrman was gracious enough to review the Biblical history sections of this book, and Frances Fitzgerald, Leah Payne, and Darren

Dochuk offered a treasure trove of illuminating details about evangelical history in the twentieth century.

Thanks to Chris Huth for giving me a (profoundly detailed) breakdown of the science behind my inability to float as a child.

And thanks to the Economic Hardship Reporting Project, whose grants supporting my reporting on the Christian right helped keep this freelance writer from having to get a day job.

Goddamn, I'm lucky.

Notes

AUTHOR'S NOTE

x   "I attack ideas": Justice Antonin Scalia, "Justice Scalia on the Record," *60 Minutes,* CBS, April 27, 2008.

INTRODUCTION: Midwestern Gothic

3   "Tell all the Truth": Emily Dickinson, *The Poems of Emily Dickinson* (Cambridge, MA: Belknap Press of Harvard University Press, 1998).

8   poison our water: "How Animal Feeding Operations Can Affect Water During a Flood," CDC, Feb. 5, 2024, cdc.gov/agricultural-water/about/animal-feeding-operations-contaminated-water-flood.html.

8   Iowa's profoundly high cancer rate: Leo Horrigan et al., "How Sustainable Agriculture Can Address the Environmental and Human Health Harms of Industrial Agriculture," *Environmental Health Perspectives* 110, no. 5 (2002): 445–56.

8   second only to Kentucky's: Natalie Krebs, "Report Finds Iowa Has Fastest Growing Rate of New Cancer in U.S.," *Iowa Public Radio,* Feb. 20, 2024.

9   suicide rate in Iowa spiked 400 percent: "The Farm Crisis," narrated by Harry Smith, Iowa PBS, July 1, 2013.

11   socioeconomic issues can be resolved: J. D. Vance, *Hillbilly Elegy* (New York: Harper, 2016), 92–4.

12   the equivalent of over twenty dollars an hour: Binyamin Appelbaum, "This Senator Has Got the Math Wrong About a $15 Minimum Wage," *The New York Times,* Feb. 25, 2021.

12   Incomes for middle-to-low wage earners: Lawrence Mishel et al., "Wage Stagnation in Nine Charts," Economic Policy Institute, Jan. 6, 2015.

12   to abandon the Democratic Party: Vance, *Hillbilly Elegy,* 139.

15   held by 26 percent of the Republican Party: "The Persistence of QAnon in the Post-Trump Era: An Analysis of Who Believes the Conspiracies," Public Religion Research Institute, Feb. 24, 2022.

15 primary motivating force: Jude Joffe-Block, "Four Years After the Capitol Riot, Why QAnon Hasn't Gone Away," Morning Edition, Dec. 2024, npr.com.

17 William McCall Calhoun, Jr.: Andrew L. Seidel, "Attack on the Capitol," in *Christian Nationalism and the January 6, 2021, Insurrection,* Baptist Joint Committee for Religious Liberty and the Freedom From Religion Foundation, Feb. 9, 2022, 38.

17 "slight, if any, moral or social consciousness": Tim Elfrink, "He Wore a QAnon Shirt While Chasing Police on Jan. 6. Now He Says He Was Deceived by 'a Pack of Lies'," *The Washington Post,* June 8, 2021.

17 bans on abortion and on transgender health care: Jonathan Weisman, "Why Iowa Turned So Red When Nearby States Went Blue," *The New York Times,* Jan. 8, 2024.

18 public-education funding to private Christian schools: Samantha Hernandez, "Iowa Is Now Paying for More Than 27,000 Students to Attend Private Schools. Here's Why," *Des Moines Register,* Jan. 23, 2025.

18 Iowa voters have swung: Weisman, "Why Iowa Turned So Red."

18 one of the worst "brain drains" in the nation: Hannah Molayal, "The 'Exodus' of College Graduates Out of Iowa," *Iowa State Daily,* Sept. 11, 2023.

18 75 percent of rural homeowners: Weisman, "Why Iowa Turned So Red."

18 "They're sitting with your children in schools": "Former President Trump Holds Rally in Mason City, Iowa," C-SPAN, Jan. 5, 2024.

18 "Iowa way of life is under siege": Jared McNett, " 'Iowa Way of Life Is Under Siege' Trump Warns in Sioux City Rally," *Sioux City Journal,* Nov. 4, 2022.

23 Ayn Rand filed for Social Security: Scott McConnell, *100 Voices: An Oral History of Ayn Rand* (New York: New American Library, 2010), 520–1.

CHAPTER ONE: Turn and Face the Strange

27 evangelists like Billy Sunday and Bob Jones, Sr.: Randy Moore, "Racism and the Public's Perception of Evolution," *Reports of the National Center for Science Education* 22, no. 3 (May–June 2002).

36 more than two million people would claim: Bill Sherman, "Famed Preacher Kathryn Kuhlman Died Here 40 Years Ago," *Tulsa World,* Feb. 20, 2016.

36 only to have her spine collapse the next day: James Randi, *The Faith Healers* (New York: Prometheus Books, 1989), 228.

36 rented hundreds of wheelchairs: Don Stewart, *Only Believe: Eye Witness Account of the Great Healing* (Shippensburg, PA: Destiny Image, 1999), 115, 130.

CHAPTER TWO: Unfortunate Son

42 "What is wrong with this world?": Quoted in Christopher D. Cantwell, "Billy Graham on the Communist Threat," YouTube, Oct. 23, 2012, https://www.youtube.com/watch?v=-SpyppSVrmA.

42 "Well, the Bible says": Cantwell, "Billy Graham."

45 "God hates sin": Billy Graham, "God Hates Sin," for Hour of Decision, Billy Graham Evangelistic Association, 1957.

46 "puff Graham": Ben Bagdikian, *The Media Monopoly* (Boston: Beacon Press, 2000), 39.

46 Pew and Bell despised FDR: Darren E. Grem, "*Christianity Today,* J. Howard Pew, and the Business of Conservative Evangelicalism," *Enterprise & Society* 15, no. 2 (June 2014): 337–79.

46 National Association of Evangelicals was formed: Grem, "*Christianity Today,*" 347.

47 "battle is between communism and Christianity": "Soul of a Nation," episode 5, *God in America,* PBS, Oct. 13, 2010.

47 from a record low of 49 percent: "Soul of a Nation," episode 5.

47 "When communism conquers a nation": "Soul of a Nation," episode 5.

CHAPTER THREE: **Get Your Jesus Freak On**

56 "get big or get out": Michael Carlson, "Obituary: Earl Butz," *The Guardian,* Feb. 4, 2008.

59 "The most important thing in my life": Jimmy Carter, "Interview with 'Leaders of National Religious Broadcasters' and 'World Religious News,'" interview by Jimmy Waters et al., The American Presidency Project, Oct. 9, 1976.

62 Frisbee was a teenage runaway: David Di Sabatino, director and producer, *Frisbee: The Life and Death of a Hippie Preacher,* documentary, 2005.

62 vision of himself leading thousands of hippies: David W. Stowe, *No Sympathy for the Devil: Christian Pop Music and the Transformation of American Evangelicalism* (Chapel Hill: University of North Carolina Press, 2011), 23–9.

63 would die of AIDS in 1993: Greg Laurie and Ellen Vaughn, *Lost Boy: My Story* (Delight, AR: Gospel Light, 2008), 81–3, 85–9, 106.

CHAPTER FOUR: **Revelation Romance**

66 bestselling nonfiction book of the 1970s: David Stout, "Hal Lindsey, Author of 'The Late Great Planet Earth,' Dies at 95," *The New York Times,* Dec. 2, 2024.

67 disagreed with Lindsey: Chuck Smith, *End Times: A Report on Future Survival* (Costa Mesa, CA: Maranatha House, 1978), 35–6.

73 "Are you ready for Armageddon?": Jeffrey Lamp, "The Hal Lindsey Effect: Bob Dylan's Christian Eschatology," *Dylan Review* 3, no. 1 (2021).

CHAPTER FIVE: **The Camel and the Needle's Eye**

76 "The Jesus Movement revival was over": Mark Allen Powell, *Encyclopedia of Contemporary Christian Music* (Peabody, MA: Hendrickson Publishers, 2002), 10.

77 "civil wrongs": Max Blumenthal, "Agent of Intolerance," *The Nation,* May 28, 2007.

77 "preachers are not called to be politicians": Michael Duffy, "Jerry Falwell, Political Innovator," *Time*, May 15, 2007.

77 "a terrible damn problem": John Dean, *Conservatives Without Conscience* (New York: Viking Press, 2006).

79 *Christianity Today* conducted a symposium: "Evangelical Scholars Endorse Birth Control," *Christianity Today*, Sept. 27, 1968, 33.

79 "physical health of the mother": "Resolution on Abortion," Southern Baptist Convention, June 1, 1971.

79 "best for the mother and for the future": David Roach, "How Southern Baptists Became Pro-Life," *Baptist Press*, Jan. 16, 2015.

79 *Newsweek* called 1976: Kenneth Woodward, "Born Again! The Evangelicals," *Newsweek*, Oct. 25, 1976.

80 turned the tide of the election: Douglas E. Kneeland, "Clark Defeat in Iowa Laid to Abortion Issue," *The New York Times*, Nov. 13, 1978.

81 "soup kitchen of the welfare state": Ronald Reagan, "A Time for Choosing," speech, Ronald Reagan Presidential Library, Oct. 27, 1964.

83 13.5 percent by 1980: Federal Reserve Bank of Minneapolis, "Consumer Price Index 1913–," https://www.minneapolisfed.org/about-us/monetary-policy/inflation-calculator/consumer-price-index-1913-.

83 echoed by historian Fareed Zakaria: Fareed Zakaria, "Fareed's Take: Politics is Causing Inflation," CNN, Jan. 16, 2022.

85 "many of the [Bible's] prophecies": John Herbers, "Religious Leaders Tell Of Worry On Armageddon View Ascribed To Reagan," *The New York Times*, Oct. 21, 1984.

CHAPTER SIX: **Blood on the Scarecrow**

90 went from 6.8 million: "The Farm Crisis," Iowa PBS.

91 cancer rates in Iowa: Leo Horrigan, et al., "Sustainable Agriculture," 445–56.

91 Suicide rates in Iowa spiked 400 percent: "The Farm Crisis," Iowa PBS.

92 2 percent of farmers joined these efforts: "The Farm Crisis," Iowa PBS.

99 brain scans of Christians: Benedict Carey, "A Neuroscientific Look at Speaking in Tongues," *The New York Times*, Nov. 7, 2006.

CHAPTER EIGHT: **Prophets of Profit**

102 "spirit with which you give": Oral Roberts, *The Miracle of Seed-Faith* (Tulsa: Oral Roberts Evangelistic Association, 1982), 121.

103 American evangelists touring developing nations: Philip Jenkins, *The Next Christendom: The Coming of Global Christianity* (Oxford, UK, and New York: Oxford University Press, 2011), 99.

108 A 2011 Gallup poll: Alyssa Davis, "With Poverty Comes Depression, More Than Other Illnesses," Gallup, Oct. 2012.

109 living below the poverty line: Anandi Mani, et al., "Poverty Impedes Cognitive Function," *Science* 341, no. 6149 (Aug. 2013): 976–80.

109 A study from Emory University: John A. Kaufman et al., "Effects of Increased Minimum Wages by Unemployment Rate on Suicide in the USA," *Journal of Epidemiology and Community Health* 74, no. 3 (March 2020), 219–24.

113 third-most-popular tourist attraction: Megan Rosenfeld, "Heritage USA & the Heavenly Vacation," *The Washington Post*, June 14, 1986.

113 fathered a child out of wedlock: David Di Sabatino, director, *Fallen Angel: The Outlaw Larry Norman*, Jester Media, documentary, 2009.

114 conservatives who disproportionately enjoyed: Julia Naftulin, "Why Conservative Men May Be Attracted to Cuckolding, According to a Researcher Who Studies the Kink," *Business Insider*, April 16, 2021.

115 According to a study in the *Journal of Sex Research*: Yaniv Efrati, "God, I Can't Stop Thinking About Sex! The Rebound Effect in Unsuccessful Suppression of Sexual Thoughts Among Religious Adolescents," *The Journal of Sex Research* 56, no. 2 (April 2018): 146–55.

115 "repression of sexual thoughts": Eric W. Dolan, "Attempts to Suppress Sexual Thoughts Could Result in an Increase of Those Thoughts," *PsyPost*, May 24, 2018.

CHAPTER NINE: **Reaping the Whirlwind**

118 "They have been taught to believe": Jerry Falwell, *Listen, America!* (New York: Doubleday, 1980), 18.

119 Reagan would cut twenty-two billion dollars: Claire Bond Potter, "The Shadow of Ronald Reagan Is Costing Us Dearly," *The New York Times*, Nov. 11, 2021.

119 fewer manufacturing jobs: "All Employees, Manufacturing (MANEMP)," Federal Reserve Bank of St. Louis Economic Data, updated July 3, 2025.

119 relaxing of antimonopoly laws: Louis Galambos, "The Monopoly Enigma, the Reagan Administration's Antitrust Experiment, and the Global Economy," in *Constructing Corporate America: History, Politics, Culture*, ed. Kenneth Lipartito and David B. Sicilia (Oxford, UK, and New York: Oxford University Press, 2007), 159.

119 wages drop by as much as 300 percent: Nick Reding, *Methland: The Death and Life of an American Small Town* (New York: Bloomsbury, 2009), 69.

122 "Satanism is cause for concern": Quoted in Geraldo Rivera, *Devil Worship: Exploring Satan's Underground*, NBC, Oct. 25, 1988.

INTERLUDE: **God-Fearing Child**

129 twelve thousand claims of Satanic ritual abuse: Daniel Goleman, "Proof Lacking for Ritual Abuse by Satanists," *The New York Times*, Oct. 31, 1994.

129 creations of Anton LaVey: Graham Harvey, "Satanism in Britain Today," *Journal of Contemporary Religion* 10, no. 3 (1995): 283–96.

CHAPTER TEN: The Wages of Sin

133 angry with the Jews: "Oberammergau Passion Play: A Brief History," American Jewish Committee.

CHAPTER NINETEEN: Pure

179 Clinton administration's "safe sex" education: Douglas B. Kirby and Nancy L. Brown, "Condom Availability Programs in U.S. Schools," *Family Planning Perspectives* 28, no. 5 (Sept./Oct. 1996): 196.

180 churchgoers admitted to having sex before marriage: Janet E. Rosenbaum and Byron Weathersbee, "True Love Waits: Do Southern Baptists? Premarital Sexual Behavior Among Newly Married Southern Baptist Sunday School Students," *Journal of Religion and Health* 52, no. 1 (March 2013): 263.

180 True Love Waits abstinence pledge: Clyde Haberman, "How an Abstinence Pledge in the '90s Shamed a Generation of Evangelicals," *The New York Times*, April 6, 2021.

180 sex education programs began receiving federal funding: "A History of Federal Funding for Abstinence-Only-Until-Marriage Programs," SIECUS, 2019, siecus.org.

180 Title V "Abstinence-Only-Until-Marriage Program": John S. Santelli et al., "Abstinence-Only-Until-Marriage: An Updated Review of U.S. Policies and Programs and Their Impact," *Journal of Adolescent Health* 61, no. 3 (Sept. 2017): 273–80.

181 "programs should be abandoned": Santelli et al., "Abstinence-Only-Until-Marriage," 400.

181 a 1992 Christian Coalition fund-raising letter: The Associated Press, "Robertson Letter Attacks Feminists," *The New York Times*, Aug. 26, 1992.

CHAPTER TWENTY: Martyr Me, Manson

187 teacher-led prayer in school was banned: *Engel v. Vitale* (1962), National Constitution Center, https://constitutioncenter.org/the-constitution/supreme-court-case-library/engel-v-vitale.

187 See You at the Pole: Steve Fitschen, "See You at the Pole: Your Right to Participate," National Legal Foundation, Feb. 7, 2018.

CHAPTER TWENTY-TWO: A Is for Apologetics

196 "God created humans in their present form": Art Swift, "In U.S., Belief in Creationist View of Humans at New Low," *Gallup News*, May 22, 2017.

198 "I pledge allegiance to the Christian flag": "The Christian Flag: History, Meaning, and Pledge of Allegiance," christianity.com, Jan. 12, 2024.

INTERLUDE: **Highway to Hegemony**

209 "franchise capital of Iowa": Kevin Hardy, "Are Lost Factory Jobs Driving Iowans to Trump?" *The Des Moines Register,* Sept. 22, 2016.

211 less likely to shop at Walmart: Rebekah Peeples Massengill, "Why Evangelicals Like Wal-Mart: Education, Region, and Religious Group Identity," *Sociology of Religion* 72, no. 1 (2011): 50–77.

212 Walmart employees cost the U.S. government $6.2 billion: "The Walmart Tax Subsidy: Walmart's Wage Hike to $10/Hour Still Requires Large Taxpayer Subsidies," Americans for Tax Fairness, April 2015.

214 On average, a high-school dropout: Jason M. Breslow, "By the Numbers: Dropping Out of High School," *Frontline,* PBS, Sept. 21, 2012.

214 around sixty-three times more likely: Breslow, "By the Numbers."

215 the income of the average CEO: Josh Bivens and Jori Kandra, "CEO Pay Slightly Declined in 2022," Economic Policy Institute, Sept. 21, 2023.

215 top income-tax rate was 91 percent: "Federal Income Tax Brackets and Maximum Tax Rates: 1950–1980," Stanford University, May 24, 2012.

215 a million hourly workers in America: U.S. Bureau of Labor Statistics, "Characteristics of Minimum Wage Workers, 2022," *BLS Reports,* Aug. 2023.

216 40 percent of workers: Sara R. Collins et al., "On The Edge: Low Wage Workers and Their Health Insurance Coverage," The Commonwealth Fund, April 2003.

CHAPTER TWENTY-FIVE: **God's Pyramid of Debt**

229 "hire half the working class": Philip S. Foner, *History of the Labor Movement in the United States,* Vol. 2 (New York: International Publishers, 1955), 50.

CHAPTER TWENTY-EIGHT: **The Fruit of Knowledge**

245 "Seventy-five percent of kids": Kent Hovind, writer, *Creation Seminar,* season 1, episode 5, "The Dangers of Evolution," 2003.

CHAPTER TWENTY-NINE: **It's Work**

250 Known at the time as "the Evangelical Vatican": Liam Adams, "How Christians Are Rebuilding a Relationship with Colorado Springs," *Christianity Today,* July/Aug. 2021.

250 Known as "the Colorado Model": William Schultz, "How Colorado Did a 180 on Gay Rights," *The Washington Post,* Dec. 17, 2018.

251 and paying for gay sex: The Associated Press, "Haggard Admits 'Sexual Immorality,' Apologizes," NBC News, Nov. 2, 2006.

251 George Rekers was discovered: James Esseks, "George Rekers: An Ex-Expert Witness," ACLU, May 18, 2010.

CHAPTER THIRTY: Boy on Fire

254 "Father, I am going to": Billy Graham, *Just As I Am: The Autobiography of Billy Graham* (New York: Harper Collins, 1997), 139.

257 Malcolm Gladwell's ten-thousand-hours rule: Malcolm Gladwell, "Complexity and the 10,000-Hour Rule," *The New Yorker,* Aug. 21, 2013.

INTERLUDE: Hounded by Fox

260 decision to jettison the old one: Michael M. Grynbaum, "Fox News Drops 'Fair and Balanced' Motto," *The New York Times,* June 14, 2017.

261 In 1960, a new policy: Jeffrey K. Hadden, "Policing the Religious Airwaves: A Case of Market Place Regulation," *Brigham Young University Journal of Public Law* 8, no. 2 (March 1994): 407.

262 a "professional mudslinger": Fred W. Friendly, "What's Fair on the Air?," *The New York Times,* March 30, 1975.

263 Ailes later worked: Tim Dickinson, "How Roger Ailes Built the Fox News Fear Factory," *Rolling Stone,* May 25, 2011.

CHAPTER THIRTY-ONE: Monetizing Trauma

270 Arne Cheyenne Johnson: Laura Zornosa, "The True Story Behind the Netflix Documentary *The Devil on Trial,*" *Time,* Oct. 18, 2023.

271 fifty-seven-year-old Robert Dear: "Robert Dear Indicted by Federal Grand Jury for 2015 Planned Parenthood Clinic Shooting," U.S. Department of Justice Archives, Dec. 9, 2019.

272 assaults against abortion providers: Alison Durkee, "Attacks on Abortion Providers Surged in 2021, Report Finds as Supreme Court Overturns Roe v. Wade," *Forbes,* June 24, 2022.

CHAPTER THIRTY-TWO: Think of the Children

274 sufferings of pioneer life: Marion L. Starkey, *The Devil In Massachusetts: A Modern Enquiry into the Salem Witch Trials* (New York: Alfred A. Knopf, 1949), 6.

274 Religious trauma syndrome has been widely discussed: Sumeet Singh et al., "Religious Trauma Syndrome: The Futile Fate of Faith," *Industrial Psychiatry Journal* 33, suppl. 1 (Aug. 27, 2024): 309–10.

275 "depression, anxiety, guilt, and addictive or compulsive behaviors": Alyson M. Stone, "Thou Shalt Not: Treating Religious Trauma and Spiritual Harm with Combined Therapy," *Group* 37, no. 4 (2013): 323–37.

275 a movement of "exvangelicals": Stef W. Kight, "The Exvangelicals," *Axios,* Sept. 19, 2021.

276 their 1999 Hell House: Jim Yardley, "Church's Haunted House Draws Fire," *The New York Times,* Oct. 29, 1999.

CHAPTER THIRTY-THREE: Exercising Demons

284 "Family pathology rolls": Terrence Real, *I Don't Want To Talk About It: Overcoming The Secret Legacy of Male Depression* (New York: Simon & Schuster, 1997), 10.

CHAPTER THIRTY-FIVE: God's Plan for Your Investment Portfolio

290 nearly half of evangelical Protestants: David Masci and Gregory A. Smith, "5 Facts About U.S. Evangelical Protestants," Pew Research Center, March 1, 2018.

290 the "Great Commission": Mathew Schmalz, "What Is the Great Commission and Why Is It So Controversial?," *The Conversation,* Feb. 8, 2019.

CHAPTER THIRTY-SIX: The Swamps of Sadness

296 highest rates of methamphetamine use: Iowa Department of Public Health, "Iowa Substance Abuse Brief," no. 9 (Oct. 2019): 1.

297 "Deterioration in job quality": Angus Deaton and Anne Case, *Deaths of Despair and the Future of Capitalism* (Princeton University Press, 2020), 7.

298 "opposite of addiction": Johann Hari, *Chasing The Scream: The First and Last Days Of The War On Drugs* (London: Bloomsbury Publishing, 2015), 174.

301 represent a tiny fraction: Randy A. Aussenberg, "Errors and Fraud in the Supplemental Nutrition Assistance Program (SNAP)," Congressional Research Service, Sept. 28, 2018.

CHAPTER THIRTY-EIGHT: Mama, I'm Coming Home

319 earning less than fifteen dollars an hour: Suzie Coen, "$15 an Hour Isn't Enough: U.S. Workers Need to Earn a Living Wage," *The Hill,* Aug. 25, 2023.

CHAPTER THIRTY-NINE: Beach Buddhist Bingo

334 One of the hallmarks of PTSD: "What Is Posttraumatic Stress Disorder (PTSD)?," American Psychiatric Association, March 2025.

336 Dalai Lama once said: Dalai Lama [Tenzin Gyatso], "Establishing Harmony Within Religious Diversity," The Office of His Holiness the Dalai Lama.

About the Author

Josiah Hesse, author of *Runner's High* and the Carnality series, is a freelance journalist out of Denver, Colorado, covering everything from politics, science, and crime to art, pop culture, and evangelical culture and theology. He is a regular contributor to *The Guardian* and *Vice,* and his work has appeared in *Esquire, Newsweek, Men's Health,* and *Politico,* among other publications.

A Note on the Type

This book was set in Arno, a typeface designed by Robert Slimbach in 2007. Its namesake is the Arno River, which flows through Florence. Inspired by the humanist letterforms of the fifteenth and sixteenth centuries, Slimbach designed Arno with the vitality and readability of Venetian and Aldine book typefaces in mind.

Typeset by Scribe,
Philadelphia, Pennsylvania

Design by Betty Lew